VOLUME 562

MARCH 1999

THE ANNALS

of The American Academy *of* Political
and Social Science

ALAN W. HESTON, *Editor*
NEIL A. WEINER, *Assistant Editor*

THE EVOLVING WORLD
OF WORK AND FAMILY:
NEW STAKEHOLDERS, NEW VOICES

Special Editors of this Volume

MARCIE PITT-CATSOUPHES
BRADLEY K. GOOGINS
*Boston College
Chestnut Hill
Massachusetts*

 SAGE Periodicals Press *THOUSAND OAKS LONDON NEW DELHI*

40877951

The American Academy of Political and Social Science

3937 Chestnut Street   Philadelphia, Pennsylvania 19104

3 8471 00168 2862

Origin and Purpose. The Academy was organized December 14, 1889, to promote the progress of political and social science, especially through publications and meetings. The Academy does not take sides in controverted questions, but seeks to gather and present reliable information to assist the public in forming an intelligent and accurate judgment.

Meetings. The Academy occasionally holds a meeting in the spring extending over two days.

Publications. THE ANNALS of the American Academy of Political and Social Science is the bimonthly publication of The Academy. Each issue contains articles on some prominent social or political problem, written at the invitation of the editors. Also, monographs are published from time to time, numbers of which are distributed to pertinent professional organizations. These volumes constitute important reference works on the topics with which they deal, and they are extensively cited by authorities throughout the United States and abroad. The papers presented at the meetings of The Academy are included in THE ANNALS.

Membership. Each member of The Academy receives THE ANNALS and may attend the meetings of The Academy. Membership is open only to individuals. Annual dues: $59.00 for the regular paperbound edition (clothbound, $86.00). Add $12.00 per year for membership outside the U.S.A. Members may also purchase single issues of THE ANNALS for $12.00 each (clothbound, $16.00). Add $2.00 for shipping and handling on all pre-paid orders.

Subscriptions. THE ANNALS of the American Academy of Political and Social Science (ISSN 0002-7162) is published six times annually—in January, March, May, July, September, and November. Institutions may subscribe to THE ANNALS at the annual rate: $281.00 (clothbound, $332.00). Add $12.00 per year for subscriptions outside the U.S.A. Institutional rates for single issues: $49.00 each (clothbound, $57.00).

Periodicals postage paid at Thousand Oaks, California, and additional offices.

Single issues of THE ANNALS may be obtained by individuals who are not members of The Academy for $19.00 each (clothbound, $29.00). Add $2.00 for shipping and handling on all prepaid orders. Single issues of THE ANNALS have proven to be excellent supplementary texts for classroom use. Direct inquiries regarding adoptions to THE ANNALS c/o Sage Publications (address below).

All correspondence concerning membership in The Academy, dues renewals, inquiries about membership status, and/or purchase of single issues of THE ANNALS should be sent to THE ANNALS c /o Sage Publications, Inc., 2455 Teller Road, Thousand Oaks, CA 91320. Telephone: (805) 499-0721; FAX/Order line: (805) 499-0871. *Please note that orders under $30 must be prepaid.* Sage affiliates in London and India will assist institutional subscribers abroad with regard to orders, claims, and inquiries for both subscriptions and single issues.

Printed on recycled, acid-free paper

THE ANNALS

© 1999 *by* The American Academy *of* Political *and* Social Science

Editorial Office: 3937 Chestnut Street, Philadelphia, PA 19104.

For information about membership* (individuals only) and subscriptions (institutions), address:

SAGE PUBLICATIONS, INC.
2455 Teller Road
Thousand Oaks, CA 91320

From India and South Asia,		*From the UK, Europe, the Middle*
write to:		*East and Africa, write to:*
SAGE PUBLICATIONS INDIA Pvt. Ltd		SAGE PUBLICATIONS LTD
P.O. Box 4215		6 Bonhill Street
New Delhi 110 048		London EC2A 4PU
INDIA		UNITED KINGDOM

SAGE Production Staff: ERIC LAW, LISA CUEVAS, DORIS HUS, and ROSE TYLAK
*Please note that members of The Academy receive THE ANNALS with their membership.
Library of Congress Catalog Card Number 98-85641
International Standard Serial Number ISSN 0002-7162
International Standard Book Number ISBN 0-7619-1731-4 (Vol. 562, 1999 paper)
International Standard Book Number ISBN 0-7619-1730-6 (Vol. 562, 1999 cloth)
Manufactured in the United States of America. First printing, March 1999.

> The articles appearing in THE ANNALS are indexed in *Academic Index, Book Review Index, Combined Retrospective Index Sets, Current Contents, General Periodicals Index, Public Affairs Information Service Bulletin, Pro-Views,* and *Social Sciences Index.* They are also abstracted and indexed in *ABC Pol Sci, America: History and Life, Automatic Subject Citation Alert, Book Review Digest, Family Resources Database, Higher Education Abstracts, Historical Abstracts, Human Resources Abstracts, International Political Science Abstracts, Journal of Economic Literature, Managing Abstracts, Periodica Islamica, Sage Urban Studies Abstracts, Social Planning/Policy & Development Abstracts, Social Sciences Citation Index, Social Work Research & Abstracts, Sociological Abstracts, United States Political Science Documents,* and/or *Work Related Abstracts, Westlaw,* and are available on microfilm from University Microfilms, Ann Arbor, Michigan.

Information about membership rates, institutional subscriptions, and back issue prices may be found on the facing page.

Advertising. Current rates and specifications may be obtained by writing to THE ANNALS Advertising and Promotion Manager at the Thousand Oaks office (address above).

Claims. Claims for undelivered copies must be made no later than twelve months following month of publication. The publisher will supply missing copies when losses have been sustained in transit and when the reserve stock will permit.

Change of Address. Six weeks' advance notice must be given when notifying of change of address to ensure proper identification. Please specify name of journal. **POSTMASTER:** Send address changes to: THE ANNALS of the American Academy of Political and Social Science, c/o Sage Publications, Inc., 2455 Teller Road, Thousand Oaks, CA 91320.

THE ANNALS

of The American Academy *of* Political *and* Social Science

ALAN W. HESTON, *Editor*
NEIL A. WEINER, *Assistant Editor*

--------------------- FORTHCOMING ---------------------

See page 2 for information on Academy membership and
purchase of single volumes of **The Annals.**

CONTENTS

BOOK DEPARTMENT CONTENTS

INTERNATIONAL RELATIONS AND POLITICS

AFRICA, ASIA, AND LATIN AMERICA

EUROPE

UNITED STATES

SOCIOLOGY

ECONOMICS

PREFACE

It has taken two decades of constant effort, but pundits, researchers, workplace practitioners, and vocal advocates have successfully brought work-family issues to the attention of corporate decision makers, academics, public sector leaders, and, indeed, the public at large. The millennium promises to be an anniversary of sorts for the work-family field. In the beginning of the 1980s, the relevance of work-family issues was apparent only to a relatively small cadre of individuals. At that time, the number of work-family researchers could have comfortably gathered together at a modest conference. Twenty years ago, only a few corporations went public with their work-family policies and programs.

During the past two decades, as researchers have documented the revolutionary shifts that have occurred within families and at places of business, the number of academics and corporate practitioners who have devoted their life's work to these important social issues has mushroomed. Today, work-life initiatives are often considered to be at the core of *Fortune* 100 companies' efforts to be an employer of choice. The work-family lexicon is no longer a foreign language; rather, work-family concepts and terms have become common parlance at the workplace and at home. It is now clear to many that work and family issues are some of the more visible manifestations of a significant transformation of the social and economic spheres of our lives. The compelling nature of work and family issues is indicated by the continued media attention to changes in our work and family lives. Indeed, the imminent century marker can be seen as a time to celebrate the accomplishments made in the work-family arena.

The research literature has reflected, chronicled, and pushed forward the growth of the work-family field. Our own first work-family research was conducted in the early 1980s, a time when there were only a limited number of studies about these issues. Now, literally hundreds of researchers publish articles and reports each year, as documented in a recent volume of annotated references to research literature compiled by Lilly, Pitt-Catsouphes, and Googins (1997). Articles about work-family issues routinely appear in journals in a range of disciplines, and new journals, such as *Community, Work and Family*, have emerged.

However, as we are getting ready to face the twenty-first century, many work-family leaders are challenging one another to be more articulate about their visions, to be bolder about their hopes, and to more actively encourage meaningful dialogue about the diverse work and family experiences that are encountered every day by working families all over the globe. A number of important, fundamental questions have been raised:

1. Despite the accolades given to some of the "revolutionary" work-life concepts, are the basic assumptions we make about work and family issues reflective of a bygone era?

2. Have we continued to focus primarily on mainstream work-family issues that are most relevant to only a very narrow spectrum of today's working families?

3. Have we seriously grappled with the inherently dynamic and changing nature of work-family experiences as they unfold in people's lives?

4. Why have we not been more successful in crossing the boundaries of our current understandings so that we can penetrate the territories of the unknown?

Given the rapidly changing social, political, and economic environments of recent years, it is incumbent on the research community to delve deeper into the assumptions that have framed the field—some of which remain relatively untested. It is widely recognized that work organizations often experience ongoing periods of discontinuous change that create upheavals in workplace structures, values, and behaviors. Family structures, roles, and relationships have also been reinvented. Indeed, some would contend that the very nature of workplaces and families has been forever altered. Despite these dramatic transformations, in some areas there has been a lag in understanding, which has barely kept pace with these changes. For example, gender issues remain obstinate, even though many people are actively engaged in fresh dialogue.

It is precisely at this point in time that the field could leap forward and begin to grapple with the complexities of the work-family experiences of today and tomorrow. However, it is also possible that the approaches to research and practice could freeze, reflecting a knowledge base that is either out-of-date or misguided. Some critics have suggested that research, rather than leading the field to new avenues of discovery, has tended to follow the conventions of the practice community. Others have suggested that, in its rush to build theory, the field may be glossing over experiences that are fundamental to everyday work and life events. As a result, some of our research may have resulted in thin understandings or inadequate responses to the complex set of work and family issues.

What might prevent the field from becoming entrenched in traditions of its own invention? There are already indications that work-family researchers and practitioners have begun to listen to new sets of voices that express fresh, new perspectives about work-family experiences and possible responses. Some of these voices may seem unorthodox, but many of them have introduced creative ideas and original concepts. The challenging discourse that has begun to unfold in recent years has encouraged academics and practitioners alike to reexamine many of the early assumptions that have framed so much of our thinking about work and family issues to date.

The present volume was inspired, in part, by our concern that the work-family field might become stale before its time. However, we were equally motivated to edit this volume because of our optimism that the field is in the midst of an exciting renewal process. The articles in this issue capture some of the exciting possibilities that lie ahead as work-family leaders (practitioners, policymakers, and researchers) more carefully listen to the voices of diverse stakeholders in work and family issues. The perspectives expressed in these articles provide a wonderful counterpoint to the dogma drift.

We have been fortunate to have some of the most creative and thoughtful researchers in the work-family field contribute to this special issue. These authors demonstrate how the field can benefit from not only looking at the present but also peeking around the corner, seeking out places where work and family issues have not yet become visible to most of us. We are pleased to be able to present a number of articles that push against the existing boundaries of work-family thinking. These articles, which discuss some of the newest insights into work and family issues, are evidence that the field has the potential to usher in a millennium of radical social change—a new era in which we can build a society that actively supports healthy families and productive workplaces.

We are sure that many of the ideas introduced in these articles will help to push forward some of the new work-family discussions that are starting to emerge. For example, researchers and practitioners alike are beginning to question the advisability of depending so heavily on the now familiar family-friendly corporate model of work and family supports. Some of the authors who have contributed to this volume have challenged us to consider the possibility of locating work and family within the community domain. The shift to a community framework not only expands our basic understanding of work and family but also opens up a host of practice and policy options that may well move this field in a radically new direction.

Similarly, increasing numbers of researchers and practitioners are contextualizing work-family experiences and responses. This is visible, for instance, in the engaging discussions about the globalization of work and family issues. As new cross-cultural studies are conducted in the years ahead, we will enrich our understanding about work and family issues. We anticipate that the work-family field will be able to glean many interesting insights into the complex web of work and family dynamics as researchers, policymakers, and workplace decision makers continue to locate work and family experiences within cultural and sociopolitical systems.

ORGANIZATION AND STRUCTURE OF THIS VOLUME

This special issue of *The Annals* has been organized into five sections: diverse families; families in transition; diverse organizations; organizations in transition; and policy perspectives.

Diverse families

Perhaps one of the more egregious oversights in the work and family field is the tendency to gloss over the diversity of family structures and experiences. To date, much of the work-family research has focused on the professional dual-career couple. In aggregate, these studies have made significant contributions to the growing knowledge base and have helped to define the contours of the work-family landscape. However, some critics have suggested that other types of families have not received as much attention; consequently, the field may have developed a limited perspective about a rather small slice of life. The three articles in this section do a fantastic job of lifting up several cutting-edge issues and help to reaffirm diverse work-family experiences.

While most scholars have focused on the ways in which employment structures family life, Rosanna Hertz identifies groups of single-parent and dual-earner families who have elected to restructure employment for the sake of family life. The findings of her research help us to recognize that, despite the tendency for workplace organizations to dominate family life, some families have been able to recalibrate the delicate balance between the organization and the family and have reasserted their family priorities.

Mary Young provides a voice to a large segment of the workforce whose needs often seem inaudible: single adults without dependent children. She considers the work-life concerns of these employees within a framework of organizational justice. The findings of her research challenge us to consider whether the focus on working parents and child care issues has had unintended consequences for single adults without dependent children. This article encourages us to ask whether the design of many work-family initiatives has inadvertently expressed a bias against those without children or those who do not have primary responsibilities for dependents.

Maureen Scully and Douglas Creed argue that work-family issues might be better examined through a lens of valuing diversity, not equity. They look at yet another group of diverse families: gay, lesbian, bisexual, and transsexual (GLBT) families. Only recently have corporate decision makers begun to recognize that a range of work-life issues are important and relevant to GLBT families. This article presents a provocative and compelling argument for continuing the dialogue about the nuances of the meanings of work-life issues to employees who have different family experiences. The authors suggest that organizations can develop policies and programs that respect a variety of alternative family arrangements while still privileging special groups such as families with young children.

Families in transition

It is indisputable that changing work and family roles have contributed to the dynamic characteristics of today's American families. In many homes (and on an almost daily basis), family members interact with each other to address and negotiate work-family issues and in the process actively reinvent and reconstruct work-life roles and responsibilities. Furthermore, many families experience, endure, and respond to changes in their work lives. A variety of factors—intrafamilial interactions, life cycle characteristics, and changes in the larger social environment—all contribute to the ebbs and flows of family life.

The three articles in this section offer us opportunities to consider different aspects of the profound impact that family transitions can have. Each of these articles focuses our attention on particular family transformations; each challenges us to consider that tomorrow's work-family experiences are likely to be different from those of yesterday and today.

Paul Attewell examines data on displaced workers and finds some surprising associations between job loss or displacement, marital status, and parental status. His analysis suggests that single and divorced employees are more likely to have experienced job loss than married employees are and that parents of children under 6 years of age and single parents have a higher likelihood of displacement. These findings raise important questions and force us to look at macro labor force trends from an entirely new perspective.

The article by Suzan Lewis, Janet Smithson, and Julia Brannen, on the family and employment orientations of young people in Europe, reminds us that a new generation of workers is about to enter the job market. These young people grew up in the midst of the work and family revolution; consequently, they may have a very different set of values, expectations, and visions for roles at work and at home. The European experience provides a useful lens through which we can consider how these issues are evolving in the United States.

The third article in this section authored by Shin-Kap Han and Phyllis Moen directs our attention to the transitions experienced by families who are entering retirement. The findings of their research are presented from a life course perspective. As a result, we are encouraged to consider the developmental dimensions of work and family experiences. Han and Moen also introduce the concept of family careers. When considered in tandem with the notion of work careers, this construct facilitates a deeper appreciation of the evolution of work-family experiences as they unfold over time. In addition, this framework facilitates the assessment of the complex intersections between the work and family careers of dual-career couples, where the work and the family careers of one individual affect the work and family careers of the other.

Diverse organizations

Much of what we know in the work and family field has been derived from studies in large multinational corporations. The vast majority of U.S. workplaces, however, are not corporate firms, and most American employees do not work for these large companies. The articles in this section examine two sectors of the workplace that have been largely overlooked in the work and family field: small businesses and nonprofit organizations.

Shelley MacDermid, Leon Litchfield, and Marcie Pitt-Catsouphes draw upon theoretical understandings about organizational size and present the findings from empirical studies of small businesses. Their article reflects the burgeoning interest in the work-family experiences of employees who work for small businesses. The authors provide highlights from two of their own studies: a national survey of 276 businesses and a qualitative study that gathered information from employees who worked for small businesses.

Judith Gonyea considers how different characteristics of nonprofit and nongovernmental organizations might affect the responses of these workplaces to their employees' work-family issues. Because there is little known about the dynamics of work and family in this sector, this article provides a rich agenda for future research. In addition, the information helps us to formulate questions about using work-family policies and programs to position not-for-profit organizations as employers of choice.

Organizations in transition

Organizational transformation has resculpted not only the workplace structure but also career options, the employer-employee contract, and even the basic design of work itself. The ever changing and complex interactions between families and work organizations continue to challenge the work and family agenda.

Rosalind Barnett delineates a number of disjunctures between the common characteristics of corporate policies and programs and today's work-life experiences. In her article, we are guided through an analytic process that helps us to dig deeper into the assumptions that have configured our notions of family-friendly companies. The ideas presented in this article push us beyond a sense of complacency; they urge us to go further than the benefits approach to work-life; they challenge us to seriously consider how the experiences of today's working families may be different from the priorities that were visible a decade ago.

Susan Eaton and Lotte Bailyn take us into the world of biotechnology firms; in the process, they offer us a rare glimpse into some of the work and family issues that may become visible at companies of the future. Their in-depth study of firms in this sector introduces us to new organizational forms and alternative organizational cultures. The very important interface between career experiences and work-family issues becomes salient in the discussions in this article.

Policy perspectives

The final section confirms the essential connections between work-family research, practice, and policy. The two articles in this section encourage us to reconsider how social and economic policies—and the meaningful linkages between them—can be powerful determinants for the work-family experiences of American employees. Each of the articles in this section gets us ready to face an important reality: despite the fact that there is widespread preference in the United States for a minimalist government, many aspects of work-family experiences can be addressed only if we consider the broad social, economic, and political policy options. The policy framework helps the field to tackle the big work-family questions: What are the critical elements of family well-being? How do work-family issues connect to sustainable and thriving communities? What types of partnerships should family-friendly businesses create with employees, their families, and their communities?

While examining the experiences of welfare reform, Susan Lambert raises several interesting questions about labor and employment policies. She considers the work-family dimensions of welfare reform from two different perspectives: labor market supply and demand. This article is very effective in translating work-family issues, as they are experienced by individuals and families, to critical public issues.

This volume concludes with an important contribution by Paula Rayman and Ann Bookman. They challenge us to create an integrated research and public policy agenda for the twenty-first century and then put it into action. Their discussion helps us to carefully unravel complex conundrums related to the development of public sector policies that can promote quality work and family experiences. This article offers wonderful insights based on previous efforts to shape public policies that are responsive to the needs of working families.

FINAL COMMENTS

We want to thank everyone who has helped to bring this exciting volume to fruition. There has been a lot of behind-the-scenes work that has truly made a difference. Teri Ann Lilly, a senior research associate at the Boston College Center for Work & Family, has worked with several of the authors, connecting them to important research.

In particular, we want to express our gratitude to the authors. Each has thoughtfully reflected on new issues that need attention if the work-family field is to stay fresh and exciting. The authors have diligently met the tight deadlines and have been graciously receptive to suggestions. We are confident that the reader will be delighted to discover the many treasures wrapped in their articles. We anticipate that their work will stimulate thinking and will provide some provocative (or even contentious) ideas.

MARCIE PITT-CATSOUPHES
BRADLEY K. GOOGINS

Reference

Lilly, Teri Ann, Marcie Pitt-Catsouphes, and Bradley Googins. 1997. *Work-Family Research: An Annotated Bibliography*. Westport, CT: Greenwood Press.

ANNALS, *AAPSS*, **562**, March 1999

Working to Place Family at the Center of Life: Dual-Earner and Single-Parent Strategies

By ROSANNA HERTZ

ABSTRACT: There are two basic types of work-family strategies: workplace-based strategies and family-centered strategies. In the past, attention has been placed mostly on work policies. This article focuses on members of dual-earner and single-parent families who have actively placed family at the center of their lives. The strategies they adopt depend upon their position in the labor market as well as marital status. Some dual-earner families jointly calculate scheduling and job trajectories while utilizing benefits from both of their employees; others reluctantly coparent because of underemployment. Single mothers who have professional or technical skills try to make special accommodations with bosses or they become contract workers, while less skilled single mothers need benefits in order not to have to work several jobs. In addition, some single mothers have developed extensive networks and advocate for more community support of child rearing. Most working parents committed to keeping their families at the center have pursued nontraditional career paths. Ideologies about families and parenting may shape strategies about employment more often than workplace norms or work-family policies.

Rosanna Hertz is professor of sociology and women's studies at Wellesley College. She has been on the Wellesley faculty since 1983. Her research focuses on the relationship between family, work, and gender in order to understand the interaction and reciprocities of these areas of inquiry. She is the author of More Equal Than Others: Women and Men in Dual-Career Marriages. *Since 1991 she as been the editor of the journal* Qualitative Sociology.

NOTE: The author thanks Robert J. Thomas for his generous comments and editorial assistance and Faith I. Ferguson for sharing data collection and initial analysis on the single-mother study. She thanks Bradley Googins and Marcie Pitt-Catsouphes for detailed suggestions that improved the flow of her arguments. Wellesley College provided transcription costs for the interviews in both studies.

MOST scholars have focused on the ways in which employment structures family life. Economic resources and employment status are frequently noted as major correlates (if not predictors) of parents' beliefs about parenting and child care (for example, who should do it and how it ought to be arranged). This holds true even in studies of child care arrangements where parents' beliefs about motherhood are positioned as independent variables. While my own empirical studies look at how workplaces cause families to organize in particular ways, in each of these studies I have also encountered numerous couples and individuals who are pushing workplaces to accommodate them or who are creating their own careers and businesses in order to place children and child rearing before employment. For the sake of clarity, I will use the term "work" to refer to paid employment; work in the home is referred to as "housework." In this article, I move these couples out of the margins and into the spotlight to examine how and why they navigate the work world despite indifferent and, in some cases, hostile employment policies. I use the cases from two recent studies as examples: a study of 95 dual-earner couples and a study of 52 single, unwed mothers.[1]

THE BROADER
WORK-FAMILY CONTEXT

Family benefits (for example, flextime, on-site day care, and parental leaves) are more common now than when I wrote *More Equal Than Others: Women and Men in Dual-Career Marriages* over a decade ago.[2] However, while organizations may acknowledge that most employees have families, families have yet to exert a dramatic influence on organizational policies. In part, the lack of a strong push to make work family-friendly can be attributed to the ability of employers to make special (that is, unique or onetime) concessions to individual employees. For example, flexible work hours may be granted to valued professional or technical women (Catalyst 1997), but such concessions generally do not translate into flextime for everyone.[3] More broadly, a concept of social contract like that found in many Western European economies is notably absent in policy circles (much less in corporate personnel departments) in the United States. However, less obvious (but no less important) is the fact that not all employees utilize benefits even when they are offered; for example, men rarely make use of paternity leave benefits. As long as a core group of employees continues to advance without the use of the new family benefits, the structure and the culture of the workplace are likely to remain unchallenged. In short, employers remain the silent (and relatively intransigent) partners in the life of all families (Hertz 1986).

Without a doubt, family structure has changed dramatically, and economic and workplace factors have an important role to play in explaining the change in family structures.[4] However, there remains a great deal to be learned about the effect of family on work, on one hand, and of family ideology on work choices, on the other. For instance, it is not at all clear that women are trading home for employment as a less stressful environment (cf. Hochschild 1997). More likely, women work outside the home because they and their families cannot get by on one paycheck. Indeed, as Coontz (1992, 18-19) notes, polls show that the pressures for balancing work and family, particularly for women, are enormous and that a large percentage of women would trade a day's pay for an extra day off. Additionally, studies of shift-work families demonstrate that wives remain in the workforce after children are born but change to working shifts (Presser and Cain 1983; Presser 1988). Working opposite shifts from those of their husbands allows them to care for their children (Hertz and Charlton 1989) and does not compete with views of being a "visible" mom in ways that working days did (Garey 1995; Hertz 1997).

Our relative ignorance about the effect of family on work stems at least in part from the fact that most scholars continue to focus their research on a narrow slice of employed families: the most successful (and elite) dual-career and dual-earner couples. Left aside are couples who—for reasons of ideology or economic circumstance—may actually be placing family ahead of workplace demands. For example, insufficient attention has been paid to dual-earner couples who have faced the effects of job loss by one or both spouses. For these couples, job loss for husbands may, in fact, be causing couples to rethink the primacy of work outside the home over family. Moreover, the most under-represented category of family are

those single (never married) women and men who have families that they support. While the fastest-growing category of U.S. families may be single moms, the focus continues to be on teen mothers and not those who are active in the labor market, economically self-sufficient, and over the age of 20.

The two groups whose experiences I analyze in this article offer up an interesting comparison. The first group consists of married dual-earner couples who have put into practice an egalitarian approach to parenting. The second group consists of women who are financially self-sufficient and who intentionally became single mothers. Both groups would appear to have made conscious choices to put family ahead of employment. Therefore, they offer a valuable opportunity to examine the conditions under which family affects employment.

DUAL-EARNER COUPLES AND THE NEW PARENTING

In my most recent study of dual-earner couples and their decision-making practices (Hertz 1997), I found three general approaches to child care: the mothering approach, the market approach, and the new parenting approach. The mothering approach assumes that the person best suited to raise the couple's children is the wife, who should be with them at home. The market approach involves hiring other people to care for one's own children. The new parenting approach is exemplified by the belief that the family ought to be organized around caring for the children—with the critical distinction that both parents are full participants. While this approach was the least common of the three, it posed the strongest challenge to a traditional family division of labor and to conventional definitions of job and career.

The two groups of couples found to most often practice the new parenting approach came from very different economic and social situations. One group was made up of couples in which both spouses held middle-range managerial and professional jobs that allowed them to request more flexible work time or fewer workdays. As valued employees whose jobs did not involve extensive direct supervision, their requests for flexibility were met with individual concessions but not policy changes. Other employees were asking to be evaluated on a per project or task-completion basis. This contract with bosses allowed individuals to structure their own work schedules and pace, shifting the work culture to performance evaluation as separate from employee visibility. The arrangement did not require income reduction. A shift to a project-based evaluation afforded parents (particularly mothers but also a small but growing number of fathers) afternoons with children in order to coach sport teams and chauffeur children to enrichment activities.

The other group was the working-class, dual-earner families where husbands were underemployed. These fathers had held blue-collar jobs before those jobs were eliminated by downsizing.[5] For these cou-

ples in particular, underemployment and/or major shifts in occupation and employer became a catalyst for reshaping—if not rethinking—traditional gender-based divisions of labor. These couples were crafting strategic responses to a turbulent and shifting labor market. Tag-team parenting typified by shift workers involved parents who worked opposite shifts in order to care for children themselves. Overlapping shift workers used a neighbor or family member for transition periods.

Couples in the upper middle class (who occupied positions often at the top of organizations and tended to have the most authority and responsibility for lower-level employees) were among the least likely to restructure their employment in order to adopt the new parenting approach. Though they might have chosen to seek alternative employment, few did, reasoning that they would have had to give up salient parts of their careers in the process of redefining their work and family goals. The other groups of couples less likely to adopt the new parenting approach to child care comprised those who worked in settings that were highly structured (inflexible) or highly demanding of their time.

In the following, I discuss two different situations where coparenting strategies are used to keep family at the center. In the first group, coparenting reflects beliefs about the importance of shared parenting itself. In the second situation, coparenting evolves as an option for keeping family at the center of daily life when both parents need to work outside the home (although some of these families might choose not to coparent if their economic circumstances were different).

Reorganizing employment to maximize parenting

This group of parents shared a belief that equal parental contributions to child care represented a superior solution to the market (for example, day care) or the mothers' complete withdrawal from the labor force. They believed that men and women should work outside and inside the home and share responsibility for child rearing. Individuals attempted to modify their jobs and employment commitments in order to regulate the demands that paid work makes and, thus, to restore some semblance of control—even if it meant loss of income.

Couples emphasized that men have historically been shortchanged as nurturers. Husbands talked about achieving parity with wives in their desire to experience fatherhood. Men modified their work schedules in order to be actively involved in child care. Usually they did this by working longer hours four days a week in order to have the fifth day to care for their child. Occasionally, this fifth day included taking the child to the office for a meeting or holding the meeting at home. But this reorganization of time did not lead to a cut in pay. For her part, the wife found a new, less demanding job working part-time three days a week. Not only did the individual spouses alter their work schedules, but the total number of hours the couple worked each week was reduced because of a

belief by the couple that both parents should be child oriented as a priority.

Underemployment as a route to shared parenting

The couples previously described arranged work scheduling to fit coparenting as a core belief. In this second dual-earner couple situation, the couples emphasized their belief in keeping family at the center. It was possible to observe couples implementing the new parenting approach in practice while not forsaking the ideology that only mothers are really capable of "maternal thinking" (Ruddick 1980). Indeed, oftentimes women with underemployed husbands struggled with the idea of sharing mothering. Still, many women whose husbands settled for jobs with less than full-time hours conceded that their husbands had mastered maternal practice. Husbands, in turn, frequently remarked that this approach to parenting was one they never imagined themselves doing.

Economic downturns and corporate downsizing in the 1980s (Hodson and Sullivan 1990) and major sectoral shifts in the mid-1990s led these couples to piece together new employment and child care arrangements from which active fathering was a by-product. These couples did not consciously choose to work less (and earn less) in order to do more for their children directly. They worried about a further erosion in their economic standing. Wives commonly worked in jobs in the service sector, particularly as caregivers such as nurses. Since many wives had secure jobs with benefits and some overtime, they often brought home a larger paycheck. Unable to find a comparable job to the one they had lost, many husbands were forced to take temporary, unskilled, or part-time work; others found entry-level jobs with a new employer and industry. Retraining programs, these men reported, had not led to well-paying full-time jobs comparable to the ones they had lost, even with the booming economy of the late 1990s. Both jobs may be important to the household economy, but the larger paycheck is symbolic of an inability to fulfill beliefs about one's identity.

One father, who was 39 years old with two children and who worked part-time as a home health aide, explained how his employment history had devolved:

I think [for] *many* of the long-term unemployed, [for] people like me who don't show up in the statistics, life goes on. So you do other things, you work part-time, either delivering pizza, which I did for three years, or bagging mail for the post office, whatever. But life goes on, so you have to adjust yourself because first of all, no one's gonna hire you. Once you're over 30, no one's gonna hire you for any real job. So what's the sense? . . . Your buddy who mows lawns for a living is offering you $10 an hour. So you do what you have to do. And you just fall into a whole other world that you forget exists when you worked for a large company, working 9-5 for six years.

The wife, aged 35, was a nurse who typically worked the night shift, from 7 p.m. to 7 a.m. She worried that, if she lost her overtime, she would have to find a second nursing job. (Not only did she not want to work a second job, but she would have preferred to stay home part-time, an unlikely reality in the near future.) She explained how underemployment had affected her husband's sense of masculinity: "And of course his ego was all shot to hell. He's not the family provider he wants to be and he's not doing exactly what he wanted, what he set in his mind. All his goals are rearranged."

Couples in which the wife was employed full-time while the husband was employed part-time often wished that the wife could opt to work fewer hours outside the home. Since she was the source of medical benefits, however, these couples were unable to reduce her employment to part-time without sacrificing these benefits. While middle-class white women continued to think of themselves as having the option of staying at home or entering the labor force, ideological and structural barriers prevented men from having similar choices (Gerson 1993).

Dual-earner couples: Summary

Regardless of which path they traveled to shared child care, the practice of new parenting transformed these men into more nurturing and sensitive caregivers who were teaching their young children how to navigate the world (Coltrane 1996). Indeed, it is ironic that many of the couples who are on the cutting edge of transforming maternal thinking are doing so not because of an ideological belief but as the result of constraints associated with corporate downsizing and economic restructuring. In both instances, however, couples rethink family life, particularly caring for children, as they cobble together identities that are no longer unidimensional. Underemployed couples continue to wish their home and work time could be more evenly divided but not because they wish wives would become full-time mothers.

SINGLE MOTHERS

The single mothers I discuss in this section were all economically self-sufficient and chose to parent without a partner. The majority described themselves as strongly committed to employment prior to motherhood. They had occupations as diverse as lawyers, corporate consultants, waitresses, and aerobics instructors. Most worked within the service sector in feminized occupations (such as nurses, secretaries, social workers, elementary school teachers). The remainder were self-employed and pieced together a living wage.

While single parents in general have been glossed over by researchers interested in work and family dilemmas, these women represent a potentially valuable source of insight into the effects of family on work. There are two reasons for this. First, family was highly valued by these women. This is powerfully portrayed in the stories the women told about the lengths to which they went to build a family (for example, enduring the uncertainties of donor insemination or the bureaucratic travails of trying to adopt as a single parent). Therefore, we should expect them to be quite dedicated to shaping em-

ployment to fit family. Second, single mothers have no one immediately available to share the tasks within the home or to shoulder the burden of earning a living. They have few easy ways to expand their financial resources, and the increase in financial costs that women experience when they double the size of their households is dramatic. For instance, child care for an infant at a day care center in metropolitan Boston is $12,000 per year (family day care is $8000 per year) and medical coverage for a family plan is usually triple the cost of an individual plan. (This leaves aside diapers, formula, car seats, strollers, and clothing, just to mention major items.) Therefore, single mothers are likely to have the least slack (the least flexible alternatives) in order to adjust family to the demands of work outside the home.

Regardless of income, these women believe themselves to be part of the middle class. This belief—even when it masks structural inequalities in the labor force—is important because it symbolizes a sense of having a future, not simply getting by from one paycheck to the next. As women said repeatedly, they worked hard to ensure that they were visible middle-class consumers. Reducing their income when children arrive—for all but the wealthiest women—would mean slipping down the economic ladder and potentially losing footing within the middle class. Cutting back, therefore, was not a viable solution (Hertz and Ferguson 1998).[6]

Like the dual-earner couples described in the preceding section who practiced the new parenting approach, these single mothers come from two very different points in the economic spectrum. First, there are the women who worked in top jobs in their chosen fields and who had spent years competing with their peers in dual-earner families (or childless peers). Once they wanted to start a family, they turned away from the attractions of job success that had motivated and rewarded them. Second, there are women who worked at the bottom of the labor force hierarchy and were employed in several part-time (sometimes full-time) jobs with no medical or child care benefits when their children were born. They had to keep (or find) one job with benefits or slip down the economic ladder and collect welfare and other subsidies. Slipping to welfare dependency went against the grain of their own values: these women had worked to keep themselves independent, and many were among the last of their high school girlfriends to have children.

Unlike the dual-earner couples, however, these single mothers have fewer resources internal to the family to call on in trying to balance work and family. They are more likely to cultivate external resources—in broader kin and friendship networks—to help them put family first. The implications of this form of community building will be taken up later, in the conclusion.

In the following, I discuss the three strategies adopted by these single mothers in order to place family life at the center: financing their own "mother time"; multiple jobs; and community supports.

Women professionals: Financing their own mother time

Armed with college and advanced degrees, these women professionals typically described themselves as workaholics prior to having children—always available to work extra hours. Once children arrived, however, they had to decide whether to set a more flexible work schedule or to reduce the inflated number of hours of "face time" that their work culture expected of them (see Landers, Rebitzer, and Taylor 1996). The work culture of competition and fear of job loss made it seem essential to be in the office from 7 a.m. till late at night. Often the last to leave the office, they used employment to fill the void of a family life.

When children arrived, many of the women cut back significantly on their work hours and, at least symbolically, demonstrated greater commitment to family over work. Quite a few took extended leaves. However, unlike Swedish families who take long parental leaves, the women in my study were financing their own parental leaves and extended periods of part-time work through savings they consciously set aside years before, knowing that someday they would have children. This gave them the time to be with their children without altering their lifestyles. When the savings ran low, they turned to credit card debt or reluctantly increased their work hours. To make up for lost mother time, they might spend their lunch hour with their child at the day care provider's.

Technical or professional skills sometimes allowed women who worked in larger organizations to argue for flexible arrangements, including working a shorter workweek (with longer days), or working part of the week in the office and part from home, or cutting back to limited travel. A manager who recently decided to change firms explained how this move enabled her to be an agent in shaping her work life, but she admitted that she could do this because of her advanced technical skills:

I'm going to have one-third of the number of people reporting to me than I used to and I'm going to walk out of work at 5:15 p.m. . . . And that was a very conscious choice. I didn't want a job that was going to consume me right now because I know that my priority needs to be taking care of Ben. . . . So it's constantly this balance of how much time at work and with my child. How deep does the foot go in? Is it the toe; up to the ankle; up to the knee? How deep am I in the work world with still my arms and my head free to be with Ben and it's a balance that I anticipate continually needing to adjust as the years play out.

However, in their attempts to strike a balance between work and family responsibilities, many traded off job advancement or opportunities for more interesting work projects in order to be out of the office by dinner time. The new goal is "streamlining": trying to "become more efficient" in order to "structure their work time better." But, since many of their managers measure time in the office—not work accomplished—the women who left early reported losing out, a trade-off they were willing to make. Sometimes they started their own businesses or freelanced on a project basis as a way to set their own

work hours and avoid the stress of a work culture that may be family friendly but not woman friendly.[7] Even the women who take on piece-rate projects, which they believe gives them independence from the dictates of corporate structures, know there are only so many hours they can shave off a day and still maintain their lifestyle. Some try to increase the rates they charge; others take a part-time job that carries medical benefits (a huge expense for the self-employed) and do contract work with the remaining allocated work hours each week.

Even more create income by turning assets like space in their homes to barter for services or rent. For instance, one woman lived in a large Victorian house with her child and retired father. When he died, however, they lost his contribution to the mortgage. Assessing her life, she decided she could either find a more lucrative job and be away from her daughter all day or turn the house into a seasonal inn. Turning space into economic value gave her continued autonomy from a more structured job situation and allowed her to blur the boundaries between work and family. Other women bought triple-decker buildings and rented out two of the apartments in order to reduce housing costs. Lacking the savings to purchase a building, others took in roommates in order to cut costs.

Women working multiple jobs

Good mothering for women who hold several jobs more closely resembles the experiences of minority and immigrant women in the United

States (as well as other mothers around the world). For these women, being a good provider and having a close family member care for a child is being a good mother (cf. Glenn, Nakano, and Forcey 1994, especially the chapters by Collins and Segura). For instance, one woman who was a day care provider at a for-profit day care center worked just under the number of hours necessary for her boss to pay her benefits. She had begun working at this center as an intern in high school, and by the time she had her child (at age 26) she had worked 10 years at the same workplace. With no benefits and an unpaid maternity leave, she took off a few weeks and then returned to work. Her child spent four days a week being cared for at her mother's home and three days a week at her own home. Without her mother's help, the cost would have made it impossible to remain employed. The day care center director gave this valued employee one free day a week of child care. The child did have medical coverage through the state, while the mother remained uninsured. To earn additional money, when her child was at her mother's, she baby- sat in the evenings, and during the summer on weekends she cleaned cottages at a vacation resort. Between her mother's ability to watch her child, the free day of child care, and the extra jobs, she managed to save money.

Those at the bottom of the labor force hierarchy, typically high-school-educated women, worked long hours and often held several part-time jobs from which they derived no benefits. Prior to having a child, they cared about piecing together enough hours of work to live decently.[8] Others worked day jobs and then night jobs (for instance, during the day they worked as an administrative assistant, and then they waitressed at night or worked as phone operators for a catalogue company). Working two or three jobs in this fashion in the Boston area gave women incomes of $25,000-$30,000 a year with no benefits, making them vulnerable labor force participants.

With the arrival of a child, however, benefits become essential. Making good money without benefits might be doable without a child, but having a child can dramatically change one's financial situation from independence to welfare dependence in a matter of months. The majority of women who parent without a partner do not have the choice of leaving the labor force. Besides a brief maternity leave (and even these may be forfeited if unpaid), these women have no option but to work for income. Some women go the route of expanding their work hours by working multiple jobs, but extra hours spent at work is a disheartening trade-off for time spent with children. Moreover, they are likely to earn entry-level wages, and the extra jobs are usually seasonal or erratic.

When workplaces do not give all their employees benefits (such as health care), these women turn to government subsidies (such as Medicaid), which are a necessary but poor substitute. In my study, those women without families to help out were likely to resort to collecting welfare until they could reorganize their lives to hold a job and parent a child at the same time. Every woman in this study who received welfare also went to two-year college programs with the hopes of acquiring skills that would get them out of the cycle of multiple jobs and hired into a job with advancement and benefits.

In short, every mother in this study wanted to reduce work hours. They cut back at work if it did not lead to downward mobility. Some who found that they could not make ends meet once children grew older took the children to their extra jobs (such as housecleaning and baby-sitting). These women took these extra jobs despite their personal cost because the chosen lifestyle—for the poorest women, remaining off of state aid—required a minimum level of cash available only through paid work.

Creating a support network

Single mothers cannot expand their time available for parenting or their income to support their families by crafting an arrangement with a family partner—because there is no partner. Therefore, as I found in my study, single employed mothers are apt to create networks of external re-sources (that is, external to their household) to substitute for the flexibility afforded to dual-earner couples. For example, nearby relatives are frequently tapped for child care; when kin are not available (as happens far more frequently these days), fictive kin like godparents are woven into the family as sources of spiritual and material support. Even more creatively, single mothers often build

a "repertory family" (Hertz and Ferguson 1997) by pulling together an ensemble of people who provide some combination of emotional and psychological support, economic contributions, and performance of routine household chores and maintenance. This way, they spread the risk of losing a key person by having a network of people in their lives.

The women I found to be most likely to create an external support network were those employed in female-dominated occupations earning wages at the border of the working and middle classes. They were highly social, resourceful, and adept at relationship building. Many of these women had or sought out middle-class sponsorship—help from other women they had met through previous jobs—particularly in sustaining a modicum of middle-class social and cultural opportunities for their children, such as invitations to birthday parties, inclusion in car pools and sports leagues, and participation in community events. Finally, they were skilled at finding "pennies from heaven," that is, at establishing rapport by revealing their circumstances to people they trusted who sometimes became significant gift-givers (Hertz and Ferguson 1998).

CONCLUSION

The objective of this article was to study the effect of family on work by comparing the experiences of two distinctly different family forms: dual-earner couples who had adopted an egalitarian approach to parenting and women who had chosen to become parents without marital partners. These families, I suggested, were most likely to offer insight into the way family is made to have priority over employment. Two conclusions, deserving of additional study, should be emphasized.

First, most parents either have or evolve a belief system about how children should be raised—whether, for example, mothers should work outside the home while children are toddlers—but not all families have the means or the opportunity to enact those beliefs. Indeed, the very concept of balancing work and family may be better viewed as a euphemism for competing ideologies about child rearing. Positioning in the external labor market and, more specifically, within a particular organization's internal labor market strongly influences whether individual women and men implement (or even contemplate implementing) their ideologies about parenting. People employed in a workplace with flexible hours and benefits are freer to live out their beliefs about parenting. When flexible work schedules or work-related benefits are not available, it is far more difficult for mothers and fathers to actively parent even when they want to.

Second, ideology is important, but benefits matter. While women with professional training or job skills, regardless of marital status, may be able to negotiate individual deals for themselves on the basis of their own value or nonsubstitutability to the organization, couples with two high-status jobs have a major source of leverage not available to single mothers: that is, the cushion (or indirect advantage) that derives from the other spouse's benefits package (and paycheck). The couple can decide how to distribute their combined time between paid work and parenting, or one spouse can decide to go solo and open up a business. As long as one partner has benefits, the other can create flexibility, including staying home with children or starting up a business. Thus, while marriage may constrain the unbridled pursuit of one career to the possible disadvantage of the other, it also buffers the negative impacts of reversals in one or the other career. The practice of combining two careers—not the articulation of a nonsexist ideology—shapes decisions and informs change (Hertz 1986).

The couple can make decisions that might not be deemed optimal from the perspective of individual employers. Put differently, the couple is utilizing two work organizations even though it may appear to the employer that only the individual is making the decision. Gender is not the determining factor as to which partner might decide to try something different. Passion or vocation is more likely to be the concern between spouses when one decides to become an entrepreneur, a consistent finding in my studies of dual-earner couples since 1986. But if both spouses remain in traditional organizations, the wives will more likely (though not always, as the new parenting approach demonstrates) be the ones to ask for part-time or flexible work arrangements. Therefore, these couples are able to exercise their family and child care ideologies in ways that single mothers (divorced or unwed) with the same human capital and similar child care ideology cannot.

Unwed single mothers who have professional and managerial careers are more likely to take longer maternity leaves in order to be with their hard-won children, and they are more likely to think up creative solutions to deal with organizations that demand either on-site constant face-time or frequent client-related travel; both work cultures limit the ability of parents to parent. These women may become the new entrepreneurs because of their organizing skills. They are more likely than their dual-earner peers to believe that raising children is not solely the responsibility of parents, but that workplaces and communities need to provide an adequate supply of day care slots for children—not just model day care for a few employees. For instance, communities need to rethink lengthening the school year and providing after-school programs as an accepted reality in community life so that children can keep up with the amount of information and skills essential to successfully entering the labor force but also so that parents are not constantly forced to make ad hoc arrangements for half days and school vacations. After-school programs have become the new neighborhoods our children play in; these programs need not simply a paid staff but community volunteers— perhaps retired individuals—who can share special talents and vocations with the young. In this regard,

privatized corporate day care has been more willing to operate during hours that are more accommodating to parents. Once children enter school, parents complain about the quality of public school education (shortened school days and year), which continues to ignore the needs of employed parents. Ironically, work sites may have day care on the premises, but the supply of slots may not equal the demand for care for children under school age. Nevertheless, we have begun to find ways to enhance parents' employment when their children are very young. Through public education, communities must take the next step from kindergartens that end by 11 a.m. to schools that end by 2 p.m.

For those dual-earner parents of preschool children and for younger couples who have experienced downsizing and underemployment—similar to single mothers—the lack of benefits is crucial. Benefits are crucial for all families but particularly those who, without spouses, manage to make a living through piecing together a variety of jobs. A world in which benefits existed for everyone would give families more choice in how to position themselves in the workplace. New employment alternatives (in some cases, new employment alternatives mean unconventional jobs and employment contracts; in others "new" just means different jobs in the same organization) are important if people are to feel they have a choice. If they are unsatisfied as a couple with work arrangements, family life becomes stressful, and work, simply clocked hours to pay the bills. Remember the nurse who wanted to stay home part-time but worked extra shifts because her husband could not find a job with adequate benefits.

In this regard, the unit of analysis is the couple, not the individual work site. Cafeteria-style benefits may allow couples to choose from the alternatives provided by two different workplaces to maximize their ability to spend time with children. But, as a society, we must also acknowledge that an important and growing part of the labor force is and will be single parents who need ways to be productive employees and good mothers: this recognition may force communities to become more than empty spaces and, instead, to become places where children can be left in safe environments so mothers can become and remain self-sufficient.

The aim of this article has been to highlight families that have tended to be overlooked in research on work-family issues and to better understand why and how they may shape their work lives to fit their beliefs about family. As I have tried to show, ideologies about family and coparenting motivated employed parents to develop creative strategies to keep family at the center. At the same time, close examination of how these families put family first demonstrates that work-family policies and programs rarely address the broader meaning of balancing work and family life. Indeed, it may rest with employees to collectively alter the future of workplace cultures by placing families first—rather than waiting for policies (public or private) to address their needs.

Notes

1. The data for the dual-earner study were collected between 1993 and 1995 in Massachusetts. Husbands and wives were interviewed in-depth separately but simultaneously. A total of 36 percent of the couples were working class; the other three-fifths were middle and upper middle class. See Hertz 1997 for a more complete description of sampling and methods. The single mothers are part of an ongoing data collection. The first wave of data, collected between 1995 and 1997, was based upon in-depth interviews with 52 single mothers stratified by route to motherhood. With social class defined by education, occupation, and income, currently the sample is 24 percent working class and 76 percent middle class. See Hertz and Ferguson 1998 for a more complete description of sampling and methods.

2. For the 837 major U.S. employers that provided information about work-family benefits in the 1990-91 Hewitt Associates SpecBook (*Work and Family Benefits* 1991), child care was the most prevalent benefit: 64 percent of the employers offered some kind of child care assistance to their employees; 89 percent of those who offered child care assistance offered dependent care spending accounts; and 41 percent offered resource and referral services. Only 9 percent of the employers provided an employer-sponsored child care center. Elder care programs were more limited: only 32 percent of the employers provided assistance to their employees. Of those providing elder care assistance, 88 percent offered dependent care spending accounts.

3. Flextime is a catchall category including time alterations ranging from arriving or leaving a half hour earlier than the official start or end of the work day, to broad blocks of time away from the workplace (for example, in the middle of the day) or banking time for use as time off in the future. Flexible scheduling arrangements are offered by 54 percent of the employers in the 1990-91 Hewitt Associates SpecBook (*Work and Family Benefits* 1991). The most common arrangements offered by these employers are flextime (provided by 76 percent of the employers) and part-time employment (provided by 67 percent of the employers). But fewer employers had scheduling on an individual basis (4 percent), work at

home (15 percent), compressed work schedules (23 percent), or job sharing (31 percent).

4. In the 1950s, the archetypal family had a stay-at-home wife, who was responsible for the children and chores. Today, only 14 percent of U.S. households consist of a married couple where only the husband earns income. The dual-earner and single-parent families of today can no longer count on a family member's running the household and taking care of the needs of each member. The most visible evidence of a changing family structure is reflected in women's workforce participation. In 1993, fully 60 percent of all women with children under age 6 worked for pay. Of those women with children aged 6 to 17 years, 75 percent were employed. This represents a marked increase from 1966, when 44 percent of women with children this age were employed (Hayghe and Bianchi 1994).

5. See Bluestone and Rose 1997 on the divided labor force.

6. The median income for the 52 women in this study was $40,000 per year, which approximated the median income for all families in Massachusetts (U.S. Bureau of the Census 1993, 23-145).

7. Family-friendly policies apply to both men and women. However, since women are more likely than men to actually care for family members, women pay a price in terms of face time, overtime, and other symbolic expressions of organizational commitment. They may do the actual job just as well as men but still be perceived as less dedicated to the job or the company.

8. It is beyond the scope of this article to discuss the economics of the part-time worker, but, clearly, not offering compensation benefits reduces the organization's costs.

References

Bluestone, Barry and Stephen Rose. 1997. Overworked and Underemployed: Unraveling an Economic Enigma. *American Prospect* 31(Mar.-Apr.):58-69.

Catalyst. 1997. *A New Approach to Flexibility: Managing the Work / Time Equation*. New York: Catalyst.

Coltrane, Scott. 1996. *Family Man: Fatherhood, Housework, and Gender Equity*. New York: Oxford University Press.

Coontz, Stephanie. 1992. *The Way We Never Were*. New York: Basic Books.

Garey, Anita Ilta. 1995. Constructing Motherhood on the Night Shift: "Working Mothers" as "Stay at Home Mom." *Qualitative Sociology* 18 (4):415-37.

Gerson, Kathleen. 1993. *No Man's Land: Men's Changing Commitments to Family and Work*. New York: Basic Books.

Glenn, Evelyn, Grace Chang Nakano, and Linda Rennie Forcey, eds. 1994. *Mothering: Ideology, Experience and Agency*. New York: Routledge.

Hayghe, Howard V. and Suzanne M. Bianchi. 1994. Married Mothers' Work Patterns: The Job-Family Compromise. *Monthly Labor Review* 117(6):24-30.

Hertz, Rosanna. 1986. *More Equal than Others: Women and Men in Dual-Career Marriages*. Berkeley: University of California Press.

———. 1997. A Typology of Approaches to Child Care: The Centerpiece of Organizing Family Life for Dual-Earner Couples. *Journal of Family Issues* 18(4):355-85.

Hertz, Rosanna and Joy Charlton. 1989. Making Family under a Shiftwork Schedule: Air Force Security Guards and Their Wives. *Social Problems* 36:491-507.

Hertz, Rosanna and Faith I. Ferguson. 1997. Kinship Strategies and Self-Sufficiency among Single Mothers by Choice: Post Modern Family Ties. *Qualitative Sociology* 20(2):187-227.

———. 1998. Only One Pair of Hands: Ways That Single Mothers Stretch Work and Family Resources. *Community, Work and Family* 1(1):13-37.

Hochschild, Arlie Russell. 1997. *The Time Bind: When Work Becomes*

Home and Home Becomes Work. New York: Metropolitan Books.

Hodson, Randy and Teresa Sullivan. 1990. *The Social Organization of Work*. Belmont, CA: Wadsworth.

Landers, Renee M., James B. Rebitzer, and Lowell J. Taylor. 1996. Rat Race Redux: Adverse Selection in the Determination of Work Hours in Law Firms. *American Economic Review* 86(3):329-48.

Presser, Harriet B. 1988. Shiftwork and Childcare Among Young Dual-Earner American Parents. *Journal of Marriage and the Family* 50:133-48.

Presser, Harriet B. and V. S. Cain. 1983. Shiftwork Among Dual-Earner Couples with Children. *Science* 219:876-79.

Ruddick, Sara. 1980. Maternal Thinking. *Feminist Studies* 6(3):343-67.

U.S. Bureau of the Census. 1993. *Population Profile of the U.S. Current Population Reports*, Special Series.

Work and Family Benefits Provided by Major U.S. Employers in 1990-91. 1991. Hewitt Associates SpecBook.

ANNALS, *AAPSS*, **562**, March 1999

Work-Family Backlash:
Begging the Question, What's Fair?

By MARY B. YOUNG

ABSTRACT: This article examines current work-family practice and scholarship in light of recent demographic shifts that make employees without children under age 18 the predominant group in the workforce. One consequence of this change is work-family backlash, a controversy over the fundamental issue of what is fair. Organizational justice theory helps illuminate the deep assumptions that underlie both corporate work-life policies and employees' perceptions of their fairness, as data from a qualitative study of work-life issues show. Organizational justice theory can also make a significant contribution to work-family research.

Mary Young, D.B.A., is a researcher, consultant, and writer on workplace issues and trends. She has taught organizational behavior in the M.B.A. Program at Boston University, from which she received her doctorate.

NOTE: The author gratefully acknowledges the help of Dr. Neal Fogg at Northeastern University's Center for Labor Market Studies.

OVER the past decade, work-family has become a well-established area of both corporate practice and academic research. Yet new demographic trends have begun to challenge the field's established parameters. This article will describe how recent demographic changes raise fundamental questions about fairness in corporate policies and necessitate that researchers broaden their scope.

THE WORK-FAMILY FIELD AND CHANGING EMPLOYEE DEMOGRAPHICS

Corporate work-family programs have expanded and multiplied since the late 1980s (Galinsky and Friedman 1991). During the same time period, work-family scholarship has developed (Zedeck 1992; Lilly, Pitt-Catsouphes, and Googins 1997). Both arenas of work-family activity—corporate practice and academic research—have proceeded from two assumptions that this article will challenge.

The first assumption—that employees are, by and large, married and raising children—is increasingly out of sync with the actual demographics of the workforce. According to the Current Population Survey, the percentage of the U.S. workforce who are married declined from 72 percent in 1970 to 59 percent in 1996. The percentage of workforce members living with one or more children (under 18 years of age) has also declined, from 53 percent in 1970 to 42 percent in 1996.

These shifting trends are likely to continue. According to the U.S. Census Bureau, childless households will increase 50 percent between 1996 and 2005 (Society for Human Resources Management 1996b). A subset of that childless group, married couples with no children, is expected to increase 29 percent between 1990 and 2000 (Future of American Households 1993). A second subset, employees without spouses or children, has been called one of the fastest-growing segments of the workforce (Society for Human Resources Management 1996b). After the year 2005, according to Census Bureau projections, the most common households in the United States will be those occupied by a single person or a married couple without children (Society for Human Resources Management 1996b).

Why is the workforce undergoing these changes? A convergence of factors related to marriage and childbearing, longevity, and careers has produced the new demographic profile. Today, men and women in the United States marry an average of four years later than in 1955 (Crispell 1994) and a significant proportion of marriages (about 40 percent in the 1990s) end in divorce. For both these reasons, a larger percentage of the workforce is not married than was true a generation ago. Moreover, a growing number of adults will never marry: 44.2 million in 1994, more than twice the number in 1970 (Society for Human Resources Management 1996a). In addition, the age of women's first childbearing has risen by nearly two years—from 22.1 from 1970 through 1974 to 23.9 years in 1990-94. One in six women, according to *American Demographics*, will never have children (Crispell 1993). As an increasing number of baby boomers' offspring reach age 18, the percentage of childless, married employees in the workforce will continue to swell.[1] For all these reasons, most people will spend one, often several, periods of their adulthood unmarried and without children.

Moreover, due to increased longevity and financial need, some workers are continuing in paid employment longer than had been true in the past, thereby increasing the number of widowed and/or childless members of the workforce. For all these reasons, the married and parent segments are becoming smaller.

The second assumption challenged by the changing workforce follows logically from the first. This assumption is that family—that is, spouse, children, and other relatives—is the primary force that pulls employees mentally, emotionally, or physically away from the workplace. Recent figures belie that. Even among the 42 percent of the U.S. workforce living in a household with children, only some are parents. Some are older siblings (over age 18), adult relatives, or nonfamily members. In any case, a minority of U.S. workers are parents and/or live with children.

What about elder care? The Families and Work Institute's *1997 National Study of the Changing Workforce* found that 13 percent of U.S. wage and salary workers were currently providing special assistance to someone 65 years or older, although roughly twice as many (25 percent) had done so during the preceding year. One in five parents were pro-

viding both child care and elder care (Bond, Galinsky, and Swanberg 1998). Although the percentage of employees with elder care responsibilities is likely to increase as baby boomers age, they are currently a minority of the workforce.

Further evidence suggests that dependent care is not the only reason—and at some work sites, not even the main reason—for employees' work-life conflicts. A 1997 study of Baxter Healthcare Corporation employees (Campbell and Koblenz 1997) found that, while mothers were the most likely to work restricted work hours, it was men aged 30-39—and, at some company locations, married, dual-income employees without children, single employees, and workers under age 30—who were most likely to have searched for a job in hopes of reducing work-and-life conflicts. While 44 percent of respondents did not have children, 88 percent agreed that work and personal life responsibilities sometimes conflicted with each other. Moreover, 40 percent of those working an average of 40-45 hours per week said they were not comfortable with their work-life balance. These findings suggest that work-life conflicts are not restricted to a specific employee population but are widespread.

The Baxter study also suggests that, even among employees with child care or elder care responsibilities, these are not the primary source of work-life conflict. Less than 15 percent of survey respondents said that better child care and elder care assistance would ease their work-life conflicts. In fact, assistance with elder and child care ranked 12th on a list of 13 choices for reducing work-life conflicts. The number one response was being able to "work some days at home on a regular basis."

What are employees' most important nonwork concerns? Asked to name factors that limit their availability for work, Baxter employees listed their personal limits on how many hours they were willing to work, spouse's work, fitness, pursuit of education, a second job, and commuting—as well as child and elder care.

The preceding discussion has challenged two common assumptions on which both work-family practice and scholarship are premised: the notion that families (traditionally, one or more parents living with one or more children) are the most common household unit for members of the U.S. workforce, and the notion that dependent care is the primary work-life issue with which employees grapple. The next section will survey current work-family practice and scholarship in light of these questionable assumptions.

THE WORK-FAMILY FIELD TODAY

Employers began introducing family-friendly programs and policies in the late 1980s in response to the growing number of dual-career couples and single mothers in the workforce. Organizational researchers also responded to this trend with a new field of research, work-family, an outgrowth of scholarship in human resources and careers. While both practice and research have broadened over the past decade,

their scope remains somewhat narrow.

Practice

"Work-family programs" has evolved in recent years toward the more inclusive term "work-life programs." Many companies now offer educational programs—on elder care issues and housing-and-tenant rights, for example—that cut across employee groups. Others have expanded their offerings to meet the needs of diverse age groups, from young unmarrieds (tuition reimbursement) and young couples (financial assistance for home buying and parental leaves), to middle-age workers (investment workshops) and seniors (retirement-planning sessions). However, based on anecdotal evidence—for example, presentations and informal discussions at conferences of work-life professionals—it appears that child care continues to be the primary concern or passion of many work-life professionals. Research has found that many employees perceive that work-life programs are intended primarily for parents (Young 1997a). Parents continue to make greater use of benefits such as flexible work schedules than do nonparents (Young 1997a, 1997b; Parkinson 1996). Therefore, despite companies' adoption of more inclusive terminology and programs, actual practice appears to lag behind.

These two factors—the continued emphasis on child and other dependent care issues in organizational practice and the greater utilization of work-life benefits by parents as compared to nonparents—have given rise to a countermovement. "Work-family backlash" is the popular term describing childless employees' claim that they are penalized in the workplace in the following ways. They are expected to work additional hours and to fill in for parents whose child care responsibilities require them to leave work. They subsidize parental benefits such as dependent health care, insurance, and, at some companies, child care. While they may have equal access to elder care benefits, they may not qualify for other work-life programs such as flexible work arrangements or unpaid leaves.

First gaining voice in the early 1990s and reaching a crescendo later in the decade, work-family backlash has become a frequent topic in the popular media (for example, Shellenbarger 1997; Flynn 1996; Williams 1994). While there have been no academic studies of work-family backlash, there has been other, nonacademic research on the topic. In a survey of 78 companies conducted by the Conference Board (Parkinson 1996), 75 percent said that childless employees carry more of the workload than do parents, and 57 percent said the company was not adequately addressing childless employees' needs. While 74 percent believed that concerns about work-family backlash were exaggerated, 56 percent disagreed that childless employees harbored no resentment against employees with children. Similarly, 80 percent of respondents in a 1996 *Personnel Journal* survey agreed that single employees were being left out of work-family programs; 81 percent believed that single employees "end up carrying more of the burden than married employees" (Flynn

1996, 60). Employees without children are also less likely to ask their boss or coworkers for informal accommodations when their personal lives conflict with the demands of work, for fear they will be viewed negatively (Young 1997a; Flynn 1996; Murray 1996).

Scholarship

While "work-life" has become the standard terminology among practitioners, "work-family" remains the most common rubric used by scholars. More important than its name, however, is the continued inattention of this field of scholarship to single and childless employees, as illustrated by the following examples. In a recently published annotated bibliography of work-family research (Lilly, Pitt-Catsouphes, and Googins 1997), marriage and dependent care issues predominate. A search conducted using an electronic database for work-family researchers generated 57 entries referring to single or unmarried employees; all but three of these focused on single parents. A similar search, this time on the topic of childless people, also identified just three publications. While neither Lilly, Pitt-Catsouphes, and Googins (1997) nor the electronic database (developed and maintained by the Center for Work & Family at Boston College) claims to be an exhaustive review of the literature, they reflect scholars' overall focus on issues related to child care and, to a lesser degree, elder care. The conclusion that work-family researchers are primarily interested in so-called traditional family issues is supported by the roster of papers presented at the 1998 Academy of Management meeting. Of three relevant conference sessions, one focused on "work family research" and one was called "The Personal Becomes Professional (and Vice Versa): Managing Work-Family Relationships." A third session, titled "Work and Personal Life," offered four papers, all but one of which addressed "work-family" issues. This nearly exclusive focus on marriage and parenting runs deeper than the session titles. For example, the four papers presented in the session on "managing work-family relationships" dealt, respectively, with work and marital satisfaction, husbands' and wives' work time, dual-career couples, and work-family supportive practices.

Clearly, there is a disconnect between the growing number of employees without children—and, within that population, the growing number of people who are single— and the limited attention that both practitioners and scholars have paid to these workers. In the workplace, work-family backlash is the most palpable consequence thus far, although the Society for Human Resources Management (1996b) predicts that discrimination suits may follow. Other consequences may be more serious for employers. Research has found that employees' perceptions about the supportiveness of their workplace are strongly related to their job satisfaction, commitment, and retention (Bond, Galinsky, and Swanberg 1998). If one segment of the workforce (such as parents) views the company as supportive but a majority of the workforce (such as nonparents) feel less supported, employers may be losing a significant share of employee commitment and retention. Finally, while the consequences for work-life scholars are less serious than for employers, their failure to address changing demographics is nonetheless a significant shortcoming.

One logical approach for redressing the disconnect between current practice and research, on one hand, and employee demographics, on the other, would be additive: add new work-life programs and expand the scope of work-family studies to include a more diverse workforce. These would be positive steps. However, such measures would not address a fundamental question that underlies all work-life programs and benefits: What's fair? The remainder of this article will examine fairness through the lens of organizational justice theory. First, it will summarize basic elements of organizational justice theory. Then it will use an organizational justice framework to analyze data from a qualitative study of work-life issues at two companies. Finally, it will suggest how organizational justice theory can contribute to both practice and research in the work-life field.

ORGANIZATIONAL JUSTICE
THEORY: AN OVERVIEW

A Fair Shake for Single Workers
    —*Chicago Tribune*, 20 April 1998

Childless Workers Fume over Kids' Stuff
    —*Sunday Boston Herald*,
          14 December 1997

Employees Without Kids Say They Have Lives, Too
    —*USA Today*, 11 November 1997

Behind the headlines (such as the foregoing) and the popular depiction of work-family backlash lie several important questions: What's fair? On what basis should work-life benefits be allocated? Should all employees have equal access to flexible work arrangements and leaves, or are these special considerations made available to special populations such as parents? In short, are work-life benefits—or even work-life balance—an entitlement? Or are they special accommodations—and, if so, who should qualify for them?

Since fairness is the central issue in work-family backlash, a theory that addresses the fair distribution of resources and rewards would seem to provide a relevant framework for work-life scholarship. Organizational justice theory, long established and well developed by scholars working outside the work-family tradition—both in organizational studies (see Greenberg 1990 for a review) and in other disciplines such as law (Thibaut and Walker 1975)—offers such a framework.

Organizational justice is "a descriptive theory about how people make judgments about what is fair or unfair and what they do with those judgments" (Sheppard, Lewicki, and Minton 1992, 3). Theorists have delineated three forms of organizational justice. Two are distributive justice, which relates to the fairness of the outcomes, and procedural justice, which relates to the perceived fairness of the processes by which the outcomes are decided (Greenberg 1990). A more recent development in organizational justice theory was the identification of interpersonal treatment, or how the employee perceives that he or she has been treated (Bies 1987; Tyler 1987). Politeness, consideration, respect, and dignity are aspects of treatment that shape perceptions regarding interpersonal justice (Greenberg 1990).

Research has demonstrated the impacts of each of these forms of fairness. Across numerous studies, procedural justice was related to an individual's feelings (such as commitment) toward the organization (Lambert 1991, 1997), while distributive justice was associated with satisfaction with the outcome (Folger and Konovsky 1989). While research on interpersonal justice is limited, some studies (discussed in Greenberg 1990) found that, when promised pay was abruptly reduced, subsequent stealing and turnover varied according to the interpersonal treatment people received when the pay cut was announced. Given the fact that all of these outcomes—satisfaction, commitment, trust, retention, and employee theft—have significant impacts on organizations, justice appears to be an important consideration for employers.

Organizational justice theory has also investigated how people decide what is fair. Three principles of fairness have been identified as informing perceived fairness (Deutsch 1975, 1985): equity, equality, and need. The equity principle is the assumption that rewards and resource allocations should be dependent upon merit (for example, past performance) or rank. The equality principle holds that everyone should receive the same allocation, regardless of performance or other contingencies. The need principle calls for allocating rewards and resources on the basis of individual circumstances.

Fairness principles, it should be emphasized, operate at a tacit level. Typically, people are unaware that their perceptions reflect one or more basic assumptions about fairness that may or may not be shared by others.

The fairly common practice of distributing free turkeys to employees at Thanksgiving is an illustration of the fairness principles in action. Typically, every employee receives a turkey of roughly the same quality and size. This practice is an expression of the equality principle. If the equity principle were in use, however, executives and high performers might receive larger, free-range, fresh turkeys while average and below-average workers would have smaller, frozen birds. If the need principle were enacted, only employees with challenging personal circumstances (for example, a large family or an out-of-work spouse) would receive this benefit.

It is easy to see that different principles produce significantly different outcomes. Different principles also produce different perceptions about the fairness of any turkey-allocation process. An employee whose assumption differs from that of company policymakers might feel that both the grounds for distributing turkeys (procedural justice) and the actual outcome of the annual turkey giveaway (distributive justice) were unfair. Moreover, if the employee also felt that the company was cavalier or insensitive in explaining its turkey policy, he or she might also feel unfairly treated (interpersonal justice).

Why do individuals choose one fairness principle over others? Researchers (for example, Cohen 1991; James 1993; Lerner 1977; Mannix, Neale, and Northcraft 1995) have identified factors at many levels—contextual, interpersonal, and individual—that influence which assumptions people apply to assess the fairness of a benefit or reward.

Empirical studies have examined the fairness of pay decisions (Folger and Konovsky 1989), job title (Greenberg and Ornstein 1983), office-space assignments (Greenberg 1993), and layoffs (Brockner and Greenberg 1990). Only one study, to date, has applied the organizational justice framework to work-life benefits. Grover (1991) studied employee perceptions about the fairness of parental-leave policies. The research found that being of childbearing age, having children, and holding positive views toward women were positively related to positive views of parental-leave fairness. Grover concluded that employees who might benefit directly from such a policy—either now or in the future—or who were similar to the policy's beneficiaries viewed the need-based parental-leave policy as more fair than did other employees.

Popular descriptions of work-family backlash suggest that many employees have strong feelings—ranging from resentment to appreciation and loyalty—about the allocation of formal and informal work-life benefits. Fairness becomes a particular concern when employees perceive that expectations about work time and time away from work vary within the same organization, depending on such factors as the supervisor, the department or functional area, the hierarchical level, and the employee's gender and life status (Young 1997a). For these reasons, organizational justice theory seems particularly relevant.

APPLYING ORGANIZATIONAL JUSTICE THEORY TO WORK-LIFE POLICIES

Grover's 1991 study suggests that organizational justice theory can provide a useful framework for categorizing the underlying principles that inform work-life practice. In the following examples, which are part of a larger study (Young 1997a) and are taken from employee focus groups at an insurance company and a financial services firm, there is further evidence that employees invoke the three fairness principles to assess the fairness of work-life practices.

Equity

A financial services manager observes,

Our budgets are pretty tight now so I can't compensate people the way I'd like to. But if they have a doctor's appointment or they need to come in late, these are things I *can* control. Money I can't. My secretary has some health problems so he works on weekends and comes in at night. That's something I can control that he really, really appreciates.

Unable to reward her secretary financially, this manager grants him work-time flexibility in exchange for his good performance. In her view, the reward should be earned rather than allocated equally to everyone or awarded on the basis of need.

In another example from the same company, a group of middle managers were discussing work-time flexibility at higher levels of the organization:

Man #1: You're saying the higher up you go, the less strict the standard is about when you have to be in the office?

Man #2: I think so. It seems that way.

Man #3: I would think the higher you go up, it comes down to a dollar-and-cents type of thing, who brings in how much.

Man #2: Everything's numbers. Black and white.

Man #3: How much new business did this person bring in? How many referrals? The higher up you move I think, you kind of get away from, "Who's here at 6 p.m.?"

These men seem to agree that the freedom to monitor one's own hours (a rare privilege in this company) comes as a result of hierarchical level and achievement (making one's financial goals). Both rank-based benefits are expressions of the equity principle.

Equality

An insurance company employee noted,

One of the things my boss said was that you can move to this kind of schedule if you have a compelling reason to do that, but [not if you don't] . . . which I actually don't think is fair. I think that *everyone* should have an opportunity to work 3-4 days a week if they can afford to do it.

The employee was arguing in opposition to his boss (an advocate of the need principle) that everyone should have the same access to a flexible schedule. His views are consistent with the equality principle.

A financial services employee described a different version of the equality principle: in his work group, no one was exempt from the expectation of working late. He observed, "My boss's boss, he doesn't care. If he walks around the floor at 6:30 in the evening, he's curious who's here working. He doesn't care if you're married. He doesn't care if you're single. He doesn't care if you have kids. The fact is, ARE YOU HERE?"

As these examples illustrate, the equality principle can be applied in one of two ways: everyone gets the same desired benefit (as in the first case) or everyone gets no benefit (as in the second).

Need

One supervisor opined, "You don't have to treat everyone the same. You have to treat everyone *fairly*." This supervisor advocated that managers take personal circumstances into consideration in deciding what is fair, rather than applying the same rules to everyone. The downside of this approach was expressed by another supervisor, who argued that equality is a more expedient principle to apply.

Managers just don't want to have to deal with judging what's reasonable and what's not. . . . That takes conversation, it takes communication, it takes time, it takes flexibility—and that all takes away from . . . the real productive time in the day. If they let it in, they have to deal with it. It's easier just to say, "Don't do that."

The preceding section demonstrates how organizational justice theory can be applied to the issue of work time and work-family practices. It illustrates that the three fairness principles informed employees' perceptions. Using organizational justice theory can also produce an even more finely grained analysis of fairness perceptions regarding work-life practice.

Previous research (Deutsch 1975) has shown that the same person can invoke multiple criteria (for example, need as well as equality) in the same or different situations. The focus group data support this conclusion. In the following exchange, financial services employees debate which justice principle(s) should be applied in work-time decision making.

Man: "Everybody's situation's different, and you have to acknowledge that. What's going to affect me, or cause me to come in late sometime, is not going to affect [her] or [her] or anybody else. There may be similar circumstances, but everyone's situation is different. You need the recognition that everyone's going to have this, so . . . it's equal, even though the circumstances, the cause [is different]. [Equality principle]

Facilitator: Oh, in other words, the overall picture is equal and everyone gets the same thing. It's not dependent upon what the individual circumstances are.

Man: Right, Exactly.

Woman: (long pause with in-drawn breath) Except, if you have children, I would say for instance that may happen more often. [Need principle]

Man: Single people, too. The single people I know go to school at night or . . . [Need principle]

Woman (talking over Man): I suppose it's the ones that don't have *anything* [laughs loudly] that are the ones that are embittered. [Need principle]

Another woman: [Our department's rule] is, if you get your job done [equity principle] and as long as you're here when you can be. [Need principle]

This example not only illustrates that different employees subscribe to different principles. It also shows that the same principle (in this case, need) is subject to different interpretations. The man argues that single people, too, have needs. One woman feels that some needs take precedence over others. Finally, the dialogue illustrates a fundamental problem endemic to need-based policies: members of one group may not understand another group's needs or value them as equally deserving as their own.

Thus far, the discussion of fairness has shown that different employees apply different principles to assess fairness, each principle having different implications for their assessment of work-life practices; the same individual may invoke more than one fairness principle; and the same

principle may be subject to different interpretations. The focus group data also suggest that individuals may hold fast to personal criteria for judging fairness even when organizational guidelines specify that a different principle applies. A supervisor's comments demonstrate this point:

If you look at the guidelines [regarding release time for parents to visit their children's schools], [they are] basically for those who have children. I don't think that way. I feel that if you can do that when you have children, if somebody else wants to volunteer their time, to me it's the same type of thing.

As these examples illustrate, there is no definitive answer to the question, What's fair? The fact that fairness judgments are based on implicit and unexamined assumptions helps explain why work-life practices may vary significantly from one work group to another in the same organization (Young 1997a) and why the same practice may provoke both discord and satisfaction in different individuals.

We now move from data analysis using a fairness framework to consider organizational justice's contributions to work-life theory and practice.

CONTRIBUTIONS TO RESEARCH

As Grover's research (1991) has demonstrated, perceptions about the fairness of a specific work-family policy (parental leave) can be predicted on the basis of employees' personal characteristics. The present analysis has argued that organizational theory is also useful for identifying fundamental assumptions—above and beyond personal characteristics—that influence employees' perceptions about the fairness of work-life policies.

In addition to these contributions, organizational justice theory also suggests the following questions for future research:

1. On what basis do organizations make work-life policy? That is, what are the underlying assumptions that inform these policies? Are they consistent with the fairness principles guiding the company's other benefit programs and with the company's overall values regarding its treatment of employees?

2. Which fairness principles are reflected in the way work-life policies are implemented in this organization? Research addressing this question would explore actual practices in comparison to formal policies.

3. Which fairness principles influence individuals' work-life decisions? That is, which principles guide behaviors such as when and how much they work, when they leave work, and whether they remain with the company?

4. Do employer-valued outcomes such as commitment and tenure differ when different fairness principles are in use?

5. Are individual or group characteristics (such as marital and parental status, age) related to which principles employees apply when judging work-life policies or making personal work-life decisions? Research on this question would test previous research findings about the influence

of group identification and social comparisons on employee assessments of fairness.

CONTRIBUTIONS TO PRACTICE

Organizational justice theory can also make a useful contribution to organizations and individuals. First, organizational justice theory provides a lens through which companies can examine the assumptions underlying their policies. It can also help employers assess the appropriateness of these policies in light of changing societal values, demographic trends, and corporate social responsibility. A company that undertakes such a self-examination could then articulate more clearly its position on work-life issues to current and prospective employees and investors. Clarifying basic, underlying values—particularly when both managers and employees receive training about fairness in work-life practices—would increase consistency across work groups and company divisions.

Second, organizational justice theory can help companies avoid superficial solutions (such as simply adding more programs) without also examining deeper assumptions. Regardless of how many new benefits are added, work-life policies may continue to provoke dissatisfaction since individuals judge employers' actions against different expectations. Unless an employer's decision makers identify their own and others' guiding principles, they will continue to disagree with each other and their employees about what is, and is not, fair. Although making these principles explicit will not eradicate disagreement, it will increase alignment between the organization and its policies and between decision makers within the organization. It will also provide a new dimension for assessing person-organization fit.

Some companies may fear that making fairness principles explicit will increase conflict between various interest groups. However, the costs of not resolving the fairness controversy surrounding work-life benefits may be the greater danger. Previous research has found that both procedural justice and interpersonal treatment were related to organizationally valued outcomes such as employee commitment and retention (Lambert 1997; Greenberg 1996). When a company makes explicit the underlying fairness principles that guide its work-life policies, employees are likely to view the decision process as fairer than if the principles remained unclear and subject to multiple interpretations (procedural justice), and they are likely to feel they have been treated more fairly than if the company had not explained its grounds for decision making (interpersonal treatment).

A final practical contribution that organizational justice theory makes is to individuals. One of the most striking features of employee discussions about work-life issues is the intense emotions that they arouse among both parents and nonparents. Reframing work-life practices using a justice lens shifts the focus from interpersonal and intergroup issues to a more constructive discussion of corporate and individual values.

CONCLUSION

This article has described changes in the composition of the workforce that work-family practice and scholarship have not fully addressed. The growing number of childless or single employees challenges the fairness of many companies' work-life programs. It has given rise to a countermovement popularly known as work-family backlash. Organizational justice theory addresses the central question, What is fair? and posits that employees answer this question by applying various principles that often operate at the level of hidden assumptions. Applying organizational justice theory can help depersonalize conflicts over the fairness of work-life policies and help organizations manage these issues more effectively. Finally, organizational justice theory can make significant contributions to work-family research.

Note

1. "Childless" is defined here, as it is by the U.S. Bureau of the Census, as having no children at all or none under the age of 18.

References

Bies, Robert. 1987. The Predicament of Injustice: The Management of Moral Outrage. *Research in Organizational Behavior* 9:289-319.

Bond, James, Ellen Galinsky, and Jennifer Swanberg. 1998. *The 1997 National Study of the Changing Workforce.* New York: Families and Work Institute.

Brockner, Joel and Jerald Greenberg. 1990. The Impact of Layoffs on Survivors: An Organizational Justice Perspective. In *Advances in Applied Social Psychology: Business Settings*, ed. John Carroll. Hillsdale, NJ: Lawrence Erlbaum.

Campbell, Alice and Marci Koblenz. 1997. *The Work and Life Pyramid of Needs*. Deerfield, IL: Baxter Healthcare and MK Consultants.

Cohen, R. 1991. Justice and Negotiation. In *Research on Negotiation in Organizations: Handbook of Negotiation Research*, ed. Max Bazerman, Roy Lewicki, and Blair Sheppard. Greenwich, CT: JAI Press.

Crispell, Diane. 1993. Planning No Family, Now or Ever. *American Demographics* Oct.:23-24.

———. 1994. Marital Bust. *American Demographics* June:59.

Deutsch, Morton. 1975. Equity, Equality, and Need: What Determines Which Value Will Be Used as the Basis for Distributive Justice? *Journal of Social Issues* 31(3):137-49.

———. 1985. *Distributive Justice*. New Haven, CT: Yale University Press.

Flynn, Gillian. 1996. Backlash. *Personnel Journal* Sept.:59-69.

Folger, Robert and Mary Konovsky. 1989. Effects of Procedural and Distributive Justice on Reactions to Pay Increase Decisions. *Academy of Management Journal* 32(1):115-30.

Future of American Households, The. 1993. *American Demographics* Dec.:27-46.

Galinsky, Ellen and Dana Friedman. 1991. *The Corporate Reference Guide to Work-Family Programs*. New York: Families and Work Institute.

Greenberg, Jerald. 1990. Organizational Justice: Yesterday, Today, and Tomorrow. *Journal of Management* 16:399-432.

———. 1993. The Social Side of Fairness: Interpersonal and Informational Classes of Organizational Justice. In *Justice in the Workplace*, ed. Russell Cropanzano. Hillsdale, NJ: Lawrence Erlbaum.

———. 1996. *The Quest for Justice in the Workplace*. Thousand Oaks, CA: Sage.

Greenberg, Jerald and S. Ornstein. 1983. High Status Job Title as Compensation for Underpayment: A Test of Equity Theory. *Journal of Applied Psychology* 68:283-97.

Grover, Steven. 1991. Predicting the Perceived Fairness of Parental Leave Policies. *Journal of Applied Psychology* 76(2):247-55.

James, Keith. 1993. The Social Context of Organizational Justice: Cultural, Intergroup, and Structural Effects on Justice Behaviors and Perceptions. In *Justice in the Workplace*, ed. Russell Cropanzano. Hillsdale, NJ: Lawrence Erlbaum.

Lambert, Susan. 1991. The Combined Effects of Job and Family Characteristics on Job Satisfaction, Job Involvement, and Intrinsic Motivation of Men and Women Workers. *Journal of Organizational Behavior* 12:341-63.

———. 1997. Workers' Use and Appreciation of Supportive Workplace Policies. In *Work Force Diversity*, ed. A. Daley. Washington, DC: NASW Press.

Lerner, Melvin. 1977. The Justice Motive in Social Behavior: Some Hypotheses as to Its Origins and Forms. *Journal of Personality* 45:1-52.

Lilly, Teri Ann, Marcie Pitt-Catsouphes, and Bradley K. Googins. 1997. *Work-Family Research: An Annotated Bibliography*. Westport, CT: Greenwood Press.

Mannix, Elizabeth, Margaret Neale, and Gregory Northcraft. 1995. Equity, Equality, or Need? The Effects of Organizational Culture on the Allocation of Benefits and Burdens. *Organizational Behavior and Human Decision Processes* 63(3):276-86.

Murray, Kathleen. 1996. The Childless
    Feel Left Out When Parents Get a
    Lift. *New York Times*, 12 Dec.
Parkinson, Deborah. 1996. *Work-Family
    Roundtable: The Childless Employee*.
    New York: Conference Board.
Shellenbarger, Sue. 1997. Work-Family
    Issues Go Way Beyond Missed Ball
    Games. *Wall Street Journal*, 22 May.
Sheppard, Blair, Roy Lewicki, and John
    Minton. 1992. *Organizational Justice:
    The Search for Fairness in the Work-
    place*. New York: Lexington Books.
Society for Human Resources Manage-
    ment. 1996a. Demographic Trends.
    Workplace Visions Nov.-Dec.
———. 1996b. Single and Childless Em-
    ployees Become More Common. *Work-
    place Visions* Sept.-Oct.
Thibaut, John and Laurens Walker.
    1975. *Procedural Justice: A Psycho-
    logical Analysis*. Hillsdale, NJ:
    Lawrence Erlbaum.

Tyler, Tom. 1987. Conditions Leading to
    Value-Expressive Effects in Judg-
    ments of Procedural Justice: A Test of
    Four Models. *Journal of Personality
    and Social Psychology* 52:333-44.
Williams, Lena. 1994. Childless Employ-
    ees Demanding Equity in Corporate
    World. *New York Times*, 12 Oct.
Young, Mary. 1997a. Does Life Status
    Matter? Marital and Parent Status as
    Antecedents of Work Time and Other
    Work-Related Outcomes. Ph.D. diss.,
    Boston University.
———. 1997b. *What's Behind Work-
    Family Backlash?* Melville, NY: Wil-
    liam Olsten Center for Workforce
    Strategies.
Zedeck, Sheldon. 1992. Exploring the Do-
    main of Work and Family Concerns.
    In *Work, Families, and Organiza-
    tions*, ed. Sheldon Zedeck. San Fran-
    cisco: Jossey-Bass.

ANNALS, *AAPSS*, **562**, March 1999

Restructured Families:
Issues of Equality and Need

By MAUREEN SCULLY and W. E. DOUGLAS CREED

ABSTRACT: The families of gay employees have recently come onto the corporate radar screen. The needs they have in common with the families of straight employees can foster connection. There are also tensions between gay and straight employees about the meanings of family, deeply rooted in the culture outside the workplace and sometimes so provocative that they appear only in indirect allusions. The case of a corporate redesign of benefits surfaces both the language of these commonalities and tensions and the underlying principles of equality versus need. Providing equal benefits for all families has the advantage of honoring equally the many ways the employees define a family, but the disadvantage of creating inequalities across families of different sizes and types. A need-based distribution has the advantage of respecting differences, but the disadvantage of requiring a way to evaluate and rank relative needs, which heightens tensions. The authors discuss how these trade-offs are voiced and played out.

Maureen A. Scully is an assistant professor of industrial relations and organization studies at the Sloan School of Management at the Massachusetts Institute of Technology. She studies how workplace inequality is alternately legitimated by meritocratic ideology and contested in grassroots activism. W. E. Douglas Creed is assistant professor of organizational studies at Boston College's Carroll School of Management. He is investigating changing media representations of gay and lesbian workplace issues. They jointly study institutional processes behind the diffusion of domestic partner benefits.

GAY activism in the workplace has helped employers to recognize that there are many types of families. A variety of benefits, ranging from sick days to health care, is becoming available to gay, lesbian, bisexual, and transgendered (GLBT) employees to provide for their families and to balance work and family life. This article opens with an example of how these families have come onto the radar screen of corporations and an appeal to researchers to represent the many families that do not fit the heterosexual or nuclear family ideal in addressing work and family issues. The common needs of the families of gay and straight employees can be a point of connection that enables good working relationships and alliances of employees who want to create workplaces that value differences.

However, a simple story of the integrative aspects of family benefits does not adequately capture the complexity of very different family structures and needs. The redesign of benefits brings a clash between two distributive justice principles: equality and need. Providing equal benefits to all families has the advantage of honoring equally all the many ways that employees choose to define a family, but the disadvantage of creating inequities across families of different sizes, types, and needs. Using a need-based distribution has the advantage of honoring differences across families through tailored or proportional packages, but the disadvantage of requiring a mechanism for evaluating and ranking relative needs that might be a source of bias or contention. Simple equality elides these contentious comparisons.

This article shows how these trade-offs between equality and need are played out in ways that do not involve a neat calculus of interests. Instead, they reveal some points of tension between gay and straight employees about the meanings of family, some of which are so taboo that they rarely break the surface of conversation. Workplace concerns are embedded in a broader culture that reflects the experiences, reference points, and coded language of the dominant straight culture and the gay subculture that had to take on a dissenting role to be heard.

Some provocative remarks at a conference presentation for gay activists in the workplace provide us with a jumping-off point to explore these deeply revealing points of tension between gay and straight employees about the meanings of family. Prospects for intergroup understanding and workplace change are at stake. While there are certainly differences in family types and needs within the straight community and within the gay community, it appears to be the cross-group differences that spark feelings about family and prompt the conversation about underexamined trade-offs. A touted advantage of diversity is realized in this example: examining an issue from the perspective introduced when a new group becomes visible provides fresh angles of vision.

CONTEXT: EMPLOYEE ADVOCACY
GROUPS IN THE WORKPLACE

Gains in access to family-related benefits for GLBT employees have been made in the context of employee advocacy in the workplace. We open by briefly reviewing the nature of employee advocacy groups, the connections between them, and their use of the discourse of family.

Groups of employees have begun to mobilize in the workplace to address unequal treatment based on social identities that they share, such as race, gender, or sexual orientation. These groups are variously referred to as advocacy groups, networks, or caucuses. They take on a variety of roles; among other things, they function as a source of instrumental career advice (Friedman 1996), performer of advocacy that could be carried out by unions as well or instead (Hyde 1997), and advocate of social activism that challenges deep assumptions and power relations (Scully and Segal 1997; Scully and Creed 1998b). The projects of these groups are active and visible forms of mobilization for making changes in the workplace and importing social movement concerns into organizational contexts (Scully and Segal 1997).

The connections between diverse employee advocacy groups, as well as with employees with dominant social identities (such as white, male, or straight), are important for understanding how joint and separate agendas are balanced. There is concern that, although social identity groups are an immediate and attractive basis for collective action (Larana, Johnston, and Gusfield 1994), they can be narrow and divisive. They may be unable to integrate their different demands for the same fixed pool of social resources (Piore 1995). Among employee advocacy groups, there is sometimes collaboration under the banner of shared civil rights concerns and sometimes distancing from one another to avoid the taint of the other group's issues. For example, African American and gay employee groups sometimes have an uneasy alliance. Between employee advocacy groups and the dominant identity groups, which have not coalesced into groups per se, there are conflicts over what are seen by the advocacy group as the invisible privileges of the dominant group and what are seen by the dominant groups as special interests of the advocacy group.

Cases on how celebrating diversity is good for the workplace generally show that addressing the particular concerns of a social identity group redounds to the benefit of the broader population. Justice for the historically oppressed group is achieved along with a demonstration that diversity sheds new light on issues. For example, the Black Caucus at Xerox lobbied in the 1970s for job openings to be announced formally, in order to share insider information that favored whites, and the resulting job-posting system helped both black and white employees (Friedman 1996). More recently, GLBT employee groups have purposefully developed "straight friends" groups that work together with them in order to legitimate their concerns, broaden their base of support, and provide safe spaces for employees whose GLBT identity is not known in the workplace. Later we will discuss how GLBT initiatives have surfaced concerns of straight employees.

In an effort to find common ground, employee activists may appeal to shared and legitimated values. The appeal to broad values has been documented as a clever strategy for change agents and one that allows them to motivate change by pointing to inconsistencies that must be resolved (Dutton and Dukerich 1991; Scully and Meyerson 1997). Women's caucuses in the workplace have worked to make parenting a legitimate concern for male employees in order to build alliances and advance work-family concerns. The welfare of families seems on the surface like an irrefutable social good, but beneath the broad swells of agreement are some rocky shoals on which family-welfare efforts can founder. Opponents of work-family programs may believe in the importance of family but argue that it should be left at home. Such tensions between the private and public spheres, gendered as female and male, are well documented (for example, Okin 1989).

It is tempting for researchers to focus on the places where there are win-win opportunities for employees and corporations or for oppressed and dominant social identity groups to coalesce around broadly shared values. However, the deep fault lines within and between groups often reveal where crucial dilemmas lie, how the texture of social life is shaped and experienced, and where the potential obstacles to change might arise. Apparently easy win-win opportunities can fail to materialize where these tensions are ignored. In this article,

we analyze a critical incident showing how the references and meanings surrounding the idea of family can subtly divide gay workplace activists and their straight allies. We explore the often silenced intergroup tensions that must be addressed despite a tendency to portray diversity as about harmony and inclusion.

DATA: BEARING WITNESS TO THE REAL TALK

The data for this article are from one incident encountered as part of a broader research program on employee activism, organizational change, and the diffusion of socially responsive programs across organizations. We have been studying the emerging role of GLBT employees in the workplace. GLBT employees are the most recently visible group of employees working on issues that promote diversity and inclusiveness in the workplace. We have tracked their advocacy of domestic partner benefits (DPBs) and their strategies for seeking fair treatment and curbing homophobia in the workplace. Our research program involves interviews, case studies of corporations, and analyses of both local and national discourse (for reports of this research, see Austin, Creed, and Scully 1997; Creed and Scully 1998; Foldy and Creed in press; Scully and Creed 1998b).

The issue

A focal issue for GLBT employees is obtaining DPBs, which are benefits provided to the same-sex partners of GLBT employees, much as opposite-sex spouses of heterosexual employees receive benefits. (DPBs in some cases are also extended to unmarried opposite-sex domestic partners.) GLBT advocates have emphasized that employer-provided benefits are a substantial portion of remuneration and that it is unfair that this compensation is not available to them. They argue that, because they are legally denied the opportunity to marry, they are unfairly ineligible for equal compensation for their work. GLBT advocates make arguments about fairness, about the goodwill to be gained from GLBT employees and their allies simply by announcing a progressive policy, and about the productivity gains from employees freed from worry about family health concerns. They also emphasize what other companies are doing and the reasonableness of the costs. When DPBs are proposed, corporate human resource departments sometimes try to assess the likely positive and negative responses (Gentile and Gant 1994; Scully and Creed 1998a).

The setting

For this article, we report on a presentation we attended at a national conference for GLBT activists. In such settings, social scientists can observe the naturally occurring discussion of issues. The shared rituals and discourse reveal a subculture's shared understandings and definition of itself vis-à-vis a dominant or outside culture. As an excellent ex-

ample of what can be discovered through this approach, Katzenstein (1995) attended conferences of feminist nuns to understand the discursive politics of women's changing roles in the Catholic church and meetings of military women to understand their advocacy for equal treatment. The special case of discursive politics became apparent through her investigation of the language and tactics of subcultures within a dominant culture. An interpretive analysis of language can reveal meanings, codes, humor, and some fault lines within a community and in the ways in which the community understands and candidly expresses its relationships to outside groups.

Most of the approximately 30 sessions at the three-day national conference for GLBT activists were devoted to community activism, but about 6 sessions addressed workplace challenges. Spokespersons from companies described their experiences and some lessons learned. One session focused on the approach taken by a company with a strongly espoused commitment to diversity; we will refer to this company pseudonymously as AltiCorp.

The two presenters from AltiCorp, who openly identified themselves as a gay man and a lesbian, described with pride how AltiCorp had proceeded. One of them was from the corporate Human Resources department and thus did work related to benefits management. Members of the sizable audience of about 35 people (attendance at the conference breakout sessions ranged from 5 to 50) took notes, picked up handouts, and asked questions.

The real talk

We will focus on the overall theme of the AltiCorp presentation as well as an offhand remark. The main focus of the presentation was on the creative way in which AltiCorp approached DPBs and found in the quest for DPBs an opportunity to understand the family concerns of a broad range of gay and straight employees. We refer to this as the integrative story. During this story, an offhand remark about employees' dependents alluded to possible tensions and what we call a disruptive story. Disruptions can be painful as well as the source of energy for change and creative misalignment.

We try to understand these possible tensions in two ways. First, there are specific cultural issues behind the remark, which can be interpreted in light of the histories and experiences of GLBT people in the United States. These cultural issues may most often be alluded to in coded language or kept backstage as "hidden transcripts" (Scott 1985). Even if the cultural references in such a remark are largely unconscious or taken for granted, they might still play a role in shaping group norms (Zucker 1988). Second, there is a more general theoretical lens through which to interpret the comment: the trade-offs between equality and need. This trade-off underlies many allocative decisions related to benefits but is not often surfaced and examined. It could advance our understanding of how the benefits and burdens of

work-family programs can be distributed. Next we tell the integrative story, then the disruptive story. In the analysis section that follows, we offer interpretations.

The integrative story

The development of DPBs as an issue at AltiCorp became an occasion to look more broadly at benefits policy. We had not encountered another company in our study that had taken this approach, which made Alti-Corp's innovation stand out. At some companies, benefits administrators quietly tack DPBs onto the benefits list as an administrative move, hoping that the right people will notice and not too much of a stir will be created. In other companies, managers engage the controversy surrounding DPBs but keep the focus on DPBs and sometimes other issues specifically relevant to GLBT employees (Scully and Creed 1998b).

What is striking about AltiCorp is that the company took a broader view that became widely regarded as successful. The old adage that "success has a thousand mothers and fathers" is pertinent. The GLBT employees network, the Human Resources department, and senior executives all claim a role and narrate the story differently. The conference speakers emphasized the role of the very active GLBT employees group, which was highly organized with a formal charter and structure to guide its advocacy efforts. They showed the time line of their group's discussions and plans and pointed out that the Human Resources officials who are now advocates came on board later. The GLBT group did not work in concert with the Human Resources department when it came time to survey all employees about their family situation and benefits preferences. For their part, Human Resources representatives often rightly anticipated that questions of fairness would be raised in turn by straight employees, particularly those who were in long-term relationships but had chosen not to marry and who wondered whether DPBs would be extended to them as well. They decided that a broad-based, anonymous survey would provide good background information on such employee concerns. Moreover, there was a widespread commitment to total quality management (TQM) at AltiCorp. The GLBT employee group, chartered at a time when the language and practices of TQM were stamped on the approach of their own network, considered the survey and bigger picture to be in keeping with TQM principles, as did Human Resources officials also dedicated to TQM. Because TQM generates activist zeal among its followers (Hackman and Wageman 1995), it was a ready-made legitimating language in which to ground this approach.

The survey revealed that very few employees lived in the canonical family (consisting of a primary breadwinner whose benefits supported a spouse [in a secondary job or at home] and approximately two children) around which AltiCorp's entire and long-standing benefits package had been designed. Instead, they found that many employees had working spouses who had their own benefits packages, and for them, partner benefits (whether for same-

or opposite-sex partners) were not necessary. (Indeed, the utilization rates of DPBs, once implemented, can be low. Their immediate value is great for the partners who need them, but their symbolic value to a broader constituency is even greater [Scully and Creed 1998a].) The survey also revealed that more employees than expected were single and not using family benefits.

The presenters reported that an even more unexpected finding was that many employees had people in their lives who were not in their immediate nuclear families and whom they wished they could cover in their health plan but could not. The range of examples was wide. Not too surprisingly but largely unaddressed, employees were worried about elder care for aging parents and health benefits for parents who did not have adequate coverage of their own. In addition, employees named others for whom they felt a concerned responsibility, including handicapped siblings, elderly aunts or uncles who had helped raise them, and young nieces, nephews, or godchildren. They found employees concerned about family members who had suddenly become unemployed during the surge of layoffs and downsizing— again, people whom employees wished they could help with benefits, even temporarily.

The discovery was that there were many ways in which employees defined the members of their family, in the sense of being within the broad boundaries of their care and interdependence. The notion of a breadwinner, typically male, with a spouse and two children applied to very few employees. This canonical family is based on an outmoded experience, which even in its heyday applied largely to white, middle- and upper-class people. Various ethnic and racial groups have long held different meanings for family. Research on the childhood experiences of African American women managers (Bell and Nkomo 1998) shows a long tradition, across class lines, of widely defined families, including aunts, uncles, and a broader set of significant people who bear the affectionate title of "aunt" or "uncle." The women in Bell and Nkomo's study report feeling cared for and connected to a range of significant people as they grew up.

A pluralist view of the family relationships of employees from varied backgrounds is not, however, common in corporate approaches to work-family. The informative results of the survey at AltiCorp led Human Resources officials there to design a radical alternative for benefits: each employee would receive a fixed amount of benefits, to be deployed to whomever the employee wished (with the caveat that the Internal Revenue Service would treat DPBs and other benefits of this nonstandard type as taxable income). DPBs became one piece or one possible use of such a benefits package.

The AltiCorp presenters suggested that this approach had made DPBs less controversial when they were announced as a part of a larger policy change, although they also indicated that senior management expressly denied both that the approach was triggered by the request

for DPBs and that it was adopted as a way of limiting the controversy over DPBs. The speakers pointed with pride to how the initial request for DPBs had yielded a broadly beneficial solution.

The disruptive story

In exploring the ramifications of this creative approach, one presenter made an interesting offhand remark. The presentation had been laced with humor. Inside jokes and references drew big laughs from an audience that was presumed to be mostly GLBT advocates. The presentation style was an interesting mix of corporate seriousness and political theater. The very professional Power-Point slides would have been at home in a corporate boardroom and, indeed, were probably downloaded from a previous corporate presentation. The style was more relaxed than a corporate presentation, in the context of a friendly, off-site meeting. A lot of useful information was conveyed in dense handouts, and it was clear that a serious financial issue that affects livelihoods was at stake, but at the same time, the spirited repartee between the presenters and with the audience held the attendees' attention and made the session lively.

The discussion turned to the different ways in which employees might use their fixed benefits allotment. The presenter noted that the amount would sufficiently cover two working parents and two children and that, of course, for single people, it was a lot of discretionary money. The presenter added, "If people want to have five children, well, that's their problem." This additional remark about children, one of very few references to children even within the broad framing of family issues, is what we unpack as the "disruptive story."

On one hand, this remark should certainly not be overinterpreted as an indicator of corporate policy. It was a throwaway line in a lively and humorous session, and, in this context, it got a bit of a laugh. On the other hand, it is precisely in such off-hand remarks that one catches a glimpse of the codes and conflicts that mark group life. The use of humor, both what is considered funny and when humor erupts, is a window into the culture of work groups and how they handle stresses and uneasy contradictions (Hatch 1997; Meyerson 1990). This remark is valuable in that it provides us with a very specifically grounded point for jumping off into an exploration of trade-offs between need and equity and the issues that can integrate or disrupt group relationships and a collective change effort.

The authors' stories

We think it is appropriate at this juncture to insert our voices as authors of this article. We had very different reactions to this remark and to how we should proceed in this article to interpret it.

As a straight woman, Maureen was jolted by the remark, perhaps more from the perspective of her gender than her orientation. The punitive treatment of women with "too many children" is a significant way

in which societal benefits are gendered and poverty is feminized (Fraser 1989). At another level, the apparent dig at people who have children at all had a familiar ring from other contexts in which she had been in the small straight minority as an ally for GLBT causes. The remark felt antiheterosexual, even though many GLBT people, including the other presenter at the session, have children. The remark itself may have meant nothing, but, against a backdrop of having heard similar remarks and subtly misogynist or anti-heterosexual tones (such as jokes about "breeders," a code name for straight people), her ear may have picked up something. What interested her immediately was the rich way in which this example opened into a discussion of the issues of equality versus need as well as an opportunity to air some of the tensions that are swept under the rug in the zeal to recount successful gay-straight alliances in the workplace.

As a gay man, Doug was surprised at Maureen's strong reaction and questioned whether the remark had been intended to sting. He was particularly interested in the implications of the integrative story because accounts of GLBT activism and a visible GLBT presence serving the broader good are just gaining attention. Such accounts are very validating of the diversity aims of GLBT activists—and the very identity of GLBT employees—and can be added to the widely circulated story of how the Xerox Black Caucus created a broadly beneficial job-posting system in the early 1970s. Doug was worried that overinterpreting the offhand remark might portray the GLBT activists in too negative a light, shifting attention from their significant accomplishment and airing tensions in a harmful way. He added texture to the historical context in which family has been so painful an issue for GLBT people in order to shed light on the remark.

The process of working on this article resulted in a number of conversations in which our own concerns and viewpoints were aired. Interestingly, this article is the fourth one that we are working on in a series of collaborations derived from this research program, but it is the only one in which we have experienced tension in our own relationship and serious disagreements about how to proceed. Our collaboration as a mixed-orientation research team has generally been quite easy and added perspective to our work, but with this article, surfacing some possible tensions and negative stereotypes brought our understanding to a new level. Neither of us, by the way, has children of our own. We found that, just as we claim in this article, working on disruptive issues as they pop up—if done with respect and an appropriate attention to the cultural context in which the remarks and hurts arise—can ultimately be an enlightening project and a step toward more integrative outcomes. The following analysis reflects our process of alternately digging ever deeper into touchy and provocative areas and tempering our interpretations by using our own cultural understandings.

ANALYSIS: THE INTEGRATIVE STORY

This story shows how GLBT issues broaden the idea of family. In addressing work-family issues, researchers probe both how the restructuring of work affects families and family policies (for example, Osterman 1995) and how the restructuring of the family affects work (for example, Bailyn et al. 1996). The restructuring of the family is often posed in terms of the shift from single-breadwinner to dual-career households (Barnett and Rivers 1997; Gerson 1985; Hertz 1986; Hochschild 1989). However, AltiCorp's survey shows that we need to restructure our notion of family even more profoundly than that.

The approach taken by AltiCorp reminds both corporations and researchers that there are many types of families. The first wave of research on work-family issues focused on the salient move of women into the workforce and the implications for working mothers and then, more broadly, working parents. The picture of family life portrayed looked particularly straight, white, and middle to upper middle class. Only slowly were other intersecting and different identities added: other sexual orientations, races, classes, and combinations thereof. While it is too often and with too few situating and disclaiming notes that researchers start with people of dominant identities, the field is gradually learning to catch up and add more voices.

Early researchers had the difficult challenge of making the case that family concerns should be workplace concerns and incorporating the voices of women. For example, an excellent chapter by Hertz (1986), based on her rich qualitative data and charting new territory, was titled, "His Career, Her Career, Their Marriage." A two-parent, nuclear, heterosexual family needs increasingly to be understood as but one of many kinds of families, in a world where there are many more single heads of household and same-sex heads of household. Heterosexist language and the complexity of navigating gendered pronouns do persist, in, for example, a more recent book whose title, *She Works/He Works*, defines a particular domain (Barnett and Rivers 1997).

The request for and provision of DPBs brings attention to the many family structures of GLBT employees. After years of being invisible, gay families have come onto the radar screens of corporate officials. Same-sex domestic partners are but one dimension of the family life of GLBT employees. In addition, their families can include children from previous marriages, biological children of one partner in a same-sex union adopted by the other and jointly raised, and/or adopted children. Time off from work for adoptions, for both gay and straight employees, is a relatively new benefit.

The advocacy of GLBT employees pried open a window for viewing a more flexible and relevant terrain of benefits. By using the request for DPBs as an opportunity to define benefits more broadly, the particular concerns of GLBT employees were linked to the universal concerns of all employees. A chief executive officer of another company in our research program explained that he understood all family benefits as a way to help relieve employees' worries so that they could concentrate better and be more productive while at work; he said that as soon as he realized that some 10 percent of his employees were being excluded, it made immediate sense to him to add DPBs. He said it was rare that he could implement a policy that would make 10 percent of his workforce more validated and committed.

The work of GLBT employees on DPBs links their advocacy to the work of other employees concerned with work and family issues. Some GLBT employees who are parents have said in interviews that discussing common concerns with straight parents is a way that they normalize their experiences and help straight colleagues become more comfortable in talking with them about their everyday lives. This integrative aspect is similar to women employees' reframing of the parenting issue to bring men on board as allies in changing family policies and examining the gendering of work practices. The concern for family can be a point of connection between groups working for equal treatment.

ANALYSIS: THE DISRUPTIVE STORY

We analyze the disruptive story in two ways. First, we explore the layers of cultural meaning associated with families and children, especially for GLBT employees reacting to how the rhetoric of family has been used to insult their identity. Second, we assess the distributive justice dilemma of equal versus need-based allocation of benefits, to which the remark at the conference alluded.

Cultural strands

The offhand remark can be seen as a kind of defensive humor, whereby a historically oppressed group turns around the subtle and overt insults it has received and reflects them back at the dominant group. GLBT employees have been placed in the position of having to subvert the status quo and the ways in which they are excluded and made invisible. Provocative asides are an everyday form of resistance. The need to make such a comment specifically where family issues are concerned can be understood through three issues at large in the culture: actual and perceived exclusion from parenting, painful experiences in families of origin, and the use of pro-family rhetoric to bolster homophobia. We consider each of these in turn.

Just as discussions and policies regarding children can ease the relationship between GLBT and straight employees at work, at the same time, they exclude people who do not have children. On one hand, some GLBT people feel they cannot have children, whether because of difficulties in finding the right partner or method or state laws preventing them from adopting. On the other hand, the image of GLBT people as not having or being interested in children reflects a false bias. The alternative press has declared a "lesbian baby boom." GLBT parents march with their kids in gay pride parades to make their family ties and devotion visible.

The potential divide between those who do and do not have children clearly need not fall along straight-gay lines. Straight people who are single and/or childless, whether by choice or not, should also be included in the discussion of fair allocation of family-friendly benefits. Increasingly, single people are weighing in to describe, in conversations at work and on-line, how family-related benefits place an undue burden on them to pick up the slack when coworkers are on leave. They wonder if they will later enjoy the reciprocity that makes such burden sharing more social and equitable. If the principal work-family benefit is defined as parenting leave, then there is a chance only for a few of them, if they eventually have children and are still with that company, that they will later enjoy this reciprocity. If family and family benefits are defined more broadly, they might get their turn for a leave to care for an elderly parent or other extended-family member or even to do service work in their community. The parallel discussions among straight childless employees and GLBT employees could be linked to pursue more broad, diverse, and fair notions of work-family balancing.

The family, for many GLBT people, has been the site of their earliest feelings of stigma and their gravest worries about claiming their identity. Sharing stories of "coming out" to family members is a ritual among GLBT employees. The stories are laced with anguish, humor, and both pleasant and unpleasant surprises. The appeal to family as a value that most people can endorse and as a strategy for making policy changes in workplace benefits is problematic. Family does not have happy connotations for all people. In other stories from the press, accounts of abuse in families are also reminders that, especially for women and children, the family is not the safe haven it is portrayed to be. Thus the perspectives of GLBT people join other critical views to insert diversity and skepticism into a simple and blissful discourse of family.

Pro-family rhetoric has been part of an ideological package that includes stingingly hostile homophobic rhetoric. For example, a conservative group calling itself the Family Research Council, one of the self-proclaimed leaders in lobbying against legislation that would outlaw workplace discrimination on the basis of sexual orientation, frames its anti-GLBT efforts as part of an effort to protect the family. So-called traditional families are among the anointed of the antigay conservatives who have often held office and influenced policy in the last two decades in the United States. Arguments that could be raised to support additional need-based benefits for families with more children might accidentally have much in common with, and even seem to derive from, those used by precisely the people who have been most intolerant of and hurtful toward GLBT people.

Conservative religious beliefs about reproductively oriented sexuality as sacred and all other sexuality as sinful underlies deeply held homophobic attitudes, according to some theologians who have unpacked this rhetoric (for example, Nelson 1992, 1988). As such, not having children is upheld as a departure from divine plan or shameful by homophobic spokespersons. This stigmatizing is a likely basis for the GLBT counter-cultural retort of calling straight people "breeders." This negative slur back at heterosexual people who have kids, and "too many" kids, can be heard at GLBT cultural events, both in seriousness and as a playful way to reclaim and reframe the discourse of family. It may also remove some of the sense of loss for people who feel they will not have children, by making having children something to mock along with the bourgeois domestic sensibility.

Fighting back and recasting cultural labels is an important aspect of resistance. As GLBT parents can attest, GLBT people are far from being antifamily. But when ostensibly pro-family rhetoric, such as the strategically named Defense of Marriage Act, is commonly used to exacerbate homophobia and demonize the GLBT civil rights movement, a pro-family rationale for helping families with more children enters contested terrain.

Equality-need trade-offs

As the foregoing discussion suggests, the ways to handle benefits for families with more children point to the tension between equality and need-based allocative schemes. Equality, need, and contribution are three common and distinct distributive rules identified in the literature (for example, Deutsch and Steil 1988). The equality rule gives everyone an identical share. Distributions based on contribution or need give people proportional shares, based either on the value they bring to a social unit or their particular needs. Proportional distributions require that contribution or need can be defined, measured, and relatively ranked. Because these are difficult to do and can breed conflict, equality might be preferred as a simpler rule. But equality breeds its own conflicts by ignoring contribution or need.

In the workplace, salaries and positions are said to be distributed on the basis of contribution. Other goods, however, such as benefits, are distributed on the basis of equality or need (Martin and Harder 1988). Different "spheres of justice" have their own distributive rules that become taken-for-granted norms (Walzer 1983). Thus need would not seem fair in the United States as a basis for salary, just as contribution would not seem fair as a way to determine who can take bereavement leave.

In the case at hand, AltiCorp's approach is distinctive because the company has decided to move to an equality-based distribution of benefits. Moreover, it is using a simple equality rule: everyone gets the same fixed share. Sometimes, the language of equality is used to describe essentially need-based outcomes, such as when everyone with a child has an "equal" chance to sign up their children for benefits. The result would not be identical shares but different shares based on the number of children.

The offhand remark is interesting not only for its cultural nuances but also because it dismisses a need-based allocation. It diminishes the idea of getting more benefits for having more children (or more dependents in otherwise more broadly defined family relationships, but this article will continue to focus on children, as the specific example used in the remark). The introduction of the new equal and broadly applicable benefits was touted in the presentation as the product of taking diversity seriously. Ironically, the equality rule elides the consideration of differences by treating all families and claimants the same. In one sense, differential treatment is problematic; that very term is at the center of equal employment opportunity legislation. In another sense, appropriately differentiated treatment might actually end up being more fair and even more equal. There would not be such huge differences between the health care dollars available to single persons versus those who are part of larger family systems.

A need-based distribution of benefits has its own loaded history with respect to work-family issues. Women were discriminated against when companies gave men greater salary and/or benefits, with the rationale that married men needed the money more and had families to support. The battle today by GLBT employees to obtain benefits for their partners was played out in the 1960s when women as breadwinners tried to legitimate their need for benefits for their husbands. Ireland (1996) opens her story of becoming an activist on behalf of women by describing her own fight, when she was a flight attendant in the 1960s, to get the airline to allow her to include her husband in her health care coverage, just as male airline employees were allowed to enroll their wives. This dimension of gender equity is now taken for granted. But there may be a persistent uneasiness that a need-based determination of family benefits might backfire and be used to bolster inequality and stereotypes of who has legitimate needs.

An equality-based approach to family benefits treats every family the same and lets each family decide how thickly or thinly their benefits will be spread. A need-based approach to family benefits makes special provisions for families with more children and other dependents. A need-based distribution of family benefits hinges on this ability to define and understand what a legitimate family need looks like. GLBT employees might fear that their families, only just recognized by corporations, would lose out in this comparative rating of needs. They may have strong reasons to take a stand for straightforward equality and not venture into definitions of need. Instead of polarizing gay and straight employees over equality and need rules, there may be another way to reframe and approach the idea of need-based benefits for families, considered in the next section.

DISCUSSION: THE SOCIETAL COMMITMENT TO CHILDREN

The notion that, if families have "too many" children, it is "their prob-lem" is just one indicator of an individualistic rather than a collective stance toward social welfare. In the United States, children are regarded as a private consumption choice, verging on a luxury good in economic terms. In contrast, other nations view children as a resource and responsibility of all members of society, including those without children of "their own." For example, European countries have national policies for parental leave and child care that emphasize the national responsibility to care for children and to subsidize their needs. Even the recent Family and Medical Leave Act in the United States leaves the United States still far behind its European counterparts in the extent of support and income for parenting (Hofferth and Deich 1994).

The idea that having "too many" children is a concern only for those who have big families also reveals another fault line. There is a racist notion in the United States that African American and Hispanic families are too large and, moreover, irresponsibly so, because people should not have children if they are not personally prepared to bear all the costs. While the typical person on welfare is white and has only two children, the misguided and stereotypical picture of families that presumably are too big can encode a subtly (or overtly) racist and antiwelfare sensibility.

A focus on children as dependent on adults might be a unifying approach to a need-based benefits program rather than a divisive one. Decoupled from the righteous rhetoric about one kind of nuclear family, concern for children can be broad based.

In particular, with the "feminization of poverty" (Fraser 1989)—the trend that most of the poor in the United States are women and children and an alarmingly high percentage of all children are poor—a focus on children could open a dialogue about inequality. Because of the American belief in opportunity, the notion that people should at least be equal at the outset of their lives is an easy one to legitimate.

Can regarding children more collectively, as a societal resource, resolve some of the tension between equality and need and yield a sensible need-based approach that is still sensitive to the concerns of GLBT employees? It is the collective aspect of the support for children that has integrative value, and this potential is best realized when children are viewed not as private consumption choices but as carriers of the societal future. In AltiCorp's plan, then, an employee might be allowed to nominate any child—his or her own, a niece or nephew, a partner's or neighbor's child, or a child met through a mentoring program—to be a recipient of his or her benefits. Such an arrangement quickly turns into benefits for all children. Ultimately, the discussions over benefits provided by corporations should be rendered moot by a broader social policy of providing national health care benefits as a condition of being a citizen, rather than as a local perquisite of being employed or related to someone who is employed.

In the United States, we still tend to hold a proprietary attitude toward our own children, unhesitatingly conferring on them advantages that other children cannot have and considering this privileging as part of being a good parent. Children pose the tension between the particular and the general quite strongly. A focus on children as an integrative justice concern requires thinking beyond taken-for-granted notions.

In the kind of thought experiment that makes science fiction into good social commentary, Feldman (1998), president of the American Federation of Teachers, wrote a position paper about a fictional "child swap" society, in which children were swapped randomly between different homes as they were raised. Such a setup, she argued, would quickly ensure that all homes were provided adequate resources for nurturing children.

We might not want to admit it, but don't we take for granted that some kids are going to have much better lives than others? Of course. We take for granted that some will get the best medical treatment and others will be able to get little or none. . . .

Obviously I'm not suggesting that the United States adopt a childswap system. The idea makes me cringe, and, anyway, it's just a fable. But I like to imagine what would happen if we did.

We'd start with political figures and their children and grandchildren, with governors and mayors and other leaders. What do you suppose would happen when these people saw that their children would have the same chance as the sons and daughters of poor people—no more and no less? What would happen to our schools and healthcare system—and our shameful national indifference to children who are not ours?

She argues that a more fluid and generous idea of whose children are "ours" to care for would raise the minimum standards for all children. Although she tells a fable, there was a historical enactment of this practice in the ancient Celtic custom of having cousins or neighbors take in each other's children to ensure peace and reciprocity in the community.

Also using science fiction as social commentary, the mystery novelist P. D. James (1993) wrote a story about an imagined future in which environmental conditions had created worldwide infertility. The last cohort of children was in their teens. No more children were on the way. She unfolds what might happen in a world without children and the implications for all people, not only those who might have had or wanted children. The collective human legacy is severed. A climate of demoralization prevails. Without any sense of continuity, routine maintenance is no longer worth the bother, so infrastructures crumble. The story shows how children are a societal resource and bridge to the future and urges a collective approach to the nurturance of children.

A collective approach does not mean that providing more resources for families with more children implies that families should have more children. Other writers on responsible child rearing from a societal perspective track the worldwide decline in family size and urge people to consider their role in population growth. For example, McKibben (forthcom-

ing) makes a social and environmental case for families with one child.

In short, considering children from a societal approach can both (1) make other people's children part of one's own responsibility, as a member of society, and (2) make one's own children, if one has them, part of the community of all children and part of a broader social, and even ecological, system.

CONCLUSION

The offhand remark analyzed in this article is valuable precisely because it helps us to surface and reconceptualize the issues of equality versus need, which should be more central to theory and research on work-family issues. The integrative story presents an equality-based distribution, but the concomitant disruptive story suggests that this is an uneasy solution with lurking tensions. This article has used these stories—the real talk of people working at the cutting edge of work-family issues—to explore a broader and richer understanding of family and of collective responsibility to family members.

References

Austin, John, W. E. Douglas Creed, and Maureen Scully. 1997. Good Business or Civil Rights? Frames and Meanings for Gay Activism in the Workplace. Paper presented at the conference Organizing in a Multi-Voiced World: Social Construction, Innovation and Organizational Change, Louven, Belgium.

Bailyn, Lotte, Rhona Rapoport, Joyce Fletcher, and Deborah Kolb. 1996. Relinking Work and Family: A Catalyst for Organizational Change. Working paper #3892-96, Sloan School of Management, Massachusetts Institute of Technology, Cambridge.

Barnett, Rosalind C. and Caryl Rivers. 1997. *She Works/He Works: How Two Parent Families Are Happier, Healthier, and Better-Off*. San Francisco: Harper.

Bell, Ella and Stella Nkomo. 1998. Our Separate Ways: Life Journeys of Black and White Women Managers. University of North Carolina, Charlotte. Manuscript.

Creed, W. E. Douglas and Maureen Scully. 1998. Songs of Ourselves: Employees' Enactment of Social Identity Through Encounters with Self and Others. Working paper, Boston College, Chestnut Hill, MA.

Deutsch, Morton and Janice Steil. 1988. Awakening the Sense of Injustice. *Social Justice Research* 2:3-23.

Dutton, Jane E. and Janet M. Dukerich. 1991. Keeping an Eye on the Mirror: The Role of Image and Identity in Organizational Adaptation. *Academy of Management Journal* 34:517-54.

Feldman, Sandy. 1998. The Child Swap Society: Where We Stand. American Federation of Teachers, Washington, DC. Position paper.

Foldy, Erica and W. E. Douglas Creed. In press. Action Learning, Fragmentation, and the Interaction of Single, Double, and Triple Loop Change: A Case of Gay and Lesbian Employee Advocacy. *Journal of Applied Behavioral Science*.

Fraser, Nancy. 1989. Women, Welfare, and the Politics of Need Interpretation. In *Unruly Practices: Power, Discourse, and Gender in Contemporary Social Theory*, ed. N. Fraser. Minneapolis: University of Minnesota Press.

Friedman, Ray A. 1996. Defining the Scope and Logic of Minority and Female Network Groups: Can Separation Enhance Integration? *Research in Personnel and Human Resources Management* 14:307-49.

Gentile, Mary and S. Gant. 1994. *Lotus Development Corporation: Spousal Equivalents*. Case #9-394-197. Cambridge, MA: Harvard Business School Press.

Gerson, Kathleen. 1985. *Hard Choices: How Women Decide About Work, Career, and Motherhood*. Berkeley: University of California Press.

Hackman, Richard and Ruth Wageman. 1995. Total Quality Management: Empirical, Conceptual, and Practical Issues. *Administrative Science Quarterly* 40:309-42.

Hatch, Mary Jo. 1997. Irony and the Social Construction of Contradiction in the Humor of a Management Team. *Organization Science* 8:275-88.

Hertz, Rosanna. 1986. *More Equal Than Others: Women and Men in Dual-Career Marriages*. Berkeley: University of California Press.

Hochschild, Arlie R. 1989. *The Second Shift*. New York: Avon.

Hofferth, S. L. and S. G. Deich. 1994. Recent U.S. Child Care and Family Legislation in Comparative Perspective (Germany, France, Sweden, Hungary). *Journal of Family Issues* 15:424-48.

Hyde, Alan. 1997. Employee Identity Caucuses in Silicon Valley: Can They Transcend the Boundaries of the Firm? Paper presented to the spring meeting of the Industrial Relations Research Association, New York.

Ireland, Patricia. 1996. *What Women Want*. New York: Dutton.

James, P. D. 1993. *The Children of Men*. New York: Knopf.

Katzenstein, Mary F. 1995. Discursive Politics and Feminist Activism in the Catholic Church. In *Feminist Organi-*

zations: Harvest of the New Women's Movement, ed. M. M. Ferree and P. Y. Martin. Philadelphia: Temple University Press.

Larana, Enrique, Hank Johnston, and Joseph R. Gusfield. 1994. *New Social Movements: From Ideology to Identity*. Philadelphia: Temple University Press.

Martin, Joanne and Joseph Harder. 1988. Bread and Roses. Working paper, Stanford University, Stanford, CA.

McKibben, Bill. Forthcoming. *Maybe One: A Personal and Environmental Argument for Single Child Families*. New York: Simon & Schuster.

Meyerson, Debra. 1990. Uncovering Socially Undesirable Emotions. *American Behavioral Scientist* 33(3):296-307.

Nelson, James B. 1988. *The Intimate Connection: Male Sexuality, Masculine Spirituality*. Philadelphia: Westminster Press.

———. 1992. *Body Theology*. Louisville, KY: Westminster/John Knox.

Okin, Susan M. 1989. *Justice, Gender, and the Family*. New York: Basic Books.

Osterman, Paul. 1995. Work/Family Programs and the Employment Relationship. *Administrative Science Quarterly* 40:681-700.

Piore, Michael. 1995. *Beyond Individualism*. Cambridge, MA: Harvard University Press.

Scott, James. 1985. *Weapons of the Weak*. New Haven, CT: Yale University Press.

Scully, Marueen and W. E. Douglas Creed. 1998a. The Irony of Utilization Data. Working paper, Boston College, Chestnut Hill, MA.

———. 1998b. Switchpersons on the Track of History: Situated Agency and Contested Legitimacy in the Diffusion of Domestic Partner Benefits. Paper presented at the annual meeting of the Academy of Management, San Diego.

Scully, Maureen and Debra Meyerson. 1997. Before Isomorphism: The Dynamics of Legitimation During the Implementation of Corporate Ethics Programs. Working paper, Massachusetts Institute of Technology, Cambridge.

Scully, Marueen and Amy Segal. 1997. Passion with an Umbrella: Grassroots Activists in Organizations. Working paper, Massachusetts Institute of Technology, Cambridge.

Walzer, Michael. 1983. *Spheres of Justice: A Defense of Pluralism and Equality*. New York: Basic Books.

Zucker, Lynne, ed. 1988. *Institutional Patterns and Organizations: Culture and Environment*. Cambridge, MA: Ballinger.

ANNALS, *AAPSS*, **562**, March 1999

The Impact of Family on
Job Displacement and Recovery

By PAUL ATTEWELL

ABSTRACT: Rates of involuntary job loss (from plant closures, downsizing, and so on) have been increasing in the United States during the past 15 years. Using several cross-sectional surveys from the Current Population Survey, and longitudinal data from the Panel Study of Income Dynamics, this article demonstrates that the likelihood of job displacement differs according to marital status, the presence or absence of young children, and single-parenthood, even after controlling for employees' age, sex, race, education, industry, occupation, and other pertinent factors. Divorce is associated with the subsequent loss of their jobs. Conversely, job displacement also raises the risk of subsequent marital breakdown. Thus the waves of job displacement have not been neutral with regard to family structure. These findings are discussed in terms of theories of work-family conflicts.

Paul A. Attewell is currently a professor of sociology at CUNY Graduate Center, specializing in the sociology of work and technology, the sociology of complex organizations, and research methods. Currently, he is the principal investigator for a National Science Foundation grant project that provides graduate research traineeships in organizational effectiveness. His publications include a number of articles in various journals including Organization Science; Work and Occupations; Journal of Historical Sociology; and Sociology of Work and Occupations.

NOTE: This research was supported by a grant from the Alfred P. Sloan Foundation. I wish to thank Lincoln Quillian for his exceptional research assistance on this project.

I NVOLUNTARY job loss has been
a common feature of capitalist
economies for more than a century:
employees are laid off when businesses relocate, shrink, or fail or because of insufficient work. Despite its
ordinariness, public and scholarly
concern about job displacement in
the United States has intensified in
recent years. The total number of displaced employees increased in the
1980s, and in the 1990s displacement has grown even while the economy expanded. The locus of job loss
also shifted. The early 1980s saw an
upswing of plant closings, affecting
predominantly blue-collar workers.
From the mid-1980s on, this was supplemented by downsizing: laying off
of white-collar employees, often from
profitable companies. The downsizing movement increased job-loss
rates to historic highs among groups
such as managers and professionals,
who had previously exhibited low
rates of displacement. By 1995, the
annual number of displaced employees was at its highest level in 15
years.

One issue that has been largely
overlooked in prior research is the relationship between family structure
and job displacement. On first impression, who is laid off during a
wave of downsizing should have
nothing to do with the family situation of employees. However, this article demonstrates that the incidence
of job loss differs according to marital
status and with the presence or absence of young children, even after
controlling for employees' age, education, occupation, and other factors.
Family structure is related also to fi-

nancial recovery from job loss: individuals in certain family configura-
tions are more likely to recover than
individuals of equivalent education,
age, and work background who differ
in family structure. Job displacement is also associated with divorce:
employees are at greater risk of losing their jobs after becoming divorced. In addition, there is an increased incidence of divorce after
people lose their jobs. In other words,
the causation between divorce and
displacement runs in both directions.

These neglected familial aspects
of job loss are addressed in this article using data from several cross-
sectional studies of the U.S. labor
force and with an event-history
analysis of a longitudinal panel of
working Americans. These findings
have implications for our ideas about
work-family conflicts.

RELATED RESEARCH:
JOB DISPLACEMENT

Blue-color workers have suffered
higher rates of job displacement than
have white-collar workers for the last
20 years; however, the gap between
the two groups has narrowed since
1990 (Gardner 1995). African American workers have also suffered
higher rates of displacement for most
of this period, but again this gap has
recently narrowed to the point of dis-
appearing (cf. Kletzner 1991; Gardner 1995; Moore 1992). People with
less than a college education suffer
higher rates of displacement than
more educated workers; men are displaced in greater proportion than
women; and younger workers lose

jobs in higher numbers than older workers (although this is obscured when samples are limited to high-tenure workers).

About one-third of displaced workers find new jobs within three months, but roughly 30 percent are unemployed for a year or more (Podgursky and Swaim 1987b). Duration of unemployment has several consequences beyond immediate loss of income: the likelihood of eventual reemployment drops rapidly among those unemployed 12 months and beyond; the longer one remains unemployed, the greater the drop in wages (comparing post- versus predisplacement job); and long-duration unemployment is associated with additional bouts of displacement, after the first job loss and first reemployment (Stevens 1995). Workers with less education suffer longer spells of unemployment, as do African Americans, older workers, and workers with long tenure with an employer (Podgursky and Swaim 1987a; Kletzner 1991).

Researchers have found that reductions in earnings following displacement persist for several years, even after reemployment. Jacobson, LaLonde, and Sullivan (1993), for example, found an average loss of 25 percent of predisplacement earnings in the fifth year following displacement. Stevens (1995) documented earnings losses of 9 percent six or more years after displacement. Studies of earnings losses in the shorter term (one to three years after displacement) document that older workers suffer greater percentage earnings losses than younger workers (Bowman, Couchman, and Cole 1994) and that African Americans and less educated workers also experience greater percentage losses (Podgursky and Swaim 1989).

In these quantitative studies, the focus is on chances for reemployment and income losses. Qualitative researchers such as Newman (1988, 1993) examine the broader impact of displacement upon the individuals involved, their spouses, and their children. She emphasizes the domino effects of job loss: conflicts often develop with spouses, and children used to a middle-class existence may resent being pushed downward and become hostile to the job loser. Displaced workers face a severe loss of self-esteem, many missing their professional identities intensely, and some come to blame themselves for their situation. Displacement becomes an assault on people's expectations about life itself. Their ideas about the rewards that follow hard work are violated, and their sense of values and their own place in society are called into question. This shock may be transmitted to children, some of whom become less trusting in education as a route to mobility and security, seeking quick material success instead.

RELATED RESEARCH:
WORK-FAMILY ISSUES

The work-family literature is very diverse, ranging from studies of the effects of mothers' work upon children's intellectual development, to relationships between work, family, and adult psychological well-being, to the impacts of work roles on parenting styles. Despite this diversity, Barnett (1997, 2) identifies a theme of conflict repeated throughout this literature: "there is a universal assumption that family demands compete with those of the workplace, such that family is seen as a problem and as a barrier to maximizing the bottom line," and "there is an almost exclusive focus on conflict, both at the individual and corporate level."

This focus on conflict, competition, or strain between work and family is disputed by Barnett (1997), Bailyn (1993), and others who regard the assumption of competition or strain (or at least its overemphasis) as biasing research away from measuring the positive spillover from work to family, and as neglecting the capacity of families and firms to make work and family life reinforcing or synergistic rather than competitive.

Along with the zero-sum or competitive metaphor, studies of work-family frequently draw upon metaphors of "contagion," "spillover," and "crossover" from home to work and vice versa (Bowen and Pittman 1995). Studies by Crouter (1984); Kirchmeyer (1993); Campbell, Campbell, and Kennard (1994); and Barnett and Marshall (1992) indicate that employees acknowledge the influences of the home situation on work. Researchers disagree whether carryover of negative aspects of family life is more prevalent or consequential than carryover of positive aspects. There is also dispute as to whether men or women are more prone to carry stress from home to work: the earlier literature implied

that women would and men would not, but Bolger et al. (1989) found the opposite to be true.

The area of most immediate relevance to the present study is the impact of gender, marital structure, family obligations, and child-rearing responsibilities upon work performance. This aspect of family-work research is quite sparse. Some studies find no differences between men and women, or between employees with young children and those without, upon work commitment or performance (Barnett and Rivers 1996, 151; Duxbury et al. 1992). Others find lower commitment among women with young children (Campbell, Campbell, and Kennard 1994) or greater absenteeism among women (Scott and McClellan 1990).

In sum, work and family research has shown that the family situation can carry over into the workplace. But this literature has not determined whether or to what extent family obligations and spillovers affect productivity in the workplace or whether highly visible indicators such as absenteeism or lateness are linked to family situation. Existing research tends to focus on employees (rather than employers) as paying the cost of competing work and family commitments in terms of time crunches and higher levels of stress.

DATA AND METHODOLOGICAL ISSUES

Two different sources of data are used in this article: the U.S. Bureau of the Census's Current Population Survey (CPS), and the Panel Study of

Income Dynamics (PSID). The former is a monthly household survey of the U.S. population, with samples of approximately 100,000 respondents. Roughly every two years, the Census Bureau has added questions about job displacement to the CPS. Unfortunately, questions about parenting were not included after the 1990 and 1992 displacement surveys. Consequently, my analyses present data from the latest 1996 survey on displacement, but have to go back to 1990 and 1992 to examine the influence of being a parent on displacement.

The PSID is a longitudinal panel survey of U.S. households begun in 1968 (Hill 1992). The analyses in this article apply event-history analysis, using person-months from the period 1984-91 as the unit of analysis. For our purposes, the advantages of using the PSID are that (1) it allows longitudinal analyses that can identify temporal ordering of events such as divorce and job loss; (2) it measures employment status monthly, rather than the longer-term retrospective of the CPS; and (3) it provides data on job tenure. One weakness, however, is that the PSID measures unemployment rather than job displacement, so that persons who were displaced are mixed in with people who lost their jobs for other reasons.

Issues of definition

The basic question used to identify displaced workers in the CPS surveys asks each respondent whether he or she lost or left a job during the prior three years because his or her plant or company closed or moved,

her or his position or shift was abolished, there was insufficient work, or for another similar reason. However, the government does not count as a displaced worker everyone who answers this question affirmatively. It excludes from its count of displaced workers all persons who had worked for less than three years for their employer before being displaced and all displaced employees who expected to be recalled to work within six months. The result of this and other exclusions is that the number of persons fitting the official definition of job displacement is much smaller than the number answering yes to the basic displacement question. The equivalent of 14.10 million employees indicated that they had lost their jobs between 1993 and 1995 in the most recent survey, but the government reported that only 3.75 million persons were displaced (U.S. Bureau of Labor Statistics 1996). Clearly, the definition makes a big difference in the perceived magnitude of the phenomenon.

For this research, the tenure restrictions in defining job displacement have been dropped. In the analyses in this article, all employees who said they had been displaced and who subsequently indicated that this was due to plant closure or relocation, the abolition of a shift or position, or insufficient work are counted as displaced workers.

Variables and models

The CPS provides population weights for each respondent. I divided each respondent's population weight by the mean of all population weights to obtain what is known as a normalized weight for each respondent.

The models presented using the CPS are logistic regressions predicting displacement from marital status and presence of young children in the home, along with control variables including sex, race, age, education, industry group, occupational group, part-time status, and economic sector (for-profit, government, self-employed).

The PSID models are discrete-time event-history models, in which the units of analysis are person-months (Allison 1984; Yamaguchi 1991). The predictors include fixed factors such as sex and race, as well as time-dependent variables such as occupation, education, age, marital status, job seniority, year in which the data are collected, and so forth.

In those event-history analyses in which unemployment served as the dependent variable, only those person-months in which an individual was employed, plus the first person-month of unemployment (if any), were included in the analysis. Similarly, in those models predicting family breakup (divorce or separation), the person-months included were those in which the person was married plus the first person-month of separation or divorce (if any). The dependent variable in these event-history models is the log of the odds that a person will shift status (to unemployment or to marital breakup). The B coefficients reported for each variable represent the change in the logit for a unit increase in that predictor, while the coefficient e^B represents the odds ratio: the change in odds resulting from a unit increase in a predictor (Darlington 1990).

FINDINGS: THE CPS ANALYSES

Trends across surveys covering the last decade are first discussed in terms of simple bivariate statistics. Then multivariate models are presented, focusing on the effect of family and marital structure after controlling for other pertinent variables. This section will be followed by analyses of data from the PSID.

Gender

Across four surveys covering the period 1985-95, there is a small, consistent, and statistically significant difference between men and women employees in the proportions experiencing job displacement. For example, in the 1996 survey, only 7.6 percent of working women were displaced, compared to 9.0 percent of working men ($p < .00001$). Although a 1.4 percent difference may sound small, it is substantial when one considers population estimates. It implies that 380,000 fewer working women were displaced than would have been the case if they had experienced the same displacement rate as men. In the multivariate models that follow, this gender difference in job displacement disappears once part-time work status and other factors are controlled for.

Education

The four surveys show a consistent and statistically significant pattern in which employees with college degrees have lower risks of displacement compared to those with a high school diploma or less education. Those with graduate degrees have particularly low rates of displacement. This pattern has held for over a decade.

Age

The displaced-worker surveys exclude employees under 20 years of age, so they do not cover the youth job market, which is known to have the highest rates of job turnover. Among those over 20, younger workers are overrepresented among those who have been displaced throughout the decade, and older workers are underrepresented. For example, in the 1996 survey, 10.1 percent of workers in their twenties lost jobs, compared to 8.6 percent of those in their thirties, 8.0 percent of those in their forties, and 6.6 percent of those aged 50-64. This pattern has been the same since the mid-1980s: comparisons across the four surveys show little or no change in the age profiles over a decade. The pattern probably results from informal "last hired, first fired" practices as well as more formalized systems of "bumping" and tenure found in unionized and civil service settings. (It does not reflect young employees' propensity to shop around for jobs, since the displacement variable excludes that type of voluntary separation.)

Occupation, industry, and sector

Blue-collar workers face a higher risk of job loss than either managerial or professional workers or white-collar clerical and sales employees. However, the gap between blue-collar and white-collar displacement has narrowed over the decade, reflecting a decrease in the displacement rate of blue-collar workers and an increase in the rate for white-collar and managerial workers. This continues a pattern found by Gardner (1995) in a 1981-92 comparison. Displacement is also more frequent in the private sector, compared to government employment and self-employment, and is higher in manufacturing than in trade, where there is more displacement than in the service industries.

Marital status

Employees' risk of displacement is associated with their marital status, and the effect is statistically highly significant. In the 1996 survey, 7.5 percent of married employees were displaced, instead of the 8.4 percent that would be expected given their proportion in the labor force. This may seem like a small difference; however, it means that 603,000 fewer married employees were displaced than would be expected. Conversely, 9.4 percent of divorced employees were displaced, or 158,000 more than expected, and 10.1 percent of never-married employees were displaced, or 436,000 more than expected. A similar pattern is found across the four surveys, with the exception that in 1994 the displacement rate for never-married employees was not significantly higher.

Multivariate models

Table 1 shows that in the 1996 survey, sector, industry, and occupa-

TABLE 1
LOGISTIC REGRESSION PREDICTING JOB DISPLACEMENT, 1996 CPS SURVEY

Predictors	B	SE	p	e^B
Male	−.0547	.0388	.1584	—
White	−.0309	.0484	.5227	—
Twenties	.1314	.0524	.0121	1.1404
Thirties	.0245	.0461	.5952	—
Fifties	−.1892	.0560	.0007	.8276
Over 64	−.1258	.1154	.2760	—
Some high school education	.1714	.0722	.0176	1.1869
High school graduate	.0521	.0574	.3642	—
Some college	.1496	.0554	.0142	1.1613
Master's or doctoral degree	.0159	.0842	.8503	—
Manager	−.1572	.0532	.0032	.8545
Blue collar	.1163	.0463	.0120	1.1233
Other job	−.8307	.1452	.0000	.4357
Manufacture	.3700	.0532	.0000	1.4478
Trade	.3116	.0505	.0000	1.3656
Other industry	.4767	.0545	.0000	1.6107
Divorced	.24967	.0498	.0000	1.2835
Single	.2521	.0461	.0000	1.2867
Widowed	.3232	.1249	.0097	1.3815
Government	−1.1696	.0758	.0000	.3105
Nonprofit	−.2811	.0984	.0043	.7549
Self-employed	−5.8243	1.6221	.0003	.0030
Part-time	−.1366	.0494	.0057	.8723
Constant	−2.5479	.0845	.0000	
−2 log likelihood	25,330.672			
Model chi-square	1,087.458	23 df	p = .0000	
N of cases	44,619			
N displaced	3,894			

SOURCE: Data are from U.S. Bureau of the Census 1996.
NOTE: The reference categories for the variables are as follows: for age, the forties; for education, college graduation; for occupation, white-collar and sales; for industry, services; for marital status, married; and for sector, private sector.

tional group remain significant predictors of the likelihood of displacement, after controlling for other factors. Gender and race have no association with displacement. Those who are self-employed or employed by government or the nonprofit sector are displaced less often than those in private industry. Managers and professionals are at less risk than other occupations (even though downsizing has increased the rate of managerial and professional layoffs compared to earlier periods). Employees who did not graduate from high school and those with some college education are more likely to be displaced than college graduates. Age is associated with displacement: younger workers (in their twenties) are more likely to be displaced, and employees in their fifties are less likely to be displaced, compared to employees in their forties (the reference category.)

Part-time work was associated with lower likelihood of displacement. The odds that a part-timer would be displaced was 87 percent of the odds that an equivalently educated full-time worker in a similar industrial sector would be displaced.

Central to our focus is the fact that marital status remains significantly associated with displacement, even after controlling for education, age, gender, industry, occupation, sector, and part-time work (see Table 1). Never-married employees have 29 percent higher odds of displacement than married employees of equivalent education, age, and so on: their e^B—the odds ratio—is 1.2867. Divorced employees have 28 percent higher odds of displacement than married employees, and widows have 38 percent higher odds than married employees, net of other controls.

What does it mean that marital status is associated with job loss or displacement? For never-married employees, there is little causal ambiguity: the results imply that single employees have been displaced more often than married employees of similar age and with equivalent educational characteristics and in similar occupational or industrial locations. In the case of divorce and separation, however, the observed association is quite ambiguous in terms of causal direction: either divorced or separated employees are being laid off in larger numbers or

TABLE 2
MARITAL STATUS, PRESENCE OF CHILDREN, AND JOB DISPLACEMENT
(Percentage displaced)

	1992 CPS	1990 CPS
Marital status		
Married	9.5	7.2
Widowed	9.8	7.7
Separated or divorced	12.1	10.4
Never married	10.9	7.9
Children younger than 18 years		
With kids	10.4	8.0
No kids	9.8	7.5
Children younger than 6 years		
With young kids	11.5	8.8
No young kids	9.9	7.4
Single parent*		
Yes	12.6	9.1
No	10.0	7.6

NOTE: All the above associations are statistically significant at $p < .01$ or below.

*Single parent is defined as a never-married, separated or divorced, or widowed person who has a child of his or her own under the age of 18 in the household.

displaced employees are becoming separated or divorced after losing their jobs. The causation could plausibly run either way or in both directions at once. To resolve this ambiguity and to measure the relative sizes of the directional effects require longitudinal data, such as the PSID reported later.

Children and job displacement

Table 2 examines the relationship between marital status and parenting, on one hand, and job displacement, on the other. It shows that divorced and never-married employees had higher job loss and displacement rates than married employees. In addition, employees with children under 18 years of age in their household, employees with children under 6, and "single parents" (that is, widowed, divorced, separated, or never-married employees who are parents of children under 18) also have higher displacement rates than their counterparts.

Table 3 reports multivariate logistic regressions that examine the associations between family and displacement after controlling for education, age, industry, and sector, in addition to family and marital variables. Equation I contains all predictors except the single-parent variable. Equation II does contain the single-parent variable but omits the marital status variables. This procedure avoids multicollinearity problems.

Table 3 indicates that the association between job displacement and parental status remains significant after controlling for education, occupation, age, and other factors in both the 1992 and 1990 surveys. Being a parent of one or more young children (under 6 years of age) and being a single parent are both associated with higher odds of job displacement: 18 percent higher for those with young children in 1992, 24 percent higher for single parents. The corresponding odds in 1990 were 18 percent and 13 percent higher, respectively.

FINDINGS: THE PSID ANALYSES

Table 4 presents the results of an event-history analysis of monthly data from the years 1984-91. The sample excludes persons who were never married during the period,

since the focus is on marital breakup. The model seeks to understand whether unemployment increases the likelihood, at a later date, of marital breakup. The control variables are demographic and occupational variables, although, as might be expected, such factors have little predictive power in explaining a phenomenon as personal as marital breakup. However, those employees who had experienced prior unemployment did have statistically significantly higher rates of later breakup, net of other factors, with an odds ratio of 1.368. Employees in their twenties were also at higher risk of breakup, as were working women, compared to working men. African Americans had a higher likelihood of marital breakup than whites, and college graduates had a lower likelihood than high school graduates. Numerous other variables, including occupation and job tenure, had no association with breakup.

Table 5 presents an equivalent analysis but looks at the reverse temporal ordering. It asks whether marital breakup, along with occupational and demographic control variables, increases the likelihood of later becoming unemployed. As expected, the model is much stronger. Marital breakup is a statistically significant predictor of later unemployment, with an odds ratio of 1.31, after controlling for education, occupation, job tenure, and so on. Single parents also had a higher likelihood of subsequent unemployment. The CPS finding that employees with young children were at higher risk of

TABLE 3

LOGISTIC REGRESSION: JOB DISPLACEMENT AND FAMILY STRUCTURE, CPS SURVEYS

| | 1992 Survey | | | | | | 1990 Survey | | | | | |
| | Equation I | | | Equation II | | | Equation I | | | Equation II | | |
Predictors	B	e^B	p	B	e^B	p	B	e^B	p	B	e^B	p
Female	-0.04		ns	-0.03		ns	-0.02		ns	0.017		ns
Children younger than 6 years	0.166	1.18	<.0001	0.104	1.11	.002	0.17	1.18	<.0001	0.134	1.14	4E-04
Single parent	n.a.			0.213	1.24	<.0001	n.a.			0.122	1.13	.028
Part-time job	-0.76	0.466	<.0001	-.077	0.465	<.0001	-0.46	0.63	<.0001	-.48	0.618	<.0001
Some high school education	0.202	1.22	4E-04	0.196	1.22	4E-04	0.161	1.18	.014	0.168	1.18	.011
High school graduate	0.043		ns	0.037		ns	0.116	1.12	.039	0.122	1.13	.03
Some college	0.078		ns	0.075		ns	0.231	1.23	2E-04	0.221	1.25	1E-04
Master's or doctoral degree	-0.02		ns	-0.03		ns	-0.04		ns	-0.04		ns
Manufacture	0.573	1.77	<.0001	0.568	1.76	<.0001	0.585	1.79	<.0001	0.579	1.78	<.0001
Trade	0.428	1.53	<.0001	0.427	1.53	<.0001	0.328	1.39	<.0001	0.328	1.39	<.0001
Other industry	0.65	1.91	<.0001	0.647	1.91	<.0001	0.779	2.17	<.0001	0.78	2.18	<.0001
Managers or professional	-0.11	0.899	.011	-0.11	0.897	.01	-0.11	0.899	.028	-0.11	0.897	.025
Blue-collar	0.171	1.18	<.0001	0.175	1.19	<.0001	0.121	1.13	.003	0.131	1.14	.001
Other occupation	-0.3	0.74	.008	-0.3	0.744	.009	-0.55	0.579	1E-03	-0.54	0.585	<.0001
Government	-1.91	0.149	<.0001	-1.91	0.148	<.0001	-2.2	0.11	<.0001	-2.21	0.11	<.0001
Self-employed	-2.62	0.073	<.0001	-2.63	0.072	<.0001	-2.63	0.072	<.0001	-2.64	0.071	<.0001
White	0.066		ns	0.061		ns	0.124	1.13	.006	0.118	1.13	.009
Age (years)	0.003		ns	0.003		ns	0.001		ns	0.002		ns
Younger than 30 years	0.066		ns	0.074		ns	-0		ns	-0.02		ns
Single	0.117	1.12	.003	n.a.			0.021		ns	n.a.		
Widowed	0.193	1.21	.038	n.a.			0.183		ns	n.a.		
Divorced	0.244	1.27	<.0001	n.a.			0.357	1.42	<.0001	n.a.		
Constant	-2.55			-2.5			-2.91			-2.9		
Log likelihood	39,589			39,610			32,653			32,712		
p	<.0001	21 df		<.0001	19 df		<.0001	21 df		<.0001	19 df	
Sample size	66,315			66,315			66,652			66,652		

NOTE: The dependent variable is job displacement (yes/no).

76

TABLE 4
EVENT-HISTORY ANALYSIS PREDICTING
MARITAL BREAKUP, PSID MONTHLY DATA, 1984-91

Variable	B	Wald	p	e^B
Ever unemployed	.3133	7.33	.0067	1.368
Twenties	.7216	18.69	.0000	2.058
Thirties	.2274	2.04	.1528	—
50-64 years	−1.2838	14.99	.0001	.277
65 years and older	−3.0023	.53	.4638	—
Black	.2859	5.45	.0196	1.331
Other race	.0347	.00	.9392	—
Child younger than 6 years	.0665	.37	.5386	—
Child younger than 18 years	.0188	.03	.8682	—
Female	.4553	14.90	.0001	1.5766
Some high school education	.2666	3.09	.0789	—
Some college	−.0631	.23	.6319	—
College graduate	−.4127	4.07	.0436	.6619
Master's or doctoral degree	−.0803	.11	.7391	—
1984	.4881	5.84	.0157	1.6293
1985	.5859	9.14	.0025	1.7965
1986	.2047	.96	.3257	—
1987	.2016	.95	.3303	—
1988	−.2431	1.08	.2994	—
1989	.2088	1.03	.3105	—
1990	.4109	4.39	.0362	1.5082
Constant	−7.8571	965.97	.0000	

	Chi-square	Significance
−2 log likelihood	6,037	.000
Model chi-square	168	.000
G of fit	383,419	.000
N of cases	46,479	

NOTE: The following additional variables proved to be statistically nonsignificant: region, occupation, job tenure, part-time status. They are therefore not shown in this table.

displacement was not evident in this PSID model of unemployment, however. This difference could stem from the different dependent variable used in the PSID (unemployment versus displacement) or from differences in the control variables (the PSID provided a control for job seniority; the CPS did not).

In sum, the PSID analyses parallel the associations found in the CPS between job displacement and marital status and suggest that, in the case of divorce or separation, the causation runs both ways: divorced people are at higher risk of subsequently losing their jobs, and job loss results in a higher risk of marital breakup. The PSID did not replicate CPS findings regarding the association between parental status and displacement, however, even though this was a consistent finding across two CPS surveys.

TABLE 5
**EVENT HISTORY ANALYSIS PREDICTING
UNEMPLOYMENT, PSID MONTHLY DATA, 1984-91**

Variable	B	Wald	p	e^B
Divorced	.2709	15.36	.0001	1.311
Single parent	.2599	10.18	.0014	1.297
Female	−.1142	6.06	.0138	.8921
Twenties	.1284	4.38	.0362	1.137
Thirties	.0529	.93	.3336	—
50-64 years	−.2091	8.21	.0042	.8113
65 years and older	.0141	.00	.9494	—
Manufacturing	.3088	28.43	.0000	1.362
Other industry	.3653	37.83	.0000	1.441
Services	−.2309	14.06	.0002	.7938
Tenure Q1	.7910	237.94	.0000	2.206
Tenure Q2	.2545	19.72	.0000	1.289
Tenure Q4	−.2270	14.49	.0001	.7969
Managers and professionals	−.5270	64.99	.0000	.5904
Technical and craft	−.2280	18.29	.0000	.7961
Other white-collar	−.4363	57.59	.0000	.6464
Black	.1512	12.01	.0005	1.163
Other race	.2340	2.86	.0909	—
Child younger than 6 years	−.0459	1.26	.2623	—
Child younger than 18 years	.0347	.72	.3962	—
Some high school education	.2999	41.52	.0000	1.349
Some college	−.1676	11.05	.0009	.8457
College graduate	−.6232	51.39	.0000	.5416
Master's or doctoral degree	−.7646	38.13	.0000	.4655
1984	.0088	.01	.8984	—
1985	.0018	.00	.9790	—
1986	.0273	.16	.6864	—
1987	−.1860	6.87	.0087	.8302
1988	−.1374	3.85	.0497	.8716
1989	−.1481	4.49	.0340	.8624
1990	−.1200	3.01	.0826	—
Constant	−4.9606		.0000	

	Chi-square	Significance
−2 log likelihood	35,215	.0000
Model chi-square	1,662	.0000
N of cases	440,480	

NOTE: The following additional variables in the model proved to be statistically nonsignificant: region, part-time status. They are not shown in this table.

Recovery from job loss

After displacement, some people quickly find new jobs, and their earnings in the new jobs equal or exceed what they earned previously. Others are reemployed but at a fraction of their old earnings level. Yet others remain unemployed for long periods, while continuing to look for employment, or become so discouraged that they leave the labor force.

I examined earnings recovery for displaced employees for the 1990, 1992, and 1996 surveys by calculating new job earnings as a percentage of their predisplacement earnings. One of the more striking features of this analysis is that the pattern is bimodal, or U shaped. Many people—between a third and half of those displaced—recover fully, in terms of earnings. Between a third and a quarter of the displaced do not recover at all: they remain without a job, even a year or more after displacement. The rest are found across a broad range of reduced earnings levels in between.

This U-shaped distribution means that most displaced workers do not find jobs by lowering their earnings expectations and moving slightly down the occupational ladder. Most either get back into something roughly equivalent to their old job or slide out of the labor force or into long-term unemployment. The size of the group that fails to find new jobs is large: even during times of economic expansion, as captured by the 1996 survey, over one-quarter of displaced workers remain out of work one year or more after displacement.

A minority (roughly 20 percent) of displaced workers who find reemployment do so at greatly reduced wages—one-half or less of their old earnings. Adding these two groups together indicates that roughly one-half of displaced workers suffer dramatic downward mobility in terms of earnings (cf. Newman 1988).

Logistic regression models (not shown) were run to identify the characteristics of displaced workers who had not found jobs within the 12 months after their displacement. Demographic and human capital characteristics proved the strongest predictors of who remained unemployed and/or with zero earnings. The strongest effects are for workers in their fifties and older, who are far less likely to hold a new job one or more years after displacement. There are also racial effects in two of the three surveys: even though people of color are not at greater risk of initial displacement than whites, once displaced, people of color are less likely to find new jobs. Whites' odds of remaining unemployed one or more years after displacement are 52-58 percent of nonwhites'.

The models show that women are more likely to remain unemployed than men (they have odds of continued nonemployment between 38 percent and 90 percent higher than men). Displaced workers who had not completed high school and those who had only a high school diploma had far higher rates of long-term unemployment. Displaced single parents were also significantly more likely to remain unemployed than other displaced employees, with other factors held constant. Last, in only one of the three models, displaced workers with young children were significantly more likely to remain unemployed than those without young children.

DISCUSSION AND CONCLUSION

Job displacement has increased substantially since the mid-1980s, catching employees of every age, family situation, education, occupational group, and industry in its net.

The processes of downsizing and plant closings are to a large extent impersonal, aimed at a whole establishment or at whole parts of a firm, not at particular kinds of people. Nevertheless, we find that displacement does not fall on all groups of employees equally, even after one controls for industry, occupation, and sector.

The central finding of this article is that marital status and parental status affect the likelihood of displacement, in addition to structural and human capital predictors. These effects are statistically significant and are modest in percentage terms, though even a small percentage difference can mean differences of hundreds of thousands of employees, economy-wide. Other things being equal, single parents have higher risks of displacement, as do parents of small children, and divorced employees. In the case of divorced and separated employees, the PSID analyses indicated that those who have suffered marital breakups face a higher likelihood of job loss thereafter and that job loss itself increases the likelihood of later marital breakup. Causation appears to run in both directions.

What behavioral mechanisms could account for these family and parental effects? The survey data cannot speak to that question. I suspect, however, that these differences in rates, aggregated across the whole economy, reflect the tensions that exist between work and family obligations. Many employees with small children are exemplary workers, and many employees work productively throughout the turmoil of divorce.

Nevertheless, some parents find themselves taking days off to look after sick children or because child care arrangements fail. Other employees suffer chronic sicknesses themselves, lose time from work, or are distracted due to marital problems. Such tensions between work demands and home demands have been central to work-family research for several decades. Employers normally take these tensions in their stride. But when directives arrive from headquarters to lay off many workers, I suggest that these behaviors begin to influence who is laid off and who stays. Aggregated across millions of layoffs, they seem to result in the displacement of larger numbers of single parents, more parents of young children, and more divorced employees.

Since these same groups find it harder to regain employment after displacement, the initial job loss is the first of a series of life crises. Many suffer serious financial setbacks, and some find their marriages falling apart. Embedded in the recent waves of job displacement we see traces of the ongoing strain between job responsibilities and family commitments.

References

Allison, Paul. 1984. *Event History Analysis: Regression for Longitudinal Event Data*. Beverly Hills, CA: Sage.

Bailyn, Lotte. 1993. *Breaking the Mold: Women, Men and Time in the New Corporate World*. New York: Free Press.

Barnett, Rosalind C. 1997. *Toward a Review and Reconceptualization of the Work/Family Literature*. Genetic, Social, and Psychological Monographs. Washington, DC: Heldref.

Barnett, Rosalind C. and Nancy L. Marshall. 1992. Men's Job and Partner Roles: Spillover Effects and Psychological Distress. *Sex Roles* 27 (9-10):455-72.

Barnett, Rosalind and Caryl Rivers. 1996. *She Works/He Works: How Two-Income Families Are Happier, Healthier, and Better-Off*. New York: HarperCollins.

Bolger, N., A. Delongis, R. C. Kessler, and E. Wethington. 1989. The Contagion of Stress Across Multiple Roles. *Journal of Marriage and the Family* 51:175-83.

Bowen, Gary L. and Joe F. Pittman. 1995. *The Work and Family Interface: Towards a Contextual Effects Perspective*. Minneapolis, MN: National Council on Family Relations.

Bowman, Jan, Glennis Couchman, and Suzanne Cole. 1994. Midlife and Older Displaced Workers: A Comparison of Pre-Displacement and New Earnings. *Journal of Family and Economic Issues* 15(2):93-115.

Campbell, D. J., K. M. Campbell, and D. Kennard. 1994. The Effects of Family Responsibilities on Work Commitment and Job Performance of Non-Professional Women. *Journal of Occupational and Industrial Psychology* 67:283-96.

Crouter, A. C. 1984. Spillover from Family to Work: The Neglected Side of Work-Family Interface. *Human Relations* 37(6):425-41.

Darlington, Richard B. 1990. *Regression and Linear Models*. New York: McGraw Hill.

Duxbury, L., C. Higgins, C. Lee, and S. Mills. 1992. An Examination of Organizational and Individual Outcomes. *Optimum: The Journal of Public Sector Management* 23(2):46-59.

Gardner, Jennifer M. 1995. Worker Displacement: A Decade of Change. *Monthly Labor Review* 118(4):45-67. Also published as *Bulletin* 2464 of the U.S. Department of Labor, Bureau of Labor Statistics, July 1995.

Hill, Martha S. 1992. *The Panel Study of Income Dynamics*. Newbury Park, CA: Sage.

Jacobson, Louis, Robert LaLonde, and Daniel Sullivan. 1993. *The Costs of Worker Dislocation*. Kalamazoo, MI: W. E. Upjohn Institute for Employment Research.

Kirchmeyer, Catherine. 1993. Nonwork-to-Work Spillover: A More Balanced View of the Experiences and Coping of Professional Women and Men. *Sex Roles* 28(9):531-52.

Kletzner, Lori. 1991. Job Displacement 1979-1986: How Blacks Fared Relative to Whites. *Monthly Labor Review* 114(7):17-25.

Moore, Thomas. 1992. Racial Differences in Post-Displacement Joblessness. *Social Science Quarterly* 37(3):674-89.

Newman, Katherine S. 1988. *Falling from Grace: The Experience of Downward Mobility in the American Middle Class*. New York: Free Press.

———. 1993. *Declining Fortunes: The Withering of the American Dream*. New York: Basic Books.

Podgursky, Michael and Paul Swaim. 1987a. Duration of Joblessness Following Displacement. *Industrial Relations* 26(3):213-26.

———. 1987b. Job Displacement and Earnings Loss: Evidence from the Displaced Worker Survey. *Industrial and Labor Relations Review* 41(1):17-29.

———. 1989. Do More-Educated Workers Fare Better Following Job Displacement? *Monthly Labor Review* Aug.:43-46.

Scott, K. D. and E. L. McClellan. 1990. Gender Differences in Absenteeism. *Public Personnel Management* 19(2):229-53.

Stevens, Ann Huff. 1995. Long-Term Effects of Job Displacement: Evidence from the Panel Study of Income Dynamics. NBER Working Paper Number 5343, National Bureau of Economic Research, Cambridge, MA.

U.S. Bureau of the Census. 1996. Current Population Survey, Feb., with displaced worker supplement.

U.S. Bureau of Labor Statistics. 1996. *Worker Displacement During the Mid-1990s.* Document no. USDL96-336. Washington, DC: Department of Labor, Bureau of Labor Statistics.

Yamaguchi, Kazuo. 1991. *Event History Analysis.* Newbury Park, CA: Sage.

ANNALS, *AAPSS*, **562**, March 1999

Young Europeans' Orientations to Families and Work

By SUZAN LEWIS, JANET SMITHSON, and JULIA BRANNEN

ABSTRACT: This article explores the orientations of young people (aged 18-30) to family and employment. We draw on data collected as part of a qualitative transnational study conducted in five European countries: the United Kingdom, Ireland, Portugal, Norway, and Sweden. The young people who participated in this study were either employed, in education or training programs, or unemployed. Some of the salient social and economic trends across Europe and some national differences are first described briefly as background to the study. The meanings that these young adults attach to family, their current work-life priorities, and the work and family arrangements that they envisage for the future are then discussed. In the context of longer periods spent in education or training and the growing insecurity of work, the participants appear to live in an extended present, where current work-life priorities remain sharply in focus. As a consequence of living in an extended present, it is difficult for them to plan for future work and family arrangements. The future scenarios envisaged differ cross-nationally, reflecting social, economic, and ideological context.

Suzan Lewis is reader in psychology at the Manchester Metropolitan University and a director of the Work-Life Research Centre. Her publications include The Work-Family Challenge: Rethinking Employment *(with Jeremy Lewis). She is co-editor of the Journal* Community, Work and Family.

Janet Smithson is research fellow at the Manchester Metropolitan University.

Julia Brannen is professor of sociology at the Institute of Education, London, and a director of the Work-Life Research Centre.

NOTE: The study on which this article was based is made possible by co-funding from the European Commission (DGV); the British Council; Manchester Metropolitan University; and the Institute of Education, United Kingdom; the Universities of Bergen, Norway, Uppsala, Sweden, and Limerick, Ireland; and Midland Bank, United Kingdom. We acknowledge the important contributions of our research partners, Pat O'Connor, Ann Nilsen, Clarissa Kugelberg, and Maria Das Dores Gurreiro, to developing and carrying out this research project in their respective countries.

CORPORATE and state policies on work and family have always rested upon implicit or explicit assumptions about what constitutes a family. Yet family is a contested and changing concept. Initially, most debate on family and work issues centered on families, and especially mothers, with young children. There is now a growing recognition of other work-family scenarios, including, for example, combining employment with elder care and care of other adult dependents (Neal et al. 1993; Phillips 1995); the care of disabled children, which can involve intense demands extending well beyond the childhood years (Freedman, Litchfield, and Warfield 1995; Kagan, Lewis, and Heaton 1998; Lewis, Kagan, and Heaton 1998); and issues for lone mothers (Hertz and Ferguson 1998) and single fathers (Gregg 1994). Debates on the nature of family in relation to work-family policy and practice have also begun to focus on diversity, for example, in relation to same-sex partners, and, to some extent, have begun to consider shifts in gendered work-family priorities (Lewis and Cooper 1995).

Little attention, however, has been given in the work-family literature to the shifting orientations to family among the younger generations of workers who are entering the labor market at a time of substantial economic and social change. This generation has experienced and been actors in a number of transitions in family and economic life, and there is little reason to expect that their work-family needs and expectations should be identical to those of earlier generations; most policy is based on the latter. They are more likely than previous generations to have been raised in dual-earner or single-parent families and to have experienced increasingly diverse family forms and shifting notions of family stability and instability. Gender roles are in transition, and women's and men's orientations to work and family are changing and converging (Halpern 1995). The economic dimensions of family life are also in transition. In the context of globalization, corporate downsizing and restructuring, and technological developments, secure employment, once considered essential for stable family life, is no longer taken for granted. The incoming generation of workers in this post-job-security era have few expectations of jobs for life.

WORK AND FAMILY IN EUROPE

While there are common trends throughout the industrialized world, there are also national and regional differences in social and economic trends and structures and in their impact on work and family life. This article examines orientations to family and work among young men and women in five European states: the United Kingdom, Ireland, Portugal, and Sweden (all members of the European Union [EU]), and Norway (a country that voted at a referendum to remain independent from the EU). We draw on data from a project undertaken as part of the EU's Fourth Action Programme on Equal Opportunities for Women and Men in the European Community. A major theme within this program is the reconciliation of employment and family life, that is, seeking ways of harmonizing paid work and unpaid family work (Moss 1996).

The focus on the reconciliation of employment and family life highlights the relationships between social and economic policies. It has prompted a number of policy initiatives at the EU level, aimed at harmonizing social policy across the EU. One example is the Parental Leave Directive, which requires member states to implement legislation on parental leave and leave for urgent family reasons. Parental leave provisions apply to all workers with an employment contract and are distinct from maternity and paternity leave. The directive sets out the minimal conditions that member states must provide. Some states already have parental leave provisions far in excess of the minimum required by the directive, while others are developing legislation to meet the requirements.

Within the broader European context, there are substantial national variations in policy context as well as in economic conditions that are relevant to work and family (Lewis 1997). The five countries have been chosen to illustrate some of this variation in relation to work and family.

Differences in policy reflect different welfare state models and the assumptions that underpin them. In particular, state social policies differ in terms of assumptions made about women's work and family activities and in terms of the extent to which governments have intervened to promote certain kinds of family arrangements. Jane Lewis (1992) has char-

acterized welfare states in relation to their adherence to or departure from the male-breadwinner family model. Commitment to assumptions underpinning this model is highest in Ireland and fairly strong in Britain. The male-breadwinner model is weakest in Scandinavian countries, where social policy is based on dual-breadwinner family patterns.

In the Scandinavian countries, public supports for work and family are well established. The Swedish parental insurance scheme has long been a model for the rest of the world. Under this scheme, parental leave is paid for 450 days and can be used until the child is 8 years old. Three hundred and sixty days are paid at full salary and the rest at a standard rate. There are 180 extra days per child for the second and subsequent children. These conditions, however, are limited to those with a permanent employment contract. Others receive paid leave but only at the standard (lower) rate. Norwegian parents have the right to 42 weeks of fully paid parental leave if they have been employed for 6 of the preceding 10 months. In both Sweden and Norway, one month is to be taken by the father and cannot be transferred to the mother if he does not make use of this right. There is also child care for every family that needs it in Sweden, and good-quality child care is a high priority. Norway also has a good child care system in comparison with most European countries, although not as good as in Sweden. It has a mixture of public and private provisions, but all under state control. Interestingly, highly controversial political debates are now taking place

TABLE 1
PERCENTAGE OF FIXED-TERM CONTRACTS AMONG EMPLOYEES
UNDER AGE 25 AND AMONG ALL EMPLOYEES, 1997

	United Kingdom	Ireland	Portugal	Sweden	Norway
Employees under 25	13	19	26	42	35*
All employees	7	10	10	14	12

SOURCES: Data are from Eurostat, Labour Force Survey, as in European Commission 1997, 51, tab. 12; Norway, Bureau of Statistics.
*Mainly students working part-time during education.

in Norway about the relative priority of a cash child care allowance to support parental child care and extrafamilial child care provision to further mothers' employment (Waerness, 1998). In Portugal, there is only unpaid parental leave and a low level of public child care, while the United Kingdom and Ireland have paid maternity leave, but parental and family leave have not yet been implemented. Public child care provision is sparse in Britain and extremely rare in Ireland.

A number of economic and social trends are also relevant for understanding current work-family issues in Europe. Of the countries studied here, the employment rates of women are highest in Norway and Sweden and lowest in Ireland. There are high rates of part-time work, mostly among women, in Sweden, Norway, and Britain, although part-time hours tend to be longer in the Scandinavian countries. There is little part-time work in Ireland and Portugal. The rate of female full-time employment is highest in Portugal, while women's labor market participation, although growing, is lower in Ireland than in the other countries. Working hours are longest in the United Kingdom and Portugal. Un-

employment is an issue in many European countries. It is very low in Norway but has risen considerably in Sweden over the last decade, from 2 percent in 1990 to 11 percent in 1998 (European Commission 1998). Youth unemployment is particularly high in the four EU countries. There has also been a growth in fixed-term contracts. As Table 1 shows, in 1997, the percentage of fixed-term contracts among employees younger than 25 years was 42 percent in Sweden, 26 percent in Portugal, 19 percent in Ireland, and 13 percent in the United Kingdom. There is a low rate of official unemployment in Portugal but a highly precarious labor market and high levels of nonpermanent work. Although regulations have recently changed, at the time this study was carried out (1997) many young people were hired as independent workers, with so-called green receipts, which do not give them access to social benefits such as unemployment benefits when out of work.

Social trends relative to work and family include a decline in marriage, a rise in cohabitation, and a rise in the age at marriage for those who do marry and at the age of first child. They also include a decline in fertility, although the latter is less marked in the Scandinavian countries (European Commission 1997).

THE STUDY

The research aimed to highlight some of the major issues identified by young people in relation to current and future work and family in the five countries. To this end, focus groups and individual interviews were carried out with diverse groups of young people (aged 18-30) including unemployed young people, those in precarious employment, low-skilled workers, highly skilled workers, and university and vocational students. This age cohort was selected to fit in with European trends. Traditionally, the age range of 18-25 has been designated the period of youth for the purpose of collecting statistics and other information. However, recent European publications have extended this to the age of 29 or 30 in recognition of the extended period of the youth phase within the life course (European Commission 1997). Most focus groups were single sex, although a few were mixed. The groups included a small minority who were already parents (single and married), except in Norway, where the groups were younger (up to the age of 25 rather than 30). A total of 70 focus groups and 100 individual interviews were carried out. A focus group guide and individual interview schedule were developed collaboratively by researchers in the five participating countries. This article examines data primarily from the focus groups. Focus groups are particularly appropriate for this type of research because they not only encourage discussion on a range of topics relevant to the research, but they also permit issues perceived as important to the participant to emerge. In this way, young people themselves set some of the agenda for the research and contributed perspectives that may not have been apparent to the researchers.

The groups discussed ideas about adulthood, relationships and settling down, having children, what they value in relation to current and future work, job insecurity, career paths, gender expectations, managing employment and family life, and expectations of support for the reconciliation of work and family from the state, employers, and trade unions. Focus groups were taped and transcribed and thematically analyzed first nationally and then with respect to transnational themes.

Most cross-national research is based on large surveys that provide insights into trends but lack the richness of qualitative data. This study does not seek to extend knowledge about trends but, rather, has generated rich and unique data on young Europeans' values, experiences, needs, and expectations, from their own standpoints, which illustrate the impacts of these trends.

While many common themes emerged from the focus groups, there were also differences at many levels. Within each country, some differences emerged between those at the younger and older ends of the age range; there were some gender differences (as well as some convergence) and also some variations based on social class and ethnicity. There was a diversity of views within many of the relatively homogeneous focus groups. But there were also discernible themes, some of which reflected a national social and economic context, which formed the basis of our discussions of cross-national differences and similarities. In this article, we focus on the meanings young adults attach to family, their current work-life priorities, and the family and work arrangements that they envisage for the future.

YOUNG ADULTS' VIEWS ON FAMILY

There is a widespread recognition among young people that families are becoming more diverse and that it is increasingly difficult to identify a typical family.

I've got a sister who's just got divorced, I've got a cousin with 2 kids by 2 different women, I've got one who's just split up with his girlfriend who's got a kid, one's living with her boyfriend, they've got a kid. They've all got kids but there's only two of them that are married. Single ones, and there's seeing them at weekends and not seeing them, paying this and not paying this. (U.K. man, unemployed)

They talk about the significance of partners, siblings, friends, and even pets in their lives, about same-sex partnerships and remaining single and/or child free. Yet most also have a notion that they will, at some point in the future, "settle down," and for most this means an ideal of a partner and, usually, children.

These contradictory discourses of diversity and tradition reflect the greater concreteness with which they talk about their present lives; ideas about the future are less well formed. For most, this idea of settling down is something for the future, not yet. The transition to what have traditionally been considered adult roles of employment, a home of their own, and family formation is becoming more complex, prolonged, and filled with ambivalence in the context of longer periods spent in education and training, and difficulties in getting a foothold in the labor market. Many talk about wanting freedom or time to travel and do other things. There is a strong theme in all the countries of wanting to live their lives before settling down and considering forming new families. While traditionally the work-family field has been arguing against a conceptual separation of work and family, it seems that the young people in this study are creating a new separation between life, on one hand, and work-family, on the other.[1]

"I have thought of having children when I am around 30. My mother was young when she had me [and my older brother; she was aged] 19 and 21. No, imagine sitting with 2 children now that I am 22. A mother of 2 when I think of myself as a child!"
"That's what I think also, I want to do my things first before having children."
"So many things come first." (Swedish women, aged 20-22)

It's nice to have your ambitions fulfilled with what as far as you can go, and do what you want when the time is available to you. And, obviously, it's inevitable that you're going to settle down. (British Asian woman, student, aged 21)

However, many also talk about the precariousness or perceived insecurity of work, which makes it difficult to think about future family formation or work-family scenarios. The focus group results suggest that young adults have not given up on achieving their future goals but that current circumstances leave them at a loss regarding how to move toward achieving them, and this is a concern for many of them.

Insecure work and the difficulties in envisaging the future

The immediate barriers to planning future work and family lives, for many of these young adults, are the problems of achieving a stable enough life to be able to think about having a family, however defined, or setting up a home. Although the young adults in the study do not expect jobs for life, those who experience difficulty in finding even relatively secure jobs find it difficult to think ahead.

You don't know where you are going, like, and you can't budget because you don't know where you are going to be in 6 months' time. (Irish woman in insecure employment)

The issue of achieving independence in the context of job insecurity arises in all the countries but is particularly strong among the Portuguese groups. The young Portuguese are very concerned with the question of how to achieve financial independence, through a steady job, which would enable them to move away from their parents' home. Independence and achieving stability are seen as vital prerequisites for having a family of one's own.

From a family point of view, I think that it's vital, as Veronica said, to get stability to be able to support a child, or even a wife, because having a child is easy. It's harder to bring it up, and without those financial supports, it's very difficult, even for us, to have children in the near future. I think that stability is important; after that . . . who knows. (Portuguese man, student)

No, without having some stability, I won't have children. It's unthinkable. (Portuguese woman, student)

For the Portuguese, the issue is particularly pressing as most do not receive unemployment benefits, so they cannot achieve any sort of independent adult life without a secure job. Although young people in the other four countries studied have access to unemployment benefits, they are also concerned about achieving security before having children.

You have no security, and then you don't want to have children, because you want to give your children security. (Swedish woman, temporarily employed)

I feel ready to have children now, but I wouldn't have children without a secure income, and that scares me, because all the jobs I want are on two-year contracts. It just doesn't work out. (U.K. man, physicist, aged 29)

Many young adults in their twenties worry that they will still be studying or in insecure employment at the age they would choose to start a family.

People . . . think they ought to wait, and they want to be in a job and have a house and . . . a home and a dog and the whole package—car, too . . . but . . . the female partner knows there's a little clock ticking, which says that, if you want to have more than one, then you must begin soon. (Norwegian woman, student, aged 25)

Some of the men also mention time contraints and even the biological clock:

Five years from now, all of us will be past 30, our son will be 10 years old when we reach 40 or 50? Our biological clock is ticking. (Portuguese man, employed)

However, the changing view of marriagelike relationships also affects work-life balance. Many women are no longer expecting lifelong partners, and consequently they stress the importance of acquiring skills and qualifications.

"You've got to look after yourself these days."
"It's like who's saying he's going to be there for you, the rest of your life, whereas if you get this education, you've got more qualifications, you can get a better job."
"So qualifications are the priority really, at the moment, [rather] than boyfriends?"
"Yeah, boyfriends come and go, don't they." (U.K. women, secretarial students, aged 18)

*Current work-life priorities
in an extended present*

It can be argued that the contexts experienced by these young adults trap them in an "extended present" (Nowotoney 1994; Nilsen 1997). By this we mean that current experiences are the only reality in the thinking of many young people and that not only is the future shrouded in uncertainty (as it is for all generations), but their current situations make it particularly hard for many of this generation to plan for or think seriously about the future. Only the biological clock ticking away reminds them, women more so than men, that the future must be confronted at some stage. The extended temporal horizons of these young adults can be contrasted with the time famine or scarcity experienced by older generations in their attempts to juggle multiple commitments in demanding work and family obligations (Daly 1997; Schor 1991). While the middle-aged generation is feeling completely overwhelmed because it has taken on so much in both work and family domains, the younger generation appears to be more fatalistic because of the difficulty in getting started in either domain.

In the extended present, the work-life needs of the moment remain in sharp focus. Although most young adults in our study expect to become parents at some stage and recognize that this will have important implications for their work and family lives, and although a few already have children, it is more difficult to contemplate the time conflicts of the future or, in some cases, to empathize with those who are caught up in the time-related dilemmas confronting employed parents of young children.

In some groups, especially in the United Kingdom and Ireland, there is a view that parents receive special favors at work and that the needs for flexibility and a life outside work if employees do not have children are overlooked.

You might have other priorities that she doesn't recognize 'cause they're not as obvious. It might be just as important things; you might have to take your cat to the vet. (U.K. woman, professional)

I want a life, too. A person has other things to do apart from work. (Portuguese man, student)

Although there is evidence that workplace policies that support employees with family obligations can enhance morale more broadly, by communicating that an employer cares about its workers (Grover and Crooker 1995), these policies can also create resentment among those who do not have family obligations in some circumstances (Cooper and Lewis 1994). Among these young workers, resentment is more prevalent in the British and Irish groups, where there is a strong discourse of choice and responsibility in relation to having children. That is, there is a view that those who choose to become parents should ensure that colleagues are not inconvenienced.

It shouldn't be the other people, their colleagues, who are doing more to cover for them 'cause that would just create resentment. (U.K. man, professional)

In Sweden, there is more understanding of the predicaments of parents, particularly in lean workforces, where there are no spare workers to provide cover for the absent colleagues. This often means that already overloaded staff must carry the extra burden.

"If we were a full workforce there would be no discontent."
"Do you bring in substitutes?"
"No. If it is possible without, we don't. But those who remain have to work double. That's why people become discontented." (Swedish women, temporarily employed)

Striking a balance: Future family and work arrangements

When they do envisage future family and work scenarios, the participants talk about their goal of achieving a balanced life. Young men and women in all the groups hope to be able to work and to have a life outside work. There is much discussion about wanting more flexible or, in Britain and Portugal, shorter working hours to enable them to spend time with family.

In many of the groups, the participants—especially but not exclusively women—also talk about a gender balance in relation to parenthood and work.

I'd like to do both [work and child care], but I want my partner to do both as well, . . . it's got to be shared. (U.K. woman)

One wants to be as much as possible with the children when they grow up. As it was in the old days, the man was always at work and could only see his kids at weekends. (Swedish man)

They belong to both of you, don't they, so you should put a joint effort in. (U.K. woman, aged 18, on secretarial course)

The ways in which this balanced work-family life is conceptualized and the barriers to and supports for its realization, however, vary both within and between countries. Most think that they will be with partners (married or cohabiting), in some form of dual-earner family, if they have children. There is some discussion about single parents, but few plan for this, so we focus on the types of dual-earner family arrangements envisaged by the young people in the different contexts. These arrangements and the possibilities they offer for work-family balance reflect national context particularly in terms of social policy, availability of part-time work, and family ideology. There are, of course, some variations within countries, reflecting gender differences, occupational level, and ethnicity. Two groups of men—those in or training for blue-collar work, and the British Asian men—articulate the most traditional views about family life. However, women in all the groups, and highly educated men, are expressing new perspectives. These trends are emerging in all the countries studied, with the exception of Swedish blue-collar working men, who also express nontraditional views about family life.

In the two Scandinavian countries, most envisage a dual-earner lifestyle when they become parents, with mothers continuing to take the major responsibility for child care but with fathers planning to be involved in parenting. Parental leave, including a period of leave exclusively for the father, and the availability of publicly provided or controlled child care are taken for granted and make balanced and relatively egalitarian lives appear relatively feasible.

. . . but you have paternal leave and maternal leave, . . . so there is really no [problem]. . . . they have made it easy for people to work and have children. (Norwegian man, shipyard worker, aged 20)

Employment is considered normal for mothers, and kindergarten is regarded as good for children.

> "A lot of those who stay home with parents could have benefited from being in child care."
> "Yes, you get the social thing about being with other kids." (Norwegian women, vocational trainees)

A dual-earner family pattern with men working full-time and women part-time is also the expected norm in the United Kingdom. However, the shortage of affordable child care and the current unavailability of parental leave other than maternity leave make it more difficult to anticipate how this will be managed. While some of the British women say they will continue to work full-time after they have children, the majority plan to work part-time. This is not only because of the perceived difficulties in sustaining two full-time jobs but is also a consequence of the ambivalence about maternal employment displayed among some of the groups (Brannen 1998). This is often manifested in distrust of nurseries and also of nannies or childminders.

You shouldn't have kids unless you can give your time to them. (U.K. woman, secretarial student)

If you don't want to have kids, then, fine, don't have them. Don't have kids and then just dump them on somebody else. (U.K. man, blue-collar job)

The notable exceptions to this are two groups of lower-skilled British women who are already mothers, most of whom considered maternal employment desirable and nursery care to be beneficial for children. Some men in Britain, as in other countries, especially among the more educated, say that they would also like to work part-time but have little expectation of being able to do so.

Ideally, as I said, I would like to be able to share child care when that came along equally, either working for part of the week, or working for part of the year; I'm strongly inclined to that. Realistically, I think I'll be forced to work five days a week and leave child care to someone else. (U.K. man, computer programmer, aged 27)

There is very little part-time work in Ireland and Portugal, and little statutory support for reconciling work and family. A "one and a half earner" lifestyle is therefore not a realistic possibility in these countries. However, the family and work lives envisaged in these two countries differ markedly, as a consequence of both economic and ideological factors.

In Portugal, wages are low, and two full-time incomes are an economic necessity for most families. There is no strong tradition of women at home. Rather, it is taken for granted that mothers will continue to work full-time, and many cannot even take their full parental leave

entitlement. Grandmothers often care for small children, and, in contrast to the Scandinavian countries, this is viewed more positively than external day care.

In Ireland, in contrast, despite high levels of education among women, there is a long tradition of mothers at home and an ongoing expectation that mothers of young children should be at home with their children. As in the U.K. groups, the main exception to this view is a group of young, lower-skilled mothers. The most common Irish solution to work-family integration is therefore for the woman to give up work for some years (O'Connor 1997). Men and women in the focus groups see this as the most "natural" family strategy.

I don't have any experience of a family [in which] both parents work. If you're there day in day out with the child at home, it's more natural. I would prefer if possible if women didn't work. (Irish woman, recently graduated from university)

Children won't know what a proper family life is [if mothers work]. (Irish man)

As in Portugal, many women express a desire for part-time work but not an expectation of this. Many talk about "sacrificing" their careers if they have children.

The successful career I will have at that stage of my life, it would have to be sacrificed slightly [when I have children]. (Irish woman, university student)

David [her child] is my life now, until he's 18, and that's that. (Irish woman, mother, aged 23)

There is some discussion in all countries about the possibilities of reversing gendered family roles, particularly if women earn more than their partners. In some cases, this is viewed very positively, while in others it creates ambivalence. The Irish groups find this possible family form the most difficult to accept as a genuine alternative.

"[Society is] so traditional. We are still victims of our upbringing. I couldn't possibly, I don't think, have respect. For example, my friend and her boyfriend stayed at home to look after the children. I think in his case it's true, that he couldn't get a job."

"I agree. He was so useless he had to stay at home." (Irish women, recently graduated from university)

The role of employers

Expectations of support from employers for work and family issues is fairly low in all the countries. Some of the U.K. focus groups discuss the potential benefits to employers of providing child care or other supports.

Something like an NHS [National Health Service] employer [that] has a massive workforce of mainly young people . . . would actually benefit from having a crèche that employees had to pay for, because . . . they're gonna have people who don't have to rush away and . . . don't give up their jobs and they'll also be making money. (U.K. woman, doctor, aged 27)

Those who can articulate this business argument have higher expectations of employer supports than others. Nevertheless, the main ex-

pectations of support from employers are in the form of part-time or flexible working hours. While flexible or part-time working hours are valued and these opportunities (or lack of them) help to shape expectations about future work and family arrangements, for many of the participants flexible employment contracts are the most salient current reality. This has major implications for their experience of work and family, now and in the future.

We have argued that social policy support and working time flexibility are significant factors taken into account when young Europeans think about future family and work. However, entitlements such as the right to parental leave are dependent on having permanent employment contracts. When employment contracts are made flexible, the impact of supportive social policies is diminished in practice. For example, a pregnant woman in a temporary job in the United Kingdom explains,

'Cause I'm on a fixed-term contract, it means my maternity rights are kind of kaput basically. Even though I've been here for over five years in the same job, because this current contract ends at the end of June and I can't come back for three months after maternity leave, it means that my maternity rights are virtually nonexistent. And I don't think that's right. (U.K. woman, pregnant, aged 30)

In Sweden, too, parental insurance is dependent on employment status, although, unlike the situation in Britain, a low level of benefit is still available to those in precarious work. This can, nevertheless, cause problems.

> "But a permanent job—that's something to go back to [after maternity leave]."
>
> "Yes, you feel that way. If you have a child, you won't have a job to return to, I don't think so." (Swedish women, temporarily employed)

It is also difficult to take advantage of child care if work is very precarious. To be totally flexible and available to work when needed, full-time child care is required, but precarious work usually does not pay sufficiently to make this possible.

CONCLUSIONS AND IMPLICATIONS

This study highlights the importance of understanding both generational and national factors in debates on work and family issues. While this qualitative study does not permit generalizations about generation or national groups or subgroups, the data do illustrate the ways in which economic and social trends, and particularly the growth in insecure work, are changing the nature of work-family dilemmas for younger workers in Europe.

The age cohort studied can be conceptualized as part of a generation. Daly (1997) argues that to be part of a generation is to "share the collective consciousness of a group and to hold a stake in the interests, values and activities that represent the historical and developmental character of that group" (198). The diverse young men and women who took part in this study share the experience of being young, albeit from different vantage points, at a point in history in which previous generations' old certainties about work and family are breaking down and giving way to new realities. In this transitional period, young people both embrace new ways of living and cling to some fragments of tradition or what is known to them within their specific context.

Young people appear to live in an extended present where current work-life needs are deemed important but future work-family scenarios are more difficult to envisage. Indeed, there appears to be an emergent notion of life as separate from work and family and as something that they wish to live to the full before considering work-family possibilities. It is important for employers to recognize that younger workers, even if they are not, or not yet, parents, do have legitimate and often pressing work-life aspirations and concerns.

The future family and work arrangements that are conceptualized vary across different national contexts, with social policy, availability of part-time work, family ideology, and employment trends all contributing to the family and work arrangements that are anticipated. At the same time, differences in social policy context are being diminished with the growth of nonpermanent employment contracts. All this is a significant part of the context for multinational companies, particularly those developing work-life policies.

Previous research suggests that the management of work and family obligations is easier for those who can make realistic plans for the future, especially if this planning is associated with a high level of "multiple role realism" (Weitzman 1992). It is apparent from the present study, however, that this sort of planning is no longer an option for many young people in Europe in the context of perceived and/or actual job insecurity and precarious employment. Corporate and public policymakers will need to consider the implications of the shifting life course family and work priorities of women and men in the post-job-security era. For example, will the difficulties in envisaging family and work trajectories result in a less well-prepared generation if young people do take on family responsibilities, particularly in countries with the least public supports for work and family? Alternatively, will the longer and more ambivalent transition into adult work and family roles better equip them to reconcile work and family, at least in supportive contexts?

What does seem certain is that precarious and fixed-term employment contracts are making the very idea of reconciling paid work and family very difficult in Europe. New ways of supporting families may need to evolve to match the changes in the nature of employment. It is important that people on temporary and fixed-term contracts are not excluded (either legally or out of fear of losing their contracts if they demand too much) from the supports and entitlements (such as parental leave) currently available to permanent workers. There is also a need for child care arrangements to become more flexible to allow parents with intermittent or nonstandard labor force affiliations to utilize them.

Note

1. We are grateful for the editors' insight on this point.

References

Brannen, Julia. 1998. Reconciling Employment and Family Life: Young People's Attitudes. In *Proceedings of the International Seminar on Work, Family and Intergenerational Solidarity*. Lisbon: ISCTE.

Cooper, Cary and Suzan Lewis. 1994. *Managing the New Workforce: The Challenge of Dual Income Families*. San Diego: Pfeiffer.

Daly, Kerry J. 1997. *Families and Time*. Thousand Oaks, CA: Sage.

European Commission. 1997. *Youth in the European Union: From Education to Working Life*. Luxembourg: Office for Official Publications of the European Communities.

———. 1998. *Employment in Europe*. Luxembourg: Office for Official Publications of the European Communities.

Freedman, Ruth, Leon Litchfield, and M. E. Warfield. 1995. Balancing Work and Family: Perspectives of Parents of Children with Developmental Disabilities. *Families in Society* 76(8): 507-14.

Gregg, C. 1994. Group Work with Single Fathers. *Journal for Specialists in Group Work* 19(2):95-101.

Grover, S. and K. Crooker. 1995. Who Appreciates Family-Responsive Human Resource Policies: The Impact of Family Friendly Policies on the Organizational Attachments of Parents and Non-Parents. *Personnel Psychology* 48:271-88.

Halpern, C. 1995. In *Psychological Disorders in Young People: Time Trends and Their Causes*, ed. M. Rutter and J. Smith. New York: John Wiley.

Hertz, Rosanna and Faith Ferguson. 1998. Only One Pair of Hands: Ways That Single Mothers Stretch Work and Family Resources. *Community, Work and Family* 1(1):13-37.

Kagan, Carolyn, Suzan Lewis, and Patricia Heaton. 1998. *Caring to Work: Parents Combining Employment with the Care of Disabled Children*. London: Family Policy Studies Centre.

Lewis, Jane. 1992. Gender and the Development of Welfare Regimes. *Journal of European Social Policy* 2(3):159-73.

Lewis, Suzan. 1997. *A European Perspective of Work and Family Issues*. Chestnut Hill, MA: Boston College, Center for Work & Family.

Lewis, Suzan and Cary Cooper. 1995. Balancing the Work Family Interface. A European Perspective. *Human Resource Management Review* 5:289-305.

Lewis, Suzan, Carolyn Kagan, and Patricia Heaton. 1998. *Caring to Work*. London: Croners Reference Book for Employers.

Moss, Peter. 1996. Reconciling Employment and Family Responsibilities: A European Perspective. In *The Work-Family Challenge: Rethinking Employment*, ed. S. Lewis and J. Lewis. Thousand Oaks, CA: Sage.

Neal, M. B., N. J. Chapman, B. Ingersoll-Dayton, and A. C. Emlen. 1993. *Balancing Work and Caregiving for Children, Adults and Elders*. Newbury Park, CA: Sage.

Nilsen, Ann. 1997. Forever Young? A Life Course Perspective on Individuation. In *Proceedings of the International Seminar on Work, Family and Intergenerational Solidarity*. Lisbon: ISCTE.

Nowotoney, H. 1994. *Time: The Modern and Post-Modern Experience*. London: Polity.

O'Connor, Patricia. 1997. A Society in Transition: Socially Created Problems and Solutions (Irish Style). In *Proceedings of the International Seminar on Work, Family and Intergenerational Solidarity*. Lisbon: ISCTE.

Phillips, Judith. 1995. *Working Carers*. Aldershot: Avebury.

Schor, Juliet. 1991. *The Overworked American*. New York: Basic Books.

Waerness, K. 1998. The Changing "Welfare Mix" in Child Care and Care for the Frail Elderly. Paper presented at the conference Work and Family in Late Modernity: Reconciliation or Fragmentation? May 1998, University of Bergen, Norway.

Weitzman, U. J. 1992. A Taxonomy of Behavioural Strategies for Coping with Work-Home Role Conflict. *Human Relations* 47:211-21.

ANNALS, *AAPSS*, **562**, March 1999

Work and Family Over Time:
A Life Course Approach

By SHIN-KAP HAN and PHYLLIS MOEN

ABSTRACT: Given the fundamental changes in the institutions of both work and family, the need to focus on the work-family interface is greater than ever. Most studies, however, examine this interface in terms of individuals and at only one point in time. The authors propose a coupled-careers model, based on a life course perspective, directly addressing the multiple interfaces between work and family and between men and women as they unfold over time. This approach challenges implicit assumptions and stereotypes about work, careers, and gender that are increasingly outdated. Analysis of the data collected in the Cornell Retirement and Well-Being Study consistently shows the asymmetry between husbands and wives in their distinctive work-family interfaces over the life course. The evidence from our data leads us to believe that what is required are new, more open, and more flexible institutional arrangements for structuring the work-family interface for both men and women at all life course and career stages.

Shin-Kap Han is an assistant professor in the Department of Sociology at Cornell University and faculty associate at the Cornell Employment and Family Careers Institute.

Phyllis Moen is Ferris Family Professor of Life Course Studies at Cornell University. She is director of the Bronfenbrenner Life Course Center and also of the Cornell Employment and Family Careers Institute, a Sloan Center for the Study of Working Families.

NOTE: Research for this article was supported in part by the Alfred P. Sloan Foundation (grant #96-6-9) and the National Institute on Aging (grants #IT50 AG11711 and #P50AG1171106).

REVIEWING the field of work and family in 1977, Kanter noted that there was only a limited amount of research or theory that considered the behavior and experiences of people in both their work and family situations, looking at people in both contexts. More than 20 years later, the need to focus on the specific intersections and transactions between work and family as connected organizers of experience, systems of social relations, and life chances is greater than ever. The partition of work and family into separate (and, frequently, unrelated) domains, however, persists in research and thinking by scholars as well as in the broader community. In this article, we map out and demonstrate how a life course perspective can illuminate the web of interdependence between the public (work) and private (family) threads of adult lives, the interactions between the work-family experiences of men and women, and the contextual nature of the work-family interface over time and across multiple domains.

WORK AND FAMILY TODAY

Both the family and the workplace in the United States have been radically altered by events of the last four decades, and they are still in flux. One of the most significant changes that directly bears on occupational as well as family careers is the enormous increase in the labor force attachment of women, especially married women, including mothers with young children. For instance, the workforce participation rate of mar-ried women with children under age 6 increased rapidly in the United States in the latter half of the twentieth century from 12 percent in 1950 to 64 percent in 1995 (U.S. Bureau of the Census 1977, 392; 1996, 400). As a consequence, about half (48 percent) of all workers in the United States now come from dual-earner couples (U.S. Bureau of Labor Statistics 1994), while only 9.4 percent of workers come from so-called traditional families.

These statistical highlights document the magnitude of change in the institutions of both work and family. Clearly, the traditional male-breadwinner, female-homemaker model no longer adequately describes the ways in which the family and the workplace intersect. In fact, this model is rapidly becoming a cultural relic, producing what Riley and Riley (1994) characterize as "structural lag," as formal and informal policies and practices fail to keep pace with the changing realities of work and family life.

These fundamental shifts demand a reappraisal of the traditional paradigm of occupational careers as well as the organization of the life course in terms of the work-family interface so as to address this changing social reality. First, these changes in women's roles pose a fundamental challenge to what Kanter calls the "myth" of separate worlds (1977, 8). In modern industrial society, the myth goes, work life and family life constitute two separate and nonoverlapping worlds, with their own functions, territories, and behavioral rules. Each operates by its own laws and can be studied independently. If events or decisions in one world touch the other, they do so as external variables, not as an intrinsic part of the operation of that other world. They help shape a context, according to the myth, but little more.

Second, a corollary of the separate-worlds myth is the assumed separation of men's and women's domains. In the traditional model of the interface between work and family, work and family are separated from each other by gender. The notions of single breadwinner, family wage, and male provider have been packaged together into a template, along with the image of women as the family caretakers of husbands, children, and infirm relatives and responsible for the domestic work of the household (Moen 1992, 1994, 1998).

Third, the emphasis, by and large, has been on structure rather than process and on the study of particular states (for example, employment status, marital status) rather than lives lived simultaneously across institutional areas. The combination of these tendencies goes against considering, in a processual way, the behaviors and events, the exchanges and transactions, that link the institutions of work and family. Scholars are only beginning to consider the work-family interface as it unfolds over time and across multiple domains. This interdependence between various life roles is a central tenet of the life course perspective (Elder 1995).

These are the three key issues that we address in this article. Our goal is to extend the temporal frame of reference, examining trajectories over the life course. These trajectories encompass not only men's (and especially husbands') work careers but also those of women (and especially wives). Moreover, both men's and women's occupational pathways are located in yet another trajectory: that of the family.

We elaborate our theoretical perspective in the following section, presenting a conceptual model that seeks to capture the interdependence between men's and women's life experiences and the dynamic, temporal nature of these experiences. The section on methods follows with a brief description of the data. We then present our findings in three parts: work career, family experience, and work-family interface. Finally, we discuss the findings in broader contexts and suggest directions for future research and policy implications.

WORK-FAMILY INTERFACE IN TEMPORAL CONTEXT

The traditional model of separating work and family along the gender line was one of the ways to effectively deal with the tension between the two "greedy institutions" (Coser 1974). Men developed a comparative advantage on the job, while their wives became adept at homemaking, reproducing a gendered division of labor that frequently made sense given the constraints of managing responsibilities at work and at home (Becker [1981] 1991).

As women have increasingly entered, remained in, and/or reentered the workforce, however, most face the dilemma of what Hochschild (1989) has termed "the second shift." Not only do women continue to bear a disproportionate share of domestic work in addition to their paid work, but also they have to cope with the strains imposed by the new work-family interface. Despite all their gains in the occupational sphere, many employed women feel as if they are living "divided lives," unable to integrate the multiple parts of their lives and frequently overwhelmed with frustration and guilt (Walsh 1995, 24-25).

The ideal situation might be one where both men and women were equally involved in both spheres. However, such a new configuration entails more boundaries to be negotiated and, thus, more potential tensions and strains (as illustrated by the arrows in Figure 1). As occupational careers and domestic arrangements are currently structured, husbands and wives may find it problematic to be simultaneously successful in both their work and their private lives (Schor 1991; Hochschild 1997).

Given the increasingly blurred division between men's and women's roles and the growing tensions between work and family obligations, we start by explicitly recognizing the multiple and interlocking dimensions built into the structure of the work-family interface. In so doing, we conceptualize couples as our basic unit of interest, taking into account the two-sidedness of this unit (Blossfeld, Drobnic, and Rohwer 1996; Bernasco 1994).

Coupled careers: A life course perspective

We examine the work-family interface as it unfolds over time, focusing on the concepts of transitions and trajectories. From a life course perspective, the two are dual concepts; transitions are always embedded in the trajectories that give them distinctive forms and meanings, and trajectories are shaped by prior, and prospective, transitions (Elder 1995; Moen, Elder, and Lüscher 1995).

Our analytical framework, shown in Figure 1, takes both work careers and family (or marital) careers into account over the life course progression. The framework underscores the multiple, interlocking interfaces between men and women and work and family over time. We call this a coupled-careers model, emphasizing the interlocking nature of trajectories and transitions, within and across life stages, between both men and women and work and family.

The model generates a number of novel research questions. How does the marital trajectory interface with occupational mobility? Does one's spouse's occupational experience influence one's own career experience? We suspect that both these processes are heavily gendered, with marriage more significantly (and negatively) related to the orderliness of women's career pathways and spouses' employment more significantly (and negatively) related to the orderliness of men's.

Tracing pathways over the life course and across multiple domains is a highly complex endeavor, and

FIGURE 1
COUPLED CAREERS: MULTIPLE INTERFACE OVER THE LIFE COURSE

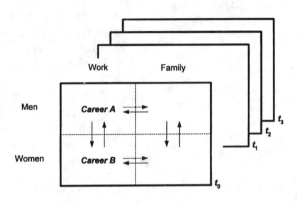

sorting them into discernible and meaningful categories is an imposing task. What is required is to take into account the incidence, timing, and duration of diverse events and their sequence. We propose a sequence analysis technique (also known as optimal matching), where the overall patterning of career pathways is both the conceptual and analytical unit. In the next section, we describe various occupational career paths followed by the men and women in our sample.

DATA AND METHODS

To illustrate the utility of the model, we analyze data collected in the first wave of the Cornell Retirement and Well-Being Study. The respondents were 458 retirees from six large manufacturing and service companies in upstate New York who were aged 50 to 72 at the time they were interviewed in 1994 and 1995. Although the experiences of these re-

tirees may not directly bear on what today's working men and women are facing, the data do help us develop a framework to examine the relevant issues and dimensions. (We are currently pursuing the topics discussed here in ongoing projects focusing on the more recent generations.)

The total sample was composed of 212 women and 246 men (46 and 54 percent of the sample, respectively) with an average age of 63 years at the time of the interviews (in 1994-95), who had spent anywhere from one month to more than 19 years in retirement. We operationalized being retired as being so designated on the lists provided by employers, which typically meant receiving a pension from one of the six companies. Respondents had been last employed in a wide range of pre-retirement jobs spanning much of the occupational hierarchy. (For more details on data, see Han and Moen 1998a, 1998b.)

The principal survey instruments included a structured interview schedule and a booklet of self-administered questions. Of special interest is the respondents' employment history, which we drew from the collection of detailed life history data. The data on employment histories of retirees provide information on transitions and trajectories over the life course in occupation, work status, and organization from age 30 until retirement. Using yearly interval as unit-time, the data were transformed into a sequence data format, that is, strings of codes. Applying an optimal matching algorithm (Abbott 1995), we empirically delineated a set of typical pathways, which we call occupational career pathway types, or "pathway types" for short. These occupational pathways will be considered in tandem with the marital trajectory as well as with the spouse's career pathway.

ANALYSIS AND FINDINGS

Charting the career pathways

The five distinctive pathway types obtained from the sequence analysis of the life history data over the prime years of work life (age 30 to retirement) can be summarized as in Table 1 with respect to the basic sequence characteristics, three aspects of employment history, and other background variables. For easy identification and reference, we call type 1 "delayed-entry career," type 2 "orderly career," type 3 "fast-track career," type 4 "steady part-time career," and type 5 "intermittent career" (Han and Moen 1998a).

Not surprisingly, we find gender highly related to the pattern of work life trajectory. Pathway type 2 seems to represent the ideal-typical career path, that is, it is stable, continuous, and upwardly mobile. About two-thirds of the respondents experiencing this traditional career path were men (see Table 1). The people (disproportionately men) composing type 3 were highly educated and upwardly mobile. They started off high on the occupational ladder and moved about quite a bit, engaging in "ladder hopping" across firms in order to advance their careers.

Those following pathway type 1 started working late in their lives, with an extended period spent out of the labor force early on. The people on this pathway consisted exclusively of women entering the labor force after their childbearing years. Although they worked typically at low-prestige jobs, these jobs were relatively stable. The people on pathway type 5 also consisted exclusively of women, and it was the least stable of all the pathways. Although it shared many of the characteristics of type 1, it distinguished itself from type 1 by a trajectory of higher mobility across organizations, mostly due to the frequent exits and reentries. Type 4 consisted of a small group of people (mostly women) working mostly part-time. Yet they showed a low level of interorganizational mobility and were relatively successful in terms of occupational prestige score and upward mobility.

Two points are worth noting. First, there seem to be highly distinct and separate career pathways for men and women. Yet the sizable presence of women in types 2 and 3 (which have been typically associ-

TABLE 1
FIVE PATHWAY TYPES AND THEIR CHARACTERISTICS

	Pathway Type				
	1 Delayed-entry career	2 Orderly career	3 Fast-track career	4 Steady part-time career	5 Intermittent career
N	46	154	160	10	21
Gender composition*[a]					
(percentage men)	0.0	64.9	61.9	30.0	0.0
(percentage women)	100.0	35.1	38.1	70.0	100.0
Education*[b]					
(mean number of years)	12.64	13.25	14.61	13.40	12.86
SEI*[b]					
(mean)	42.8	50.3	58.5	54.6	42.5
Number of organizations*[b]					
(mean)	1.5	1.2	2.8	1.7	3.7
Work status full-time*[b,c]					
(percentage)	47.4	94.6	94.4	26.2	73.7
Work status part-time*[b,c]					
(percentage)	9.3	1.5	2.3	69.6	10.6
Work status, unemployed/OLF*[b,c]					
(percentage)	43.4	3.9	3.3	4.2	15.7

NOTE: * denotes where $p < .001$. "a" denotes where likelihood ratio (L^2) test is conducted, and "b,"
F test. "c" denotes where the figure is calculated on the basis of total person-years.

ated with men's careers) suggests that the gap between men's and women's work experiences may be gradually closing. Second, men's career paths tend to be much more standardized, following only a couple of career pathways, whereas working women seem to have traveled quite diverse paths. These findings illustrate that the issues of gendered careers and the possibility of change cannot be addressed simply by contrasting stylized men's and women's career paths. Rather, a more refined perspective is needed regarding the differentiation between men and women, as well as between men and between women, within particular historical contexts.

Family experience

The men and women in our sample (all of whom worked for a significant portion of their prime adulthood) have quite different marital histories. In terms of marital stability, men tend to be better off by a large margin. For the women in our sample (who spent a considerable period of time in the labor force), the likelihood of both getting married and staying married is far lower than that for their male coworkers. Men are about 50 percent more likely to be currently married than women, whereas working women are more than seven times more likely never to have married and 34 percent more likely to have experienced a breakup in their marriage. A marital stability score, constructed from the detailed marital history, produces the same significant result, with men experiencing far greater marital stability than the women in our sample.

Interfaces: Work and marriage

How, then, do these various dimensions—men's and women's careers in both work and marriage—interact with one another? How, for instance, does gender influence the careers of men and women at work? How do family experiences enter into that relationship? How does the marital trajectory interface with occupational mobility? Does one's spouse's occupational experience influence one's own career experience?

Using log-linear analytic techniques, we first examine the relationship between gender, career pathway, and marital history. The model pictured in Figure 2 fits the observed data best. In addition to gendered career (arrow 1) and differences in marital history between men and women (arrow 2), the model posits that there is a direct relationship between work and family, that is, between career pathway type and marital history (arrow 3).

The overall pattern of the relationship between career pathway and marital history, when divided by gender, produces a picture of the gendered interface between work and family. The relationship between marital careers and occupational careers is, in fact, rather weak among men. In other words, men's occupational paths seem to have little influence on their marriage paths and

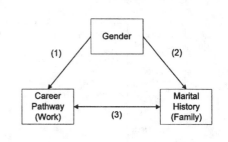

FIGURE 2
INTERFACE MODEL

vice versa. This, however, is primarily due to the lack of variance; that is, men's career pathway type is highly homogeneous and their marriage, very stable.

Among women, however, there is a strong relationship between occupational and marital careers. Those women who experienced occupational pathway type 2 (orderly career) or type 3 (fast-track career), which are the relatively smooth, orderly, and upwardly mobile career tracks, are very likely to have also experienced marital instability. As a case in point, all 14 women who never married are found in the orderly career pathway types 2 and 3, patterns that are typical for men! The opposite is true for women in type 1 (delayed-entry career) or type 4 (steady part-time career). In both cases, marital stability appears to come at the expense of success in career, or vice versa. Women in these pre-baby-boom cohorts apparently could not have it both ways. The only exceptions are the women in type 5 (intermittent career), who seemed to have suffered on both fronts, having unstable ties both to their jobs and to their marriage.

FIGURE 3
MARITAL STABILITY BY PATHWAY TYPE AND GENDER

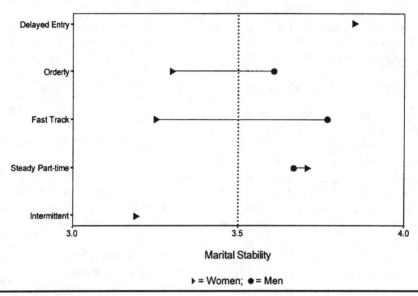

NOTE: 3.0 represents low marital stability; 4.0 represents high marital stability.

Figure 3 depicts the relationship between occupational career pathway type and marital stability by gender, corroborating the result described previously. This explains why so many women who are highly successful in their careers are so often without the families and/or children that seem to be taken for granted for upwardly mobile men.

In the early 1980s, Bernard ([1972] 1982) observed that (1) for most American couples, being married is a much better deal for the husband than for the wife, and (2) married men are healthier, happier, and saner than the unmarried, while just the opposite is true for women. This seems to hold true for the men and women in our sample. The asymmetry between the sexes operates in such a way that it forces a zero-sum game—that is, a trade-off between occupational careers and family careers—for women but not for men. That, in turn, leads to the development and persistence of unequal comparative advantage and life chances between men and women at work, at home, and in the links between the two.

His career, her career

We now turn to the situation where two occupational careers, those of the husband and wife, have to be negotiated. For the wives of the men in this sample, work patterns appeared to be tightly coupled with, and highly contingent upon, their husbands' careers. This was not the case, however, for the women in our sample; that is, their husbands' work histories were not constrained by how the women themselves worked in any patterned way. This finding, once again, documents the heavily skewed relationship between the experiences of men and women.

The ways in which husbands' and wives' careers were coupled are quite distinct. For instance, the wives of the men in the type 2 career path (the orderly career) were more likely not to have worked at all, whereas the opposite seems to be true for the wives of the men in the type 3 career path (the fast-track career). Husbands were more likely to have worked continuously, regardless of their wives' career pathway type.

Summary: The case
of Hugh and Hannah

The findings can be summarized in terms of our conceptual model (see Figure 2) as follows. First, men and women tend to be sorted into different career pathways, with men faring far better in terms of staying on orderly and upwardly mobile tracks. To put it more succinctly, career pathways tend to be gendered (arrow 1 in Figure 2). Second, working women (that is, the women in our sample) tend to suffer higher degrees of marital instability than do men (arrow 2). In addition, type of career pathway and marital history are strongly related for women (arrow 3). Among women, those on the better career tracks suffer more in terms of marital stability, and vice versa (see Figure 3). Finally, spouses' career paths are played out in tandem, with

wives' experiences contingent on their husbands' career trajectories.

The case of Hugh and Hannah clearly illustrates this complexity involved in negotiating work and family and his and hers. Hugh said,

[Work and family overlap] plays out because Hannah picks up the loose ends. If she had responsibilities away from home that required as much time as I devote away from home, then we would not have a home life. I pitch in on a more as-needed basis. . . . But by no means am I the primary person.

He acknowledged that Hannah "sacrificed her career in favor of our being able to live here." When asked if he felt that one job took precedence over the other, Hugh replied, "Yes. Not that one should have. But, out of necessity, one of the jobs had to take precedence."

Hannah was also ambivalent about the issue. On one hand, referring to her early job as an account representative at a publishing company in New York City, she said, "I loved it! It was a great career. The only reason I left was because we got married and you only commute for so long." When asked if her husband's role was discussed, she said, "Yes, I would discuss it, but he didn't always see it the same way I did. His role was he was the one making the money here and his job is most important."

On the other hand, Hannah did not feel that Hugh was not doing his share, particularly after she opened her gallery. She said, "He was forced to do more child care than he normally would have done. . . . He would be the one at home every Saturday baby-sitting. Once that [sank] in, it was done." When asked to describe her ideal family, she replied, "The ideal family? Oh, of course, the husband who comes home and fixes dinner and folds clothes. That is easy." She laughed, then continued, "There will never be that 50 percent at-home responsibility. I know my husband really feels he does a great job here, but, compared to what he would have done if he had not had to, he really does."

The picture we get here is of a family trying to cope the best they could with the multiple demands imposed on them. The findings from the statistical analysis of the data reflect those day-to-day struggles and show the typical outcome.

DISCUSSION AND CONCLUSION

Our goal has been to understand the occupational careers of American men and women who find themselves having to negotiate the two spheres of life, work and family, and also with each other over the life course. Examining couples' conjoint careers as they unfold over time is important, given the dramatic changes in women's labor force participation in the last half of the twentieth century. This transformation has created a structural lag, pointing to the need to radically alter the ways in which we structure two most fundamental institutions, work and family, and the interface between them. The work-family interface is, thus, increasingly seen as no longer just a women's issue but a challenge confronting workers, managers, and employers, if not the nation (for example, Barnett and Rivers 1996). This transfor-mation, furthermore, presents itself as a challenge to old ways of understanding career path, family stages, and gender roles, necessitating a new approach in theory, research, and policy to address the new and emerging realities of contemporary adulthood.

A broader understanding of the complexity of work-family life paths is particularly crucial given the fundamental changes in the world of work that we are currently experiencing. The United States is in the midst of major transformations in the larger opportunity structure and in the implicit as well as explicit contracts between employers and employees. During the past 15 years in particular, many companies, led by such blue-chip corporations as IBM, AT&T, GM, and Eastman Kodak, have sought to move away from the traditional model of employment where most employees—typically males—were connected to their employers on a full-time, relatively permanent basis. They are dismantling this internalized system of mutual obligations, the "implicit contract," between employees and the firm, which emerged in the post–World War II era of rising productivity and U.S. economic dominance, profoundly affecting individual workers' lives. These transformations are affecting the family as well (for example, Hochschild 1997).

In using the concept of career, however, social scientists have failed to point out that it contains a number of hidden assumptions—about the nature of the life course, jobs, and the social relations within which careers unfold. These assumptions represent a set of practices and policies that no longer fit with the realities of a changing economy, changing gender roles, blurred lines between work and retirement, and a cohort of educated, introspective baby boomers newly valuing family life and uncertain about middle age.

We challenged three of those assumptions in our analysis. First, we returned to a basic premise of the life course perspective that points to the connection between events and experiences, transitions and trajectories. Second, we questioned taking for granted the male experience as the template in career research. By documenting the mechanisms underlying the divide between men and women, we provided a new way to explore the changing reality. Third, most researchers of occupational careers focus on individuals—oftentimes men, effectively removing them from the family context. We argued for an alternative to the individual as the unit of analysis, suggesting the importance of couples, families, or households as the appropriate unit of analysis in modeling career paths. Elder's notion of "linked lives" (1994) becomes key to adequately addressing this issue, into which we explicitly incorporated possible inequality and asymmetry by gender.

We proposed a model that addresses the multiple interfaces between work and family and between men and women as they unfold over time. We found the notion of coupled careers and its proper and direct formulation critical to understanding the dynamics of the work-family interface over the life course. The asymmetry between the husbands and wives in their distinctive work-family interfaces was the most consistent finding.

By challenging old stereotypes, we hope to shed light on the question of how to design new strategies for a world in which, increasingly, both men and women work and both men and women shoulder family responsibilities. Our findings make it clear that current assumptions, policies, and practices are outmoded and inappropriate for the changing reality of work, family, and the contemporary life course. The evidence from our data leads us to believe that what is required are new institutional arrangements for structuring occupational trajectories, creating greater flexibility and more options in career development and progression for both men and women. As a nation, however, Americans have yet to achieve consensus as to what the nature of work, careers, or the work-family interface should be. This absence of consensus means that working couples will continue to confront structural lags in the policies and practices that shape and structure their life course.

References

Abbott, Andrew. 1995. Sequence Analysis: New Methods for Old Ideas. *Annual Review of Sociology* 21:93-113.

Barnett, Rosalind and Caryl Rivers. 1996. *She Works/He Works: How Two-Income Families Are Happier, Healthier, and Better-Off*. New York: HarperCollins.

Becker, Gary S. [1981] 1991. *A Treatise on the Family*. Cambridge, MA: Harvard University Press.

Bernard, Jessie S. [1972] 1982. *The Future of Marriage*. New Haven, CT: Yale University Press.

Bernasco, Wim. 1994. *Coupled Careers: The Effects of Spouse's Resources on Success at Work*. Amsterdam: Thesis.

Blossfeld, Hans-Peter, Sonja Drobnic, and Götz Rohwer. 1996. Employment Patterns: A Crossroad Between Class and Gender: A Long-Term Longitudinal Study of Spouses' Careers in West Germany. Arbeitspapier #33, University of Bremen, Germany.

Coser, Lewis A. 1974. *Greedy Institutions: Patterns of Undivided Commitment*. New York: Free Press.

Elder, Glen H., Jr. 1994. Time, Human Agency, and Social Change: Perspectives on the Life Course. *Social Psychology Quarterly* 57:4-15.

———. 1995. The Life Course Paradigm: Social Change and Individual Development. In *Examining Lives in Context: Perspectives on the Ecology of Human Development*, ed. P. Moen, G. H. Elder, Jr., and K. Lüscher. Washington, DC: American Psychological Association.

Han, Shin-Kap and Phyllis Moen. 1998a. Clocking Out: Multiplex Time in Retirement. Bronfenbrenner Life Course Center Working Paper no. 98-03, Cornell University, Ithaca, NY.

———. 1998b. Coupled Careers: Men's and Women's Pathways Through Work and Marriage in the United States. Bronfenbrenner Life Course Center Working Paper no. 98-12, Cornell University, Ithaca, NY.

Hochschild, Arlie Russell. 1989. *The Second Shift*. New York: Viking.

———. 1997. *The Time Bind: When Work Becomes Home and Home Becomes Work*. New York: Metropolitan Books.

Kanter, Rosabeth Moss. 1977. *Work and Family in the United States: A Critical Review and Agenda for Research and Policy*. New York: Russell Sage Foundation.

Moen, Phyllis. 1992. *Women's Two Roles: A Contemporary Dilemma*. Westport, CT: Auburn House.

———. 1994. Women, Work and Family: A Sociological Perspective on Changing Roles. In *Age and Structural Lag: The Mismatch Between People's Lives and Opportunities in Work, Family, and Leisure*, ed. M. W. Riley, R. L. Kahn, and A. Foner. New York: John Wiley.

———. 1998. Recasting Careers: Changing Reference Groups, Risks, and Realities. *Generations* Spring:40-45.

Moen, Phyllis, Glen H. Elder, Jr., and Kurt Lüscher, eds. 1995. *Examining Lives in Context: Perspectives on the Ecology of Human Development*. Washington, DC: American Psychological Association.

Riley, Matilda W. and John W. Riley, Jr. 1994. Structural Lag: Past and Future. In *Age and Structural Lag: The Mismatch Between People's Lives and Opportunities in Work, Family, and Leisure*, ed. M. W. Riley, R. L. Kahn, and A. Foner. New York: John Wiley.

Schor, Juliet. 1991. *The Overworked American: The Unexpected Decline of Leisure*. New York: Basic Books.

U.S. Bureau of the Census. 1977. *Current Population Survey*. Washington, DC: Department of Commerce.

———. 1996. *Current Population Survey*. Washington, DC: Department of Commerce.

U.S. Bureau of Labor Statistics. 1994. *Employment and Earnings Characteristics of Families*. Washington, DC: Department of Labor.

Walsh, Elsa. 1995. *Divided Lives: The Public and Private Struggles of Three Accomplished Women*. New York: Simon & Schuster.

Organizational Size and
Work-Family Issues

By SHELLEY M. MacDERMID,
LEON C. LITCHFIELD, and MARCIE PITT-CATSOUPHES

ABSTRACT: Although the number of small businesses has grown significantly, and the majority of American workers are employed by smaller companies, very little attention has been given to conducting research studies about work-family issues in these companies. This article presents information about other business studies that have focused on organizational size, and it highlights several research traditions that can be used to develop future studies of company size and work-family issues: organizational theories, and studies of community and school size. Studies that explore organizational and employee perspectives on work-family issues in smaller businesses are presented. Finally, recommendations are made for future studies to explore the relationship between organizational size and work-family issues, including the suggestion that multilevel studies be conducted that combine both organizational and employee perspectives.

Shelley M. MacDermid is associate professor and director of the Center for Families at Purdue University. She is currently a faculty fellow of the Boston College Work-Family Roundtable.

Leon C. Litchfield is the director of research at the Center for Work & Family at Boston College.

Marcie Pitt-Catsouphes is the director of the Center for Work & Family at Boston College.

111

DESPITE the fact that the majority of businesses in the United States have fewer than 20 employees, most work-family research has focused on the experiences of employees in larger corporations. Since it is unclear to what extent observations about work-family issues in larger firms can be generalized to employees and their families in smaller companies, researchers may not have an accurate picture of work-family issues in the typical American workplace.

BACKGROUND

During the past three decades, significant public attention has been directed to changes that have affected two of our most fundamental social institutions: work and family. Specifically, there have been dramatic shifts in the demographics of American workers during this period. For example, nearly three-quarters (68 percent) of American women with children under age 6 are currently in the labor force (Spain and Bianchi 1996, 152). In addition, single parents and dual-earner couples compose 44 percent of the total workforce (Friedman 1990).

In response to these changes, employers across the country have begun to establish programs designed to help employees fulfill their responsibilities at home and work (Kalleberg, Knoke, Marsden, and Spaeth 1996a, 11; Eichman and Reisman 1991, 1). Surveys conducted by Hewitt Associates (1996) indicate that the number of workplaces offering work-family supports continues to increase at a steady rate. In con-

junction with the employer response to these issues, the field of work-family research has also rapidly grown (see Lilly, Pitt-Catsouphes, and Googins 1997). Studies have shown that while unresolved work-family conflicts may be associated with employee problems (Emlen and Koren 1984; Fernandez 1986; Burden and Googins 1987; Googins, Griffith, and Casey 1994), work-family programs may result in positive outcomes, including improved worker commitment and greater employee participation in business strategies (Dorman 1995, 22; Gonyea and Googins 1993; Lambert 1993).

Need for studying work-family issues in small businesses

An examination of statistics related to company size makes a strong case for the dominance of small businesses and for the importance of studying work-family issues in these types of companies. Examples include the following:

1. The U.S. Bureau of the Census (1993) reports that of the 6.3 million establishments in the country, 89.6 percent have fewer than 20 employees.
2. The number of businesses with fewer than 20 employees has steadily risen, from 3.0 million in 1982 to 5.6 million in 1990 (Oppenheimer 1994, 20).
3. In addition to the number of businesses, the percentage of individuals in smaller companies has also increased. For example, a study conducted by the National Bureau of Economic Research found that 44 percent of business jobs were in com-

panies employing 100 or fewer workers (cited in Oppenheimer 1994, 20).

4. In recent years, small businesses have been responsible for creating most of the new jobs in the country. During the period 1988-90, small businesses (employing fewer than 20 workers) created 4 million new jobs, whereas medium (21-499 employees) and large firms (500 or more employees) each lost 500,000 jobs (Oppenheimer 1994, 20).

5. Small businesses have become important contributors to the nation's economy, accounting for 44 percent of all sales and 38 percent of the U.S. gross national product (Eichman and Reisman 1991, 2).

Although small businesses have grown in terms of the number and percentage of American workers, there has not been an accompanying movement on the part of organizational researchers to study small companies (Kalleberg, Knoke, Marsden, and Spaeth 1996a, 16). As Arthur and Hendry (1990) observed, "The significance of small to medium sized business units (SMBUs) has received little explicit attention in mainstream management literature. Yet . . . in the US, such business units account for over 80 percent of the private, non-agricultural, non-construction workforce" (233).

In addition to a lack of information about employees in smaller companies, there is also an absence of research comparing the work and family needs and responsibilities of those in smaller and larger companies. By considering organizational size as a comparison variable, researchers can explore how and why the experiences of workers in companies of varying sizes are different.

Several factors have contributed to the failure of work-family researchers to examine the experiences of small businesses and their employees, including the difficulty of getting small businesses to participate; the expense of collecting data from a large number of small employers; and lack of interest by the large corporations that often sponsor or support work-family research. While work-family studies in small businesses are the exception rather than the norm, examples of this type of research will be presented later in this article.

Definition

Before moving to other pertinent questions related to work-family issues in smaller companies, it is important to briefly discuss how researchers define a small business. As straightforward as this may seem, a number of different factors have been considered as indicators of organizational size (see Kimberly 1976, cited in Kalleberg, Knoke, Marsden, and Spaeth 1996b, 48-49). For example, the Small Business Administration has a multidimensional operational definition of small businesses that includes patterns of ownership, net worth or sales, and workforce size within specific industry sectors or business groups.

The most common indicator of workforce size has been the number of workers employed by a company.

However, no single, widely accepted cutoff point has been set to distinguish the category of small business from firms of other sizes. Rather, small businesses have been variously operationalized as including companies with less than 20, 50, 100, or 250 employees.

Another consideration in the definition of small business is the difference between a firm and an establishment, with a firm being viewed as including one or more establishments. While some researchers have found differences related to both firm and establishment size (for example, earnings and benefits) (Kalleberg and Van Buren 1996a), Villemez and Bridges (1988), in their study of occupational level and gender, concluded that establishment size was more important than firm size.

What we already know

To date, work-family researchers have given little attention to smaller workplaces. However, company size is well established as a key factor in studying other aspects of businesses, and examples of these types of study will be presented in this article. In most cases, the findings we report have emerged in multiple studies of large nationally representative samples and are generally robust to a variety of statistical controls. Virtually all evidence is correlational rather than causal, since few existing studies are longitudinal. Interestingly, while these studies address the impact of organizational size, what is less fully explained is why size is so important.

Business structure and functioning. Smaller establishments have less complicated structures than larger ones (Kalleberg and Van Buren 1996a, 49-50; Marsh and Mannari 1989, 88), and more centralized decision-making (Kalleberg, Marsden, Knoke, and Spaeth 1996, 103). Externally, small firms are more likely to rely on networks of partners than on vertically integrated hierarchical structures (Acs and Audretsch 1990b, 8).

Small businesses are generally thought to be a wellspring of new jobs and innovations (Acs and Audretsch 1990b, 7; 1990a, 10), although there is some debate about the interpretation of data in this area (cf. Brown, Hamilton, and Medoff 1990, 90). In the long term, smaller firms are less likely to be successful than larger ones, particularly if they are owned by women (Mayo and Murray 1991, 1358; Tigges and Green 1994, 302).

Job design and training. Work tasks in smaller organizations are less routinized and specialized (Dewar and Simet 1981, 19), resulting in greater autonomy for employees (Kalleberg and Van Buren 1996a, 49; Marsh and Mannari 1989, 88). However, a more fluid approach to work design may also be associated with less access to career ladders and formal dispute resolution procedures (Kalleberg, Marsden, Knoke, and Spaeth 1996, 99, 105).

Some evidence suggests that larger workplaces offer more training (Barron, Black, and Loewenstein 1987, 84; Duxbury 1997, 6), but this pattern may not be consistent across all measures of training (Knoke and Kalleberg 1996, 177).

Compensation. One of the best-known facts about small workplaces is that they pay less than large ones (Rebitzer 1986, 297). Actually, the effect of size on wages, though significant, is weaker than its effects on benefits, promotion opportunities, and job autonomy (Kalleberg and Van Buren 1996a, 56, 58, 60, 61; Mellow 1982, 500).

The compensation disadvantage of workers in smaller workplaces extends to benefits, especially those with direct costs to employers (although the discrepancy is not fully explained by ability to pay; Knoke 1996, 243, 245). Employees in small workplaces have less access to pensions and health insurance (Mehta 1995; Rebitzer 1986, 297), paid vacations, dependent care assistance, and parental leave (Bond 1996). In contrast, they have as much or more schedule control and flexibility than their counterparts in larger workplaces, particularly on an informal, day-to-day basis (Bond 1996; Duxbury 1997, 4). Benefits, in turn, appear to moderate employees' behavior. For example, in one national study, turnover was lower in larger firms than smaller ones, but only among employees who had access to pensions (Even and MacPherson 1996, 724).

Workers' opportunities. Job tenure and attachment are positively related to the size of firms (Brown and Medoff 1989, 1041, 1044; Evans and Leighton 1988, 316) and plants (Evans and Leighton 1988). Across workplaces, larger employers may use their compensation advantage to discriminate in favor of employees they consider stable and desirable (for example, married men, unmarried women, non-parents) (Barth, Cordes, and Haber 1987, 566; Peterson 1989, 411). Within workplaces, the evidence is mixed; while the relative informality of smaller workplaces may make it easier for employers to discriminate between workers (Villemez and Bridges 1988, 254), managers perceive greater earnings inequality in larger establishments (Kalleberg and Van Buren 1996b, 225).

Workers' evaluations of their experiences. Employees of smaller workplaces have reported lower job demands, more autonomy, higher supervisor support, better social climate, less stress, more satisfaction overall, and less burnout (Bond 1996). Although not all of these patterns hold consistently (Duxbury 1997, 5-7; Marsden, Kalleberg, and Cook 1996, 313), there does seem to be some agreement between researchers that size is not related to workers' reports of commitment to their jobs (Bond 1996; Duxbury 1997, 7).

A study by Dekker, Barling, and Kelloway (1996) found that satisfaction in smaller workplaces was higher only for areas over which organizations exerted less control (for example, supervisor competence). In contrast, satisfaction was higher in larger workplaces for areas they were more likely to control (for example, pay, promotion opportunities).

What we don't know

To date, labor market segmentation theory has emerged as the best explanation for the effects of organizational size. Increasing size is thought to increase the costs of monitoring and screening workers, to which employers respond by using more pay and benefits to recruit and retain better (that is, more cheaply monitored) workers (Barron, Black, and Loewenstein 1987, 87-88; Garen 1985, 715), who, in turn, are more satisfied. It also has been suggested that larger employers have to pay workers more to compensate for less favorable working conditions (Acs and Audretsch 1990b, 16; Kwoka 1980, 378; Schmidt and Zimmerman 1991, 705).

These explanations have not been entirely satisfactory. Even when all of the foregoing factors are taken into account statistically, the effects of organizational size rarely fade from significance (Villemez and Bridges 1988, 246-50), and they are often among the strongest single predictors of organizational and individual outcomes (Brown and Medoff 1989, 1056; Dekker, Barling, and Kelloway 1996, 204). Kalleberg and Van Buren (1996a, 63) suggest that size itself may be explanatory, indicating that the sheer number of employees may affect workers' experiences and opportunities. In the next section, we turn to other research traditions that can be applied to the study of work-

family relationships as a function of organizational size.

WHERE MIGHT WE GET GOOD ANSWERS?

While few studies have focused specifically on organizational size and work-family issues, three research traditions exist that may prove useful in nurturing new ways of thinking about smaller workplaces. These are organizational theories, studies of community size, and studies of school size.

Organizational theories

Two theoretical perspectives about organizations seem particularly appropriate for examining the responsiveness of small businesses to work-family issues: structural theories and systems or contingency theories.

Structural theories. Theories of organizational structure focus on the characteristics of organizations and their component parts. Structural theorists have been primarily interested in six features: (1) size and complexity; (2) hierarchy, reporting relationships, authority, and decision making; (3) rules, procedures, and practices; (4) patterns of communication; (5) industry, technology, and work processes; and (6) tasks, positions, and job responsibilities (Gordon 1991, 531; Kalleberg, Knoke, Marsden, and Spaeth 1996a, 9).

Structural theories devote particular attention to the relationships between organizational characteristics. Since structural theorists assume that organizations are goal directed and rational, they attempt to understand and predict how organizations structure themselves as a means for moving toward organizational goals (Kalleberg, Knoke, Marsden, and Spaeth 1996a, 9). Studies of organizational structure have already been useful in comparing and contrasting smaller and larger companies. There may also be aspects of structure unique to smaller workplaces that have not yet been identified and explored. For example, informal, rather than formal, means of assessing and rewarding workers or managing family-friendly practices and procedures may be understudied.

Systems theories. In contrast to structural theories, which concentrate on the internal characteristics of organizations, systems theories focus on the dynamic relationship between organizations and their environments. Several important assumptions associated with this view of social systems can be applied to companies of different sizes.

As social systems, organizations establish boundaries that define and distinguish them from their environments. Organizations also interact constantly with their environments. When organizational boundaries are rigidly set between the employees ("us") and the rest of the environment ("them"), it can be more difficult for employers to appreciate the relevance of work-family issues to the company (Parsons 1982). Small and large workplaces likely differ in the permeability of their boundaries

and in the types of resources that flow most easily across these boundaries (Aldrich 1979, 219).

Studies of community size

Differences between small (rural) and large (urban) communities have been studied for decades. Hypotheses propose that urban residents risk isolation as a result of disruption in their social networks or environmental overload, with negative implications for their well-being and personal functioning.

In fact, according to national data, residents of large urban communities report slightly lower well-being and less satisfaction with their relationships with friends than do rural residents (Palisi and Canning 1986, 373). However, urban residents also report greater tolerance (Wilson 1991, 119). There are differences in social relationships as a function of community size, but they are minimal and apply more to strangers and acquaintances than to close friends. For example, urbanites are less likely to help strangers (Korte 1980, 46; Steblay 1987, 352) or the elderly (Amato 1993, 258). Low-income individuals also are more isolated in urban areas (Fischer 1982, 252; Houghland, Kim, and Christenson 1979, 608).

There is also limited evidence that urban newcomers report more feelings of fear and distrust than their rural counterparts, making the transition from stranger to friend more difficult (Franck 1980, 61, 66). In general, interacting with and assisting others appear to be more discretionary in urban environments, and giving may depend more upon receiving (Amato 1993, 258). Urban-rural differences seem to be primarily related to characteristics of the environment (Steblay 1987, 352), although they are also partially explained by the characteristics of people who choose to live in cities (Stinner et al. 1990, 494).

These findings suggest that social interactions and relationships within workplaces may be an important locus of differences between small and large settings. A recent study of the banking industry offers some support. In small banks, workers who felt closer to their coworkers reported less difficulty managing the demands of work and family life. In large banks, however, workers had to reach a certain level of closeness before they reported any reduction in difficulty (MacDermid et al. 1994, 165). Another small study showed that friends reported less closeness when they worked together in more formal organizations (Bridge and Baxter 1992, 216).

Studies of school size

Another large literature exists that explores the impact of school characteristics on student performance. A classic study by Barker and Gump (1964) examined schools in terms of the number and diversity of the "behavior settings"—opportunities to engage in a particular activity with others who have similar interests—that they contained. Large schools had 65 times as many students but only 8 times as many settings and 1.5 times the variety of settings of small schools. Thus students in large schools experienced more crowded conditions and, possibly as a result, were less than half as likely to participate in activities as their counterparts in small schools (Barker and Gump 1964, 90; Morgan and Alwin 1980, 248).

More recent results consistently suggest that students and teachers are more engaged, both behaviorally and psychologically, in small schools than in large ones. For example, small schools experience fewer problems with absenteeism and tardiness, attendance, teacher reports of inattentiveness or noncompletion, and lack of preparation (Finn and Voelkl 1993, 264-65). Students in smaller schools are more satisfied with opportunities to develop competence, to be challenged, and to engage in important actions. They also report feeling more welcomed and supported (Finn and Voelkl 1993, 265), more responsible, and more obliged to participate (Barker and Gump 1964, 133, 197). Teachers in smaller high schools report less conflict (Beck 1974, 528) and a stronger sense of community (Newmann, Rutter, and Smith 1989, 234).

Characteristics of smaller schools that may be linked to the greater engagement of students include less rigid social groupings, smaller social distance (that is, less hierarchy), more flexible views of time, more participatory decision making, less emphasis on control, and a higher sense of efficacy among teachers (Gregory and Smith 1987, 24-46). Garbarino (1980, 21, 23) argues that smaller schools have better "social control" than large schools, making it more difficult for academically marginal students to fall through the cracks. Although some work has been done to extend this perspective to organizations (for example, "manning" theories in Wicker 1984 and others), this perspective has not been fully explored.

WORK-FAMILY RESEARCH IN SMALLER COMPANIES

Despite interesting conceptual possibilities from these diverse areas of study, relatively little research attention has been devoted to work-family issues in smaller workplaces. In the following section, we offer evidence from studies that have been conducted in this area from two different perspectives: organizational and employee.

Organizational perspectives

A survey that asked about a range of work-family issues was distributed by the Center for Work & Family at Boston College to company representatives with human resource responsibilities. Using a national random sampling strategy, nearly 200 businesses (n = 188) with fewer than 50 employees were surveyed, along with a comparison group of larger companies (n = 88).

Comparisons between companies with fewer than 50 employees and those with 50 or more employees revealed some interesting findings. First, employees in smaller and larger companies faced many of the same work and family issues, with three of the top five areas being identical. Respondents listed being "late or absent in order to take care of family members" as the personal or family issue that occurred most frequently among their employees.[1] The two issues listed next most often were having "family responsibilities interfere with work performance" and having "employees ask for time off to take care of family responsibilities." Given the frequency with which these issues were reported (once every two weeks in small companies and 1 percent of larger companies each year), they are not issues that companies can afford to ignore.

In each of the other areas studied (challenges; priorities; policies or practices; and benefits or options), there were significant differences between the two groups. When respondents were asked to use a five-point scale (ranging from "not at all" to "a great extent") to rate whether they were experiencing challenges, there were differences between the respondents in smaller and larger companies for most of the items included in the survey. In general, participants from small companies reported fewer challenges than those in larger companies. For example, while 84 percent of those in larger companies reported coworkers not getting along as a problem, this was true for only half of the respondents in small companies. Larger companies were also more apt to report experiencing challenges with providing effective supervision, compliance with the Occupational Safety and Health Administration, sexual harassment complaints, and employees' disabilities.

When asked about the importance of priority areas for their business, interviewees in small companies were nearly three times as likely as those in larger companies to rate "helping employees balance their work and family responsibilities" as being "very important" to their business. However, relative to other priorities, those in both types of companies were less apt to rate this priority as "very important."[2] It was also interesting that the three priority areas most frequently rated as "very important" were identical in smaller and larger companies: caring for employees "as people," encouraging each employee to "take the initiative" for quality work, and encouraging two-way communication with employees.

Large businesses were more apt to offer most of the policies and practices to all employees than were small businesses. However, part-time work and being allowed to periodically adjust work hours were more available to employees in small companies than in large companies. While it was hypothesized that small companies might offer such policies and practices more informally than larger companies, this was not the case. With the exception of part-time work, large businesses were actually more apt to allow certain accommodations on a case-by-case basis than were small companies.

Similar differences were discovered when comparing small and larger companies with respect to benefits. For all but 1 of the 22 benefits listed, larger companies were more apt to offer the benefit to all employees. The one benefit that was more available to all employees in small companies was on-the-job training.

Information from the Center for Work & Family study was useful in determining the organizational perspective of small businesses regarding work-life challenges, priorities, personal or family issues, and responses and for comparing them to that of larger businesses. Overall, small and large businesses seem to report similar manifestations of personal and family issues among their employees. However, while those in small companies were less apt to report work-family challenges, they were more apt to view the issues listed in the survey as priorities. Neither type of company perceived helping employees to balance their work and family responsibilities as a high priority.

Finally, as expected, larger companies offered more in terms of policies, benefits, and options for getting work done and balancing it with home responsibilities. While it was anticipated that small companies might be more apt to offer benefits on an informal basis, for the most part this was not confirmed.

Employee perspectives

Although understanding the organizational perspective on work-life issues is important, especially in small businesses where there have been few research studies, it is becoming increasingly recognized that a complete picture of work-life issues must include feedback from the true recipients of work-life programs— the employees themselves. Only a few studies, however, have compared the work-family conflicts experienced by employees in small and large workplaces, and the results have been mixed (Duxbury 1997, 3; MacDermid et al. 1994, 163). The largest and most representative study to date indicates that individuals working for employers with fewer than 50 employees reported less work-family conflict than individuals with 500 or more colleagues (Bond 1996).

Since it seems likely that small firms are not just quantitatively but also qualitatively distinct (Storey 1990, 43), interactions between organizational size and other factors may be more important than simple mean differences. Two small comparative studies of married mothers working in the banking industry (MacDermid and Williams 1997, 562; MacDermid et al. 1994, 164-65) found that women who worked in large workplaces and perceived benefits as more available reported less spillover from work to marriage. Women who worked in small workplaces and were closer to coworkers reported less difficulty managing the demands of work and family and less spillover from work to marriage and home management.

Workplace size also moderated the relationships between work conditions and workers' parenting behavior. In large workplaces, structural and hierarchical features of work (such as schedule demands, supervision, and benefits) were linked to parents' evaluations of their children's behavior and the priority they placed on children's independence. In small workplaces, processual features of work (such as substantive complexity and relationships with coworkers) were related to parents' reports of nurturing behavior.

EMERGING DIRECTIONS

More than ever before, workers are facing complex choices and difficulties in attempting to balance their work and family responsibilities. While the number of small businesses has grown significantly, and the majority of American workers are employed by smaller companies, very little attention has been given to conducting research about work-family issues in these companies. This article presented other business research that has focused on organizational size, and it highlighted several research traditions that could be used to develop future studies of company size and work-family issues. In addition, studies that explored organizational and employee perspectives on work-family issues in smaller businesses were presented.

In considering future research in this area, more multilevel studies are needed that include both organizational and employee perspectives. While a few research studies have combined individual- and organizational-level data (Villemez and Bridges 1988; Peterson 1989; Kalleberg, Knoke, Marsden, and Spaeth 1996b), they did not address work and family issues. Of these studies, the National Organizations Study (NOS) conducted in 1991 (and reported by Kalleberg, Marsden, Knoke, and Spaeth in 1996) deserves mention for the model the researchers employed to collect information from a representative sample of American companies (including companies of various sizes). This methodology has already been influential (see the many citations to the work of Kalleberg et al. in this article) and has been used as a basis for studies by national research organizations such as the Families and Work Institute.

The NOS collected data as a follow-up to the General Social Survey. It used a more comprehensive approach that the researchers term an "unrestricted diverse organizational survey" design. This approach improves on other designs by studying a diverse population of organizations and by collecting data at different levels (that is, organizational and individual perspectives). Its one disadvantage appears to be that it does not collect data from more than one employee in each of the organizations surveyed.

Something different appears to be happening in smaller businesses around the country. As indicated in the few studies that have asked employees in smaller companies about their experiences, workers report having fewer work-family conflicts. In addition, relationships with coworkers seem to be particularly important in smaller companies, with good coworker relationships related to fewer problems with work-family balance and to positive parenting behaviors. Yet these differences seem to extend beyond simply having fewer workers in the workplace and the availability in smaller companies of fewer formal programs and policies to help employees balance their work and home lives. It may be that employees in smaller companies are experiencing a different kind of work environment from those in larger workplaces and that interaction patterns, relationships, and even the ways in which work gets done are qualitatively different.

Comprehensive studies of work-family issues in companies of different sizes may need to include information about individual employees and their relationships with their supervisors, their coworkers, and company owners. While we would expect that at least some of these relationships would differ by the size of the organization and that there might be less social distancing in smaller companies (especially between employees and their supervisors and/or owners), data have not been collected that measure these relationships.

Future studies should provide information about both the employees' experiences and the programs and policies in companies of all sizes. By combining these types of data, researchers could examine these issues in a more comprehensive way, which would lead to a much richer database than has previously existed in the past. It is studies such as these, using methodologies such as that of the 1991 NOS directed at balance issues facing workers in all types of companies, that can truly move the work-family field forward. As indicated in the data presented in this article, the number of smaller businesses is rapidly expanding, and some feel that these companies are the wave of the future. By conducting more detailed, multilevel studies of smaller businesses, we may indeed be forecasting what the experiences of the majority of Americans will be like in the next century.

Notes

1. Due to the nature of smaller and larger businesses, different tracking systems were used to record the occurrence of personal and family issues. On average, those in smaller companies reported that this problem had occurred 1.4 times (per workplace) during the past week, while larger companies indicated that 1.2 percent of their workforce had been out for this reason during the previous year. Given the size of some of these larger companies, this is not an insignificant problem.

2. For smaller businesses, there were only three other areas that received fewer "very important" ratings than helping employees to balance their work and family responsibilities; for larger companies, this was true for only one other area.

References

Acs, Zoltan J. and David B. Audretsch. 1990a. *Innovation and Small Firms.* Cambridge: MIT Press.

——. 1990b. Small Firms in the 1990s. In *The Economics of Small Firms: A European Challenge*, ed. Zoltan J. Acs and David B. Audretsch. Dordrecht, Netherlands: Kluwer Academic.

Aldrich, H. E. 1979. *Organizations and Environments.* Englewood Cliffs, NJ: Prentice Hall.

Amato, Paul R. 1993. Urban-Rural Differences in Helping Friends and Family Members. *Social Psychology Quarterly* 56(4):249-62.

Arthur, Margaret B. and C. Hendry. 1990. Human Resource Management and the Emergent Strategy of Small to Medium Sized Business Units. *International Journal of Human Resource Management* 1(3):223-50.

Barker, Roger G. and Paul V. Gump. 1964. *Big School, Small School: High School Size and Student Behavior.* Stanford, CA: Stanford University Press.

Barron, John M., Dan A. Black, and Mark A. Loewenstein. 1987. Employer Size: The Implications for Search, Training, Capital Investment, Starting Wages, and Wage Growth. *Journal of Labor Economics* 5(1):76-89.

Barth, James R., Joseph L. Cordes, and Sheldon E. Haber. 1987. Employee Characteristics and Firm Size: Are There Systematic Empirical Relationships? *Applied Economics* 19:555-67.

Beck, E. M. 1974. Conflict Change and Stability: A Reciprocal Interaction in Schools. *Social Forces* 52(June):517-31.

Bond, T. E. 1996. Work-Life Sensitivities in Small Business: Preliminary Research Findings. Presentation at a conference by the Families and Work Institute, New York.

Bridge, Kennan and Leslie A. Baxter. 1992. Blended Relationships: Friends as Work Associates. *Western Journal of Communication* 56(Summer):200-225.

Brown, Charles, James Hamilton, and James Medoff. 1990. *Employers Large and Small.* Cambridge, MA: Harvard University Press.

Brown, Charles and James Medoff. 1989. The Employer Size-Wage Effect. *Journal of Political Economy* 97(5):1027-59.

Burden, Diane and Bradley Googins. 1987. *Balancing Job and Homelife Study.* Boston: Boston University, School of Social Work.

Dekker, Inez, Julian Barling, and E. Kevin Kelloway. 1996. Work Force Size and Multifaceted Job Satisfaction: A Cross-National Study. *Journal of Social Psychology* 136(2):201-8.

Dewar, Robert D. and Donald P. Simet. 1981. A Level-Specific Prediction of Spans of Control Examining the Effects of Size, Technology, and Specialization. *Academy of Management Journal* 24(1):5-24.

Dorman, P. 1995. Idaho Benefits Survey: Implied Compliance with the Pregnancy Discrimination Act. *Social Science Journal* 32(1):17-34.

Duxbury, Linda. 1997. Balancing Work and Family: A Study of Canadian Small Business Employees. Carleton University. Summary report.

Eichman, C. and B. Reisman. 1991. *Not Too Small to Care: Small Businesses and Child Care.* New York: Child Care Action Campaign.

Emlen, A. C. and P. E. Koren. 1984. *Hard to Find and Difficult to Manage: The Effects of Child Care on the Workplace.* Portland, OR: Portland State University, Regional Research Institute for Human Services.

Evans, David S. and Linda S. Leighton. 1988. Why Do Smaller Firms Pay Less? *Journal of Human Resources* 24(2):299-318.

Even, William E. and David A. MacPherson. 1996. Employer Size and Labor Turnover: The Role of Pensions. *Industrial and Labor Relations Review* 49(July):707-28.

Fernandez, John P. 1986. *Child Care and Corporate Productivity: Resolving Work / Family Conflicts.* Lexington, MA: D. C. Heath.

Finn, Jeremy D. and Kristin E. Voelkl. 1993. School Characteristics Related to Student Engagement. *Journal of Negro Education* 62(3):249-68.

Fischer, Claude S. 1982. *To Dwell Among Friends: Personal Networks in Town and City.* Chicago: University of Chicago Press.

Franck, Karen A. 1980. Friends and Strangers: The Social Experience of Living in Urban and Non-Urban Settings. *Journal of Social Issues* 36(3):52-71.

Friedman, Dana. 1990. Corporate Response to Family Needs. *Marriage and Family Review* 15:77-98.

Garbarino, James. 1980. Some Thoughts on School Size and Its Effects on Adolescent Development. *Journal of Youth and Adolescence* 9(1):19-31.

Garen, John E. 1985. Worker Heterogeneity, Job Screening, and Firm Size.
Journal of Political Economy 93(4):715-39.

Gonyea, Judith and Bradley Googins. 1993. Linking the Worlds of Work and Family: Beyond the Productivity Trap. *Human Resource Management* 31:209-26.

Googins, Bradley, Margaret Griffith, and Judith Casey. 1994. *Balancing Job and Homelife: Changes over Time in a Corporation.* Boston: Boston University, Center for Work & Family.

Gordon, Judith R. 1991. *A Diagnostic Approach to Organizational Behavior.* Boston: Allyn & Bacon.

Gregory, Thomas B. and Gerald R. Smith. 1987. *High Schools as Communities: The Small School Reconsidered.* Bloomington, IN: Phi Delta Kappa Educational Foundation.

Hewitt Associates. 1996. *Salaried Employee Benefits Provided by Major U.S. Employers in 1990 and 1995: A Comparison Study.* Lincolnshire, IL: Hewitt Associates.

Houghland, James G., Kyong-Dong Kim, and James A. Christenson. 1979. The Effects of Ecological and Socioeconomic Status Variables on Membership and Participation in Voluntary Organizations. *Rural Sociology* 44(3):602-12.

Kalleberg, Arne L., David Knoke, Peter V. Marsden, and Joe L. Spaeth. 1996a. Organizational Properties and Practices. In *Organizations in America: Analyzing Their Structures and Human Resource Practices,* ed. Arne L. Kalleberg, David Knoke, Peter V. Marsden, and Joe L. Spaeth. Thousand Oaks, CA: Sage.

———, eds. 1996b. *Organizations in America: Analyzing Their Structures and Human Resource Practices.* Thousand Oaks, CA: Sage.

Kalleberg, Arne L., Peter V. Marsden, David Knoke, and Joe L. Spaeth. 1996. Formalizing the Employment Relation. In *Organizations in America: Analyzing Their Structures and Hu-*

man Resource Practices, ed. Arne L. Kalleberg, David Knoke, Peter V. Marsden, and Joe L. Spaeth. Thousand Oaks, CA: Sage.

Kalleberg, Arne L. and Mark E. Van Buren. 1996a. Is Bigger Better? Explaining the Relationship between Organizational Size and Job Rewards. *American Sociological Review* 61(Feb.):47-66.

―――. 1996b. The Structure of Organizational Earnings Inequality. In *Organizations in America: Analyzing Their Structures and Human Resource Practices*, ed. Arne L. Kalleberg, David Knoke, Peter V. Marsden, and Joe L. Spaeth. Thousand Oaks, CA: Sage.

Knoke, David. 1996. Cui Bono? Employee Benefit Packages. In *Organizations in America: Analyzing Their Structures and Human Resource Practices*, ed. Arne L. Kalleberg, David Knoke, Peter V. Marsden, and Joe L. Spaeth. Thousand Oaks, CA: Sage.

Knoke, David and Arne L. Kalleberg. 1996. Job Training in U.S. Organizations. In *Organizations in America: Analyzing Their Structures and Human Resource Practices*, ed. Arne L. Kalleberg, David Knoke, Peter V. Marsden, and Joe L. Spaeth. Thousand Oaks, CA: Sage.

Korte, Charles. 1980. Urban-Nonurban Differences in Social Behavior and Social Psychological Models of Urban Impact. *Journal of Social Issues* 36(3):29-51.

Kwoka, John E. 1980. Establishment Size, Wages, and Job Satisfaction: The Trade-Offs. In *The Economics of Firm Size, Market Structure, and Social Performance*, ed. John J. Siegfried. Washington, DC: Federal Trade Commission, Bureau of Economics.

Lambert, Susan. 1993. Workplace Policies as Social Policy. *Social Service Review* 67:237-60.

Lilly, Teri Ann, Marcie Pitt-Catsouphes, and Bradley Googins. 1997. *Work-Family Research: An Annotated Bibliography*. Westport, CT: Greenwood Press.

MacDermid, Shelley M. and Margaret L. Williams. 1997. A Within-Industry Comparison of Employed Mothers' Experiences in Small and Large Workplaces. *Journal of Family Issues* 18(Sept.):545-66.

MacDermid, Shelley M., Margaret L. Williams, Stephen Marks, and Gabriela Heilbrun. 1994. Is Small Beautiful? Work-Family Tension, Work Conditions, and Organizational Size. *Family Relations* 43(2):159-67.

Marsden, Peter V., Arne L. Kalleberg, and Cynthia R. Cook. 1996. Gender Differences and Organizational Commitment. In *Organizations in America: Analyzing Their Structures and Human Resource Practices*, ed. Arne L. Kalleberg, David Knoke, Peter V. Marsden, and Joe L. Spaeth. Thousand Oaks, CA: Sage.

Marsh, Robert M. and Hiroshi Mannari. 1989. The Size Imperative? Longitudinal Tests. *Organization Studies* 10(1):83-95.

Mayo, John W. and Matthew N. Murray. 1991. Firm Size, Employment Risk, and Wages: Further Insights on a Persistent Puzzle. *Applied Economics* 23(Aug.):1351-60.

Mehta, Stephanie N. 1995. Many Small Companies Drop Retiree Health Benefits. *Wall Street Journal*, 22 Aug.

Mellow, Wesley. 1982. Employer Size and Wages. *Review of Economics and Statistics* 64(Aug.):495-501.

Morgan, David L. and Duane F. Alwin. 1980. When Less Is More: School Size and Student Social Participation. *Social Psychology Quarterly* 43(2):241-52.

Newmann, Fred M., Robert A. Rutter, and Marshall S. Smith. 1989. Organizational Factors That Affect School Sense of Efficacy, Community, and

Expectations. *Sociology of Education* 62(Oct.):221-38.

Oppenheimer, M. 1994. Small-Minded: Despite the Hype, Smaller Isn't Better in the Business World. *Dollars and Sense* Nov.-Dec., 20-21, 39-40.

Palisi, Bartolomeo J. and Claire Canning. 1986. Urbanism and Social Psychological Well-Being: A Test of Three Theories. *Sociological Spectrum* 6:361-78.

Parsons, Talcott. 1982. *Talcott Parsons on Institutions and Social Evolution.* Chicago: University of Chicago Press.

Peterson, Richard R. 1989. Firm Size, Occupational Segregation, and the Effects of Family Status on Women's Wages. *Social Forces* 68(2):397-414.

Rebitzer, James B. 1986. Establishment Size and Job Tenure. *Industrial Relations* 25(3):292-302.

Schmidt, Christoph M. and Klaus F. Zimmerman. 1991. Work Characteristics, Firm Size, and Wages. *Review of Economics and Statistics* 73(Nov.):705-10.

Spain, Daphne and Suzanne M. Bianchi. 1996. *Balancing Act: Motherhood, Marriage, and Employment Among American Women.* New York: Russell Sage Foundation.

Steblay, Nancy Mehrkens. 1987. Helping Behavior in Rural and Urban Environments: A Meta-Analysis. *Psychological Bulletin* 102(3):346-56.

Stinner, William F., Mollie Van Loon, Seh-Woong Chung, and Yongchung Byun. 1990. Community Size, Individual Social Position, and Community Attachment. *Rural Sociology* 55(4):494-521.

Storey, David J. 1990. Firm Performance and Size. In *The Economics of Small Firms: A European Challenge*, ed. Zoltan J. Acs and David B. Audretsch. Dordrecht, Netherlands: Kluwer Academic.

Tigges, Leann M. and Gary P. Green. 1994. Small Business Success Among Men- and Women-Owned Firms in Rural Areas. *Rural Sociology* 59(2):289-310.

U.S. Bureau of the Census. Program Research and Methods Branch. Economic Planning and Coordination Division. 1993. Unpublished data.

Villemez, Wayne J. and William P. Bridges. 1988. When Bigger Is Better: Differences in the Individual-Level Effect of Firm and Establishment Size. *American Sociological Review* 53(Apr.):237-55.

Wicker, Alan W. 1984. Behavior Settings Reconsidered: Temporal Stages, Resources, Internal Dynamics, Context. In *Handbook of Environmental Psychology*, ed. Daniel Stokols and Irwin Altman. New York: John Wiley.

Wilson, Thomas. 1991. Urbanism, Migration, and Tolerance: A Reassessment. *American Sociological Review* 56(Feb.):117-23.

ANNALS, *AAPSS*, **562**, March 1999

The Nonprofit Sector's Responsiveness to Work-Family Issues

By JUDITH G. GONYEA

ABSTRACT: Although researchers have explored the growth and impact of family-supportive policies in the business sector, there has been a curious lack of attention to the development of family-responsive policies in the nonprofit sector. This article suggests possible explanations for the dearth of such studies, reviews the existing literature, and offers directions for future research examining the kinds of work environments and policies that attract and retain high-quality employees in nonprofit organizations. Such research is critical as a growing number of workers, both men and women, are seeking ways to balance a desire for meaningful work with a wish for fuller family or personal lives.

Judith G. Gonyea is associate professor and chair of the Social Welfare Research Department at the Boston University School of Social Work. In 1995, she coauthored (with Nancy Hooyman) the book Feminist Perspectives on Family Care: Policies for Gender Justice. *She was also the guest editor of a special issue of* Research on Aging *(1994) devoted to the topic of work and elder care.*

OVER the past three decades, social scientists have increasingly challenged Parsons's conceptualization of family and work as two distinct and separate spheres (1952). Rejecting a formalist dichotomy between economic and noneconomic activity, researchers have pursued the study of the interface between family life and the workplace by exploring such phenomena as "family-job spillover" and "work-family balance." Correspondingly, throughout the past 20 years, work-family policies and programs have gained an enormous presence in American corporations and now represent a highly visible and well-entrenched part of corporate human resources. What were once viewed as curious business experiments are now basic benefits in many *Fortune* 500 and *Fortune* 1000 companies. To a large extent, the dramatic expansion of family-friendly organizations is the result of companies' creation of work-family manager or work-life manager positions whose functions are to inform and advise corporate leadership about the shifting landscape of employee demographics and personnel policies. Similarly, media attention, such as from the *Wall Street Journal's* weekly work-family column and *Working Mothers* magazine, has heightened public interest in how American companies are responding to employees' family responsibilities. In fact, it could now be said that, in the 1990s, work-family policies and programs have settled into a relatively comfortable niche in corporate America.

Although researchers have explored the growth and impact of family-supportive policies in the business community, there has been a curious lack of attention to the development of such policies in the nonprofit sector. Past studies have focused almost exclusively on the for-profit or public sectors. Further, much of the work-family research has been conducted in larger companies that typically employ several thousand employees. Very little is known about if, and how, nonprofit organizations—or even small for-profit firms—have modified their work environments in response to employees' family needs. This article therefore begins with a discussion of the importance of studying the nonprofit sector and offers several possible explanations for the lack of such research. The focus then shifts to examine what specifically is known about the family-supportive policies and programs in nonprofit organizations. Finally, an agenda to guide future work-family research in the nonprofit domain is offered.

THE IMPORTANCE OF STUDYING
THE NONPROFIT SECTOR

As defined by U.S. tax law, the nonprofit sector (which is also referred to as the independent sector, the voluntary sector, or the civil society sector) consists of two major groups of tax-exempt organizations: 501(c)(3) charitable organizations and 501(c)(4) social welfare organizations. For purposes of discussion, however, nonprofit organizations are typically classified into seven subsectors: health services and hospitals; education and research; social and legal services; religious organiza-

TABLE 1

NONPROFIT, BUSINESS, AND GOVERNMENT SECTORS' SHARES OF THE U.S. ECONOMY

	Nonprofit	Business	Government
Percentage of all U.S. organizations (1992)	4.2	93.8	0.4
Percentage of national income (1994)	6.9	78.0	15.1
Percentage of U.S. paid workforce (1994)	6.7	75.0	17.3

SOURCE: Hodgkinson et al. 1996, 25, 28.

tions; civic and social organizations; arts and culture; and foundations. In 1994, almost half (46 percent) of the total employment in the nonprofit sector was in the health services subsector, followed by the education and research subsector (21 percent) and social and legal services (16 percent) (Hodgkinson et al. 1996). Although smaller than the business and government sectors, the nonprofit sector nonetheless has a significant presence in the U.S. economy (see Table 1). In 1992, there were slightly more than 1 million nonprofit organizations, representing 4.2 percent of total organizations in the United States. The nonprofit sector's share of the 1994 national income was 6.9 percent, or $508.2 billion. Furthermore, in 1994, the number of full-time and part-time paid employees in the independent sector was 9.7 million, representing 6.7 percent of the total U.S. workforce (Hodgkinson et al. 1996).

In fact, the nonprofit sector is an important economic presence not only in the United States but also worldwide. Salamon and Anheier (1997) found in their analysis of 1990 data from eight countries—France, Germany, Italy, Hungary, Japan, Sweden, the United Kingdom, and the United States—that the non-

profit sector employed the equivalent of 11.9 million full-time paid employees, representing almost 1 out of every 20 jobs. Equally important, their data revealed that worldwide the nonprofit sector was the chief growth sector of the 1980s. For example, although the nonprofit sector accounts for only 6.7 percent of total employment in the United States, it accounted for 13.0 percent of the job growth, or approximately one out of every eight new jobs during the 1980s (Salamon and Anheier 1997). Much of this growth can be attributed to the shift of most nations' economies to services where, as Ben-Ner and Van Hoomissen (1990) note, nonprofit organizations have traditionally had a significant presence. In fact, a number of demographic, social, and economic trends suggest that there will be a growing need for the type of services nonprofit organizations have historically provided, including care for young children (with women's increased entry into the paid labor force) and frail elders (with longer life expectancies). Moreover, Ben-Ner and Van Hoomissen suggest that the redistribution of income or the widening of the gap between the haves and have-nots in American society will continue to fuel the growth of the nonprofit sector:

The redistribution of income in favor of wealthier families and individuals . . . and from younger people to the elderly . . . had a double yet generally positive effect on the demand for services. The improved position of comparatively wealthy segments of society enhanced their demand for, among other things, certain types of health, education, and social services. The rise in poverty increased demand for other types of services—those addressed to alleviation of poverty (especially social services) and those directed to individuals and families with little ability to pay. (112)

Despite its importance and dramatic worldwide growth, Salamon and Anheier (1997) note that the nonprofit sector or "civil society sector remains one of the best kept secrets of modern social development" (61). Further, they offer three reasons that the nonprofit sector has "remained an uncharted subcontinent on the social landscape of modern society":

1. Empirically, national and international data systems on economic life have either overlooked or excluded the nonprofit sector from their analyses.
2. Conceptually, given the diverse array of organizations that fall within the nonprofit sector, it is often not studied in totality.
3. Ideologically, both the political Left and the political Right have minimized the nonprofit sector albeit for different reasons—the Left being concerned that too positive a view of the nonprofit sectors' capabilities will reduce support for the government's role in protection of the vulnerable and the Right being concerned that the growth of the nonprofit sector undermines the argument that state expansion displaces nonprofit groups (60).

Analysis of the U.S. Bureau of Labor Statistics (BLS) data underscores Salamon and Anheier's first point that "data systems used to gather information about the structure of economic life have systematically overlooked this sector or simply defined it away" (1997, 60). BLS reports typically compare employee wages and compensation (including the availability of family-responsive benefits) by company size, type of industry, occupational group, and full- and part-time work status, but they do not analyze nonprofit, or independent, sector status. The BLS data document that access to family-friendly benefits is unevenly distributed among American workers. For example, while 84 percent of full-time employees at medium-sized and large private establishments in 1995 had access to unpaid time off, only 45 percent of their counterparts in small private establishments did (U.S. Bureau of Labor Statistics 1998). The BLS also reveals that family benefits are more available to professional and technical employees as compared to clerical and sales employees and blue-collar and service employees (see Table 2).

Given these dramatic differences in worker benefits by industry and employee characteristics, it is unfortunate that the BLS data do not examine worker characteristics, wages, or compensation by nonprofit sector status. In fact, the lack of attention to the nonprofit sector is

TABLE 2
**ELIGIBILITY FOR FAMILY BENEFITS AT MEDIUM-SIZED AND LARGE PRIVATE FIRMS,
BY OCCUPATIONAL CATEGORY FOR FULL-TIME EMPLOYEES, 1995 (Percentage)**

	Professional or Technical	Clerical or Sales	Blue-Collar or Service
Employer-provided child care funds	7	4	2
On-site child care	8	2	1
Adoption assistance	18	12	6
Flexible workplace	5	2	1

SOURCE: U.S. Bureau of Labor Statistics 1998.

ironic given that, as reflected in Table 3, almost one-third (31 percent) of the nonprofit sector's funds come from public sources (government) (Hodgkinson et al. 1996).

In addition to the BLS tracking of family benefits, a number of consulting firms and academic institutes, including Work/Family Directions, Catalyst, the Conference Board, the Families and Work Institute, and the Boston College Center for Work & Family, have been created to provide services, advocacy, and research in this area. Yet, here also one finds that information on the nonprofit sector is missing. To a certain degree, this absence reflects the fact that a significant portion of the research conducted by these centers or institutes is funded by large corporations whose primary interests are in the for-profit sector. For example, Catalyst's study of flexible work arrangements "was funded by a consortium of companies: American Brands, Inc., AT&T, Chubb & Son, Inc., Intel Corporation and Metropolitan Life" (Catalyst 1993, 7). Of the 70 surveyed companies (which included the five identified funders), only 2 employed fewer than 1000 workers. Almost half (49 percent) of the

surveyed firms had over 10,000 employees (Catalyst 1993). Similarly, Boston College's Center for Work & Family's study of contingent work arrangements in family-sensitive corporations, funded by a corporate foundation, "distributed surveys to the thirty-three members of its Work and Family Roundtable. The Roundtable is a national membership group consisting of corporations that have demonstrated leadership and commitment to work-family issues. . . . The [21] respondent companies were predominantly large corporations with an average U.S. work force of 43,797 employees (ranging from 4,000 to 185,000)" (Christensen 1995, 18-19). The Conference Board's study, *Juggling the Demands of Dependent Care* (1997), was based on a sample of 83 companies that were members of the Work-Family Advisory Panel. The respondent companies' average employee population was 35,000.

Although the literature (including the previously identified surveys) suggests there has been a substantial expansion of work-family policies, questions emerge when we attempt to extrapolate these data to nonprofit organizations or even

TABLE 3

SHARE OF TOTAL ANNUAL FUNDS FOR THE NONPROFIT SECTOR, BY SOURCE OF REVENUE, 1992

Source	Percentage
Private contributions	39.1
Government sector payments	31.3
Private sector payments	18.4
Other revenue	11.2

SOURCE: Hodgkinson et al. 1996, 5, Fig. 2.

small for-profit firms. Lack of data on small organizations is a significant gap, as 98 percent of all U.S. companies have fewer than 100 employees and these firms provide 41 percent of all U.S. jobs (Employee Benefit Research Institute 1996). Similarly, the vast majority of nonprofit organizations employ fewer than 100 workers. Most 501(c)(3), or charitable, organizations are very small. With the clear exceptions of the Aspen Institute, the Ford Foundation, and the Packard Foundation, few foundations have defined research on the nonprofit sector as part of their mission or as a priority area. Given their relatively small staffs and budgets, few nonprofits have engaged in studies of their own organizations.

FAMILY-RESPONSIVE WORK
ENVIRONMENTS IN THE
NONPROFIT SECTOR

A series of literature searches were undertaken using PSYCHLIT, SOCIOFILE, ABI, and NEXIS to identify any sources published since 1985 that address the issue of work-family policies and programs in the nonprofit sector. Despite the extensiveness of the search process, only

four studies were identified (Fischel-Wolovick et al. 1988; Fernandez 1990; Galinsky and Stein 1990; Hohl 1996). Fischel-Wolovick and her colleagues describe the process of introducing alternative work schedules—job sharing and a compressed workweek—into the social work department of an 1100-bed hospital that already had flextime. As part of a pilot project, a single job-sharing position was created in the Inpatient Medical Services unit, and six social workers were selected to participate in a compressed workweek. Fischel-Wolovick et al. report:

At this time, we have had two years of experience with job sharing and compressed workweek. Although no formal evaluative tool has yet been developed to measure results objectively, the general response to the flexible work schedules has been very positive. We measured worker productivity by (a) the number of cases opened monthly, and (b) the number of direct services (interviews with a patient or family group) provided. The monthly average of new cases opened and the number of direct services have both increased. . . . The medical and nursing staffs have adjusted well to job sharing and the compressed workweek. Their responses have been positive. (100)

Fischel-Wolovick and her colleagues note that the introduction of the alternative work schedules occurred in an organization that values participatory management and where conflict resolution and problem solving are viewed as the responsibility of both administrators and staff.

Arguing that "family-sensitive policies can attract employees to human services organizations," Fernandez (1990, 53) examines the advantages and disadvantages of 10 options: resource and referral services; on- or near-site child care; dependent care account; cafeteria-style fringe benefits; special rates at child care facilities; maternity leave; paternity leave; flexible use of sick days; flextime; and job sharing. Fernandez presents data on the availability of these family-sensitive options among the members of the Urban Affairs Partnership, "a not-for-profit group of 90 corporate, religious, university, and neighborhood leaders who have joined together to focus on the human and social concerns in the Philadelphia region." She notes that "most of the corporate members are large (93% over 100 employees)" (51). Only 33 partnership employers completed the survey, and no information is presented by Fernandez as to their for-profit or nonprofit status. Nevertheless, the reported availability of the family-sensitive options was as follows: maternity leave, made available by 94 percent of employers; information and referral, 58 percent; flextime, 46 percent; flexible sick days, 42 percent; paternity leave, 42 percent; dependent care account, 24 percent; job sharing, 18 percent; on-site child care, 9 percent; cafeteria benefits, 3 percent; and child care discounts, 3 percent. Clearly, caution must be taken in generalizing these findings, as organizations committed to participating in a partnership to improve the urban environment may not be representative of many for-profit or even nonprofit organizations.

Fernandez concludes her article by stating,

With a shrinking pool of employable people, employers are going to find it increasingly essential to compete successfully for productive and dependable employees. Since salaries in the human services are frequently relatively low, "family sensitive" fringe benefits and personnel policies can be a determining factor in attracting and retaining productive and loyal employees in such a competitive environment. (1990, 65)

Galinsky and Stein (1990) compared the development of work-family programs in five corporations and five universities that are leaders in the sciences. The five companies—IBM, Merck, Digital, Johnson & Johnson, and AT&T—are generally regarded as progressive leaders in the work-family realm. The five universities were seen as competing with the firms in the recruitment and retention of top scientists—the Massachusetts Institute of Technology (MIT), Stanford, the University of California at Berkeley, Harvard, and the University of Texas at Arlington. Few differences existed between the corporations and universities in terms of child care support, parental leave, or flextime. The availability of part-time work with benefits did, however, vary between the for-profits and the universities. All five universities offer part-time jobs with benefits. Galinsky and Stein report that "these policies are well established at Stanford and widely used at Harvard, MIT, Berkeley, and [the] University of Texas." They note that the use of part-time labor is less extensive in the corporations and that experiences at some companies "indicate that women who choose to work part-time may fall into a lower career track" (376). Thus it appears that for-profit firms did not use part-time employment as creatively as did the academic organizations.

The most recent and rigorous research conducted on family-responsive initiatives in the nonprofit sector is Hohl's statewide survey (1996) of the use of flexible work arrangements by nonprofit organizations in Illinois. From an original sample of 245 nonprofits employing 20 or more persons, Hohl received completed surveys from 156 organizations (a 64 percent response rate). Hohl explored the availability of eight types of flexible work arrangements: compressed workweek; flextime; job sharing; joint appointments; part-time work; phased retirement; reduced workweek;[1] and telecommuting. Follow-up in-person interviews were also conducted with 30 organizations that had the "most extensive and formal" policies. Hohl found that 84 percent of the 156 surveyed nonprofits offered one or more of the eight different flexible work arrangements. She notes that "although this percentage is slightly lower than Christensen's (1989) survey of large for-profit firms, in which 93 percent of respondents offered at least one of six alternatives, it is substantially higher than current national figures of 61 percent (U.S. Bureau of Labor Statistics, 1991)" (74).

Hohl's data also revealed that the three most common flexible work arrangements available organization-wide were part-time work (69 percent), reduced workweek (48 percent), and flextime (33 percent), whereas the most frequently available flexible work arrangements in selected units were flextime (42 percent), job sharing (38 percent), and joint appointments (32 percent). Yet, even among the 30 organizations that had more extensive flexible work arrangements, only a small percentage had written policies on the use of these options. Hohl comments that the lack of written policies may reflect the fact that only 7 of the 30 organizations offered these options as part of "proactive and strategic plans"; in the remaining 23 agencies, the availability of flexible work arrangements appeared to be "reactive and incremental" (Hohl 1996, 78, 80). In fact, the follow-up interviews revealed that the percentages of employees in the various types of arrangements were low. Hohl also notes that although part-time work was the most frequently available option, in contrast to findings of others, only 10 percent of the 30 organizations offered any paid benefits to part-time staff. Finally, Hohl's research suggests that while competition for personnel is often a catalyst for the introduction of flexible work arrangements, once they are implemented, administrator and supervisor support is often key to the arrangements' success.

An additional resource providing information on family-friendly initiatives in the nonprofit sector is *What Works! The Working Women Count Honor Roll Report* (1997), by the Women's Bureau of the U.S. Department of Labor. Although the Women's Bureau did not use a random, or probability, sample, it signed

TABLE 4
**WOMEN'S BUREAU HONOR ROLL: NUMBER OF
HONOR ROLL PROGRAMS, BY TYPE OF ORGANIZATION**

| Organization Type | Honor Roll Program | | | | total |
	Pay or benefits	Valuing women	Family friendly	Multiple programs	
Business	17	138	41	111	307
Nonprofit	27	56	89	84	256
Government	4	25	13	25	67
Labor union	6	7	4	8	25
Other	6	30	42	37	115

SOURCE: U.S. Department of Labor, Women's Bureau 1997, 9.

up more than 1300 organizations in order to address the workplace concerns of women. More than 840 of these applicants were approved for inclusion on the Women's Bureau's Honor Roll based on an evaluation of the organizations' efforts to increase opportunities and remove barriers for women in three areas: pay and benefits (for example, part-time worker benefits; gender-neutral job evaluations); balancing work and family (for example, child and dependent care, paid leave); and respect and opportunity on the job (for example, overcoming sexual discrimination and harassment; training).

Although the Women's Bureau may have, in fact, oversampled the nonprofit sector, it is significant that the nonprofit organizations were responsible for one-third of all Honor Roll–qualifying initiatives (see Table 4). As the Women's Bureau notes,

Different types of organizations tend to favor different types of programs. Close to half of the Honor Roll programs instituted by business (representing 40 percent of the total programs) are in the category of balancing work and family. . . . Nonprofits, which are responsible

for 33 percent of all Honor Roll initiatives, are equally likely to develop family-friendly policies, to value women, and [to] meet the multiplicity of their needs. Programs initiated by state and local governments are most likely to fall into the family-friendly and multiplicity categories. In contrast to other institutions, labor unions are almost as likely to negotiate for and implement pay and benefits programs, family-friendly policies, and multiple initiatives. (1997, 9)

Due to the relatively few studies, the extent to which nonprofit organizations have modified their work environments in response to employees' work-family conflicts remains largely unknown. There are, however, several reasons to believe that the nonprofit sector may be more responsive to employees' family needs than either the for-profit or the public sectors. First, nonprofits are often held to higher societal expectations and ethical standards of fairness than the for-profits. Jeavons (1992) notes that

the higher standards that we expect of these organizations encompass more than just greater honesty and extend beyond values related to their immediate and primary enterprise or mission . . . people expect nonprofit service organizations to maintain and promote a more generally humane, caring, or socially progressive set of values in every facet of their behavior. (408)

Second, a larger percentage of workers in the nonprofit sector are women. In 1994, 68 percent of paid employees in the independent sector were women, as compared to 44 percent among all employees (excluding agricultural workers) in the other sectors (Hodgkinson et al. 1996). As family care still is predominantly a woman's role, nonprofits may have a greater stake in addressing employees' work-family conflicts. Third, the independent sector has historically served as a sector of access not only for women but also for persons of color. In 1994, 15 percent of paid employees in the nonprofit sector were African American, compared to 10 percent of employees (excluding agricultural workers) in the other sectors (Hodgkinson et al. 1996). As the issue of creating a diverse workforce is often linked to the work-family issue, once again nonprofit organizations may have a greater commitment to the creation of a family-responsive work environment. Finally, as employers are more likely to extend family-supportive benefits to higher-status employees, and professionals compose a large percentage of the staff in nonprofits, we might expect to find greater responsiveness in the independent sector. As indicated in the *Nonprofit Almanac 1996-1997*, the independent sector has a major presence in occupations that require skilled workers or individuals with college educations. More than one-third of nurses and managers in health services and over one-quarter of physicians, clinical laboratory technicians, social workers, educational administrators, and postsecondary teachers are found in the independent sector (Hodgkinson et al. 1996).

Yet, at the same time, there is some anecdotal evidence that suggests that a double standard may exist between the kinds of vision nonprofit organizations hold for society and their treatment of their own staff. For instance, a 1991 *Chronicle of Philanthropy* article reports that a number of nonprofit employees felt that the organizations pay so poorly and/or make such demands on their time as to make their family lives very difficult (Green 1991). Mirvis's 1990 replication of his 1977 survey comparing employee attitudes in the three sectors also revealed some significant shifts (Mirvis 1992). Although, as in the earlier survey, he found that people working in the nonprofit sector gain more satisfaction from their jobs and have more trust in their management than their counterparts in business and government, nonprofit employees are just as concerned that their employers will "take advantage of them." Moreover, in contrast to the 1977 survey, the 1990 data revealed that people working in the nonprofit sector are no more psychologically committed to their organizations than employees in the other two sectors.

Although there is a great deal of variation in the wages paid across sectors of the economy, various surveys place nonprofit employees' salaries between 7 percent and 35 percent lower than those of their for-profit counterparts. For example, the *Nonprofit Almanac* reports the wage differential of physicians, psychologists, public relations specialists, and management-related occupations in the independent sector as being 10 to 25 percent lower than those of their peers in the for-profit sector (Hodgkinson et al. 1996). Comparing employees with similar educational, occupational, and demographic characteristics, Preston (1989) estimates that the average full-time income of nonprofit workers is 15 percent lower than the average full-time income of for-profit workers. However, Preston (1990) notes,

While the variation in the nonprofit wage differential by industry and occupation is significant, it is relatively small compared to the variation in the wage differential by gender. The loss of wages experienced by full-time white-collar men who choose nonprofit work is much more severe (–41 percent and statistically significant in the WAJC [1980 Worker Assessment of Jobs' Nonmonetary Characteristics] data) than the loss experienced by full-time white-collar women (–6 percent and not statistically significant in the WAJC data). (19)

In fact, Preston suggests that one of the reasons for the historically greater representation of women in the nonprofit sector is that (unlike men) they were not required to make such a large salary sacrifice relative to comparable employment elsewhere. She cautions, however, that her analysis of the U.S. labor market in the 1980s suggests that this lack of

sacrifice may no longer be true: "Opportunities and wages for women are improving steadily in the for-profit sector, while they are not changing visibly in the nonprofit sector" (Preston 1990, 26). Preston cautions that this relative decline in wages may result in labor shortages in the nonprofit sector if nonprofit organizations do not engage in policies to attract workers. She suggests,

There are a number of policies that nonprofit managers can consider to remedy the situation. The most obvious is to raise wages. As an alternative, the nonprofit manager can improve other aspects of compensation or job attributes. Job attributes can be tailored to the types of employees whom the manager hopes to attract. For example, if the nonprofit manager wants to hire well-educated young females, an attractive job package would include flexible hours, good health and maternity benefits, and perhaps even day care benefits. (27)

In their study of careers in Australia's third sector, Onyx and Maclean (1996) note that women seek employment in the nonprofit sector for most of the same reasons that men do. They found, however, that the women were also attracted to employment that is flexible and close to home, allowing them the opportunity to balance their family commitments with their desire for meaningful work. Like Preston, Onyx and Maclean argue, "Women provide a highly committed and skilled labor force for third-sector organizations. In order to fully tap that potential, organizations need to provide the flexibility and development opportunities that women require" (344).

FUTURE RESEARCH
DIRECTIONS

This article underscores the need for more research to understand the kinds of work environments and policies that attract and retain high-quality employees to the nonprofit sector. Such research is critical as a growing number of professionals, both men and women, are seeking ways to balance a desire for meaningful work with a wish to be more engaged in or accessible to their families and/or have fuller personal lives. As Hohl (1996) notes, more than half of the administrators she interviewed indicated that they expected their organizations to offer a greater variety of flexible work arrangements and that employees would use them more extensively in the future.

The question of whether organizations in the nonprofit sector are more family-friendly than organizations in the other two sectors currently remains unanswered. As Salamon and Anheier (1997) note, the nonprofit sector "is still largely hidden from view . . . a largely invisible subcontinent on the landscape of twentieth century social reality" (60). Future research into the extent to which nonprofit organizations have become more responsive to their employees' family needs can, however, be informed or guided by the research being done in the for-profit and public sectors.

Of particular interest is Osterman's study (1995) of how various for-profit organizations' employment strategies are associated with firms' adoption of work-family programs. Based on data from 874 establishments, Osterman finds that firms

that pursued high-commitment work systems (measured by organizations' employment goals, the level of employee work discretion, and adoption of specific work policies) were more likely to adopt work-family programs, even after controlling for internal labor market structures and wage and other benefit levels. Osterman comments that this finding is significant in that throughout the past decade there has been a notable shift in the American workplace. Many U.S. companies are attempting to move away from the traditional workplace (that is, tight divisions of labor and narrowly designed specialized jobs) to self-managed teams or problem-solving groups often consisting of cross-sections of employees. Depending on the definition of "high-commitment work system" used, various surveys have estimated that 25 to 40 percent of American companies are now using some of these innovative practices to reorganize the workplace.

Nonetheless, Osterman (1995) cautions, "One limitation is that this paper deals only with private-sector establishments and that the considerations that underlie adoption of work-family programs in the government and nonprofit sectors may be quite different from those discussed here" (696). In fact, there is considerable merit to expanding Osterman's research to the nonprofit sector. A significant portion of nonprofit organizations might well be viewed as "high-commitment work systems," in which an emphasis is placed on having employees "engage themselves and offer their ideas and knowledge with a degree of authenticity that, by its very nature, is not enforceable and which therefore requires a substantial element of volunteerism on the part of the workforce" (686).

Central to future investigations is the issue of how one defines "family supports" or "family benefits" in the workplace. Family benefits have most frequently been divided into three categories: leave policies (maternity or paternity leave, disability leave, sick leave, vacation); child and elder care assistance (such as referral services, subsidies, on- or near-site care); and work schedule and personnel policies (such as flextime, part-time work, telecommuting). However, it is increasingly being argued that although these options may alleviate some problems of the work-family dilemma, they do not address the broader issue of the way work is organized. Hall (1990), for instance, notes that offering these options may allow a company to look progressive without actually changing the work environment or culture. In fact, in most companies, family-responsive policies have simply been superimposed on a traditional work culture (Gonyea 1997). Thus, Daly (1996) argues, the majority of employees have been receiving contradictory messages from their employers. On one hand, companies are saying that they recognize that employees must be attentive to their family needs. On the other hand, the message is that company commitment and work performance are measured by long hours. Given this second message, it is not surprising that family-work benefits are largely underutilized by workers.

Although larger organizations are generally promoted as being more family-friendly than medium-sized or small establishments, Kalleberg and Van Buren (1996) note: "The maxim 'bigger is better' is true in the sense that employees of large organizations obtain higher earnings and more fringe benefits and promotion opportunities than do employees in small organizations. On the other hand, 'small is beautiful' if a worker desires to exercise autonomy and control over his or her work" (62). Kingston (1990) argues that the limited changes in the American workplace are the result of decisions by business leaders, policymakers, and scholars to define "family responsive" narrowly. Noting that family-responsive policies have come to be viewed as additions to the corporate welfare system either as fringe benefits (such as dependent care assistance plans, cafeteria benefit plans, or flexible benefit plans) or modifications in work schedules (for example, flextime, compressed workweeks), Kingston (1990) suggests:

This operational definition has two significant implications: it obscures the full breadth of the ways business practices shape family lives, and it constricts policy debates to a fairly narrow range of modest reforms. . . . [The failure] to link wages and job security to family welfare narrows the contours of the policy debate. (441)

Osterman (1995) also raises the issue of the need to examine the trend of companies to provide work-family benefits within a broader framework:

An optimist might read the results as suggesting that at least a substantial minority of firms are both introducing work systems that empower employees and taking more responsibility for the personal welfare of employees. A pessimist would point to cuts in other benefits . . . [and argue that] work/family plans are being introduced to gain a one-sided and uneven commitment that is in the narrow interests of employers. (697)

In fact, there has been a significant erosion in both employees' pension and health insurance coverage in the private sector—benefits that are critical to families' well-being. In 1983, 47 percent of full-time workers received pension coverage through a traditional pension plan and only 3 percent of workers participated in 401(k)-type plans. A decade later, only one-third of workers had coverage under a traditional plan, while slightly more than one-quarter of workers were covered by a 401(k) plan, and 10 percent of workers had coverage under both plans. Correspondingly, employer contributions to pension plans declined (in real dollars) from $1939 per worker to $506 per worker annually (Lehigh 1995). Similarly, we have seen a shift toward American workers' paying for their health insurance premiums, a cost once covered by companies. Whereas in 1980, 75 percent of companies paid for all of their employees' health insurance, only about one-third (35 percent) of companies now do so (Seccombe and Amey 1995).

Mirvis (1992) suggests that "there are indications that the work climate in nonprofits is becoming 'more like a business'" (39). As in the business sector, nonprofit organizations are increasingly emphasizing efficiency and cost control and are reorganizing, declassifying jobs, and/or downsizing. Clearly, the nonprofit sector has been affected by the managed care movement as a growing number of states shift the provision of health care, mental health care, and social services to managed care systems using a variety of reimbursement systems, including capitation, fee-for-service plans, and discounted rates. Pynes (1997) stresses that "the 'contract state' or 'nonprofit federalism' will become even more blurred as many local and state governments go beyond contracting out services and attempt to privatize services presently performed by public employees" (359). These services may be transferred to either nonprofit or for-profit organizations.

CONCLUSION

The trends that contributed to the dramatic expansion in the nonprofit sector during the 1980s and 1990s, particularly the growth of the service economy, will continue throughout the next decade. Previous research in the work-family field suggests that as we seek to understand what factors contribute to or constrain the development of family-responsive work environments, it is important to examine both endogenous variables (such as organizational characteristics) and exogenous variables (for example, labor market conditions, government policy). It is also critical that researchers examine organizations' comprehensive approaches to becoming more family sensitive rather than to individual family benefits or policies.

In the past three decades, there has been a continuing blurring of the distinctions between the nonprofit and public sectors and between the nonprofit and for-profit sectors. Most nonprofit service organizations depend on the government for over half of their revenues (Lipsky and Smith 1989-90). There has also been a significant increase in the involvement of for-profit organizations in the social welfare field, a shift often referred to as the "marketization of welfare." Future investigations may well reveal growing similarities between the work climates in the three sectors, including the degree to which the work environment has become family responsive.

Note

1. Hohl defined "part-time" as working less than half-time on a regular basis (typically less than 20 hours per week). "Reduced workweek" was defined as working half-time or more per week but less than full-time, on a regular basis.

References

Ben-Ner, Avner and Theresa Van Hoomissen. 1990. The Growth of the Nonprofit Sector in the 1980s: Facts and Interpretation. *Nonprofit Management and Leadership* 1:99-116.

Catalyst. 1993. *Flexible Work Arrangements II: Succeeding with Part-Time Options*. New York: Catalyst.

Christensen, Kathleen. 1995. *Contingent Work Arrangements in Family-Sensitive Corporations*. Chestnut Hill,

MA: Boston College, Center for Work & Family.

Conference Board. 1997. *Juggling the Demands of Dependent Care*. Work-Family Roundtable 7. New York: Conference Board.

Daly, Kerry J. 1996. *Families and Time*. Thousand Oaks, CA: Sage.

Employee Benefit Research Institute. 1996. *The Changing World of Work and Employee Benefits*. EBRI Issue Brief no. 172. Washington, DC: Employee Benefit Research Institute.

Fernandez, Happy C. 1990. "Family Sensitive" Policies Can Attract Employees to Human Services Organizations. *Administration in Social Work* 14: 47-66.

Fischel-Wolovick, Lisa, Connie Cotter, Ilene Masser, Emily Kelman-Bravo, Ronnie S. Jaffe, Gary Rosenberg, and Beth Wittenberg. 1988. Alternative Work Scheduling for Professional Social Workers. *Administration in Social Work* 12:93-102.

Galinsky, Ellen and Paul J. Stein. 1990. The Impact of Human Resource Policies on Employees: Balancing Work/Family Life. *Journal of Family Issues* 11:368-83.

Gonyea, Judith G. 1997. The *Real* Meaning of Balancing Work and Family. *Public Policy and Aging Report* 8(3):1, 6-8.

Green, S. L. 1991. Poor Pay Threatens Leadership. *Chronicle of Philanthropy*, 26 Mar., 1, 28-31.

Hall, Douglas T. 1990. Promoting Work/Family Balance: An Organizational-Change Approach. *Organizational Dynamics* 18:5-18.

Hodgkinson, Virginia A. and Murray S. Weitzman with John A. Abrahams, Eric A. Crutchfield, and David R. Stevenson. 1996. *Nonprofit Almanac 1996-97: Dimensions of the Independent Sector*. San Francisco: Jossey-Bass.

Hohl, Karen L. 1996. The Effects of Flexible Work Arrangements. *Nonprofit Management and Leadership* 7:69-86.

Jeavons, Thomas H. 1992. When the Management Is the Message: Relating Values to Management Practices in Nonprofit Organizations. *Nonprofit Management and Leadership* 2:403-17.

Kalleberg, Arne L. and Mark E. Van Buren. 1996. Is Bigger Better? Explaining the Relationship Between Organization Size and Job Rewards. *American Sociological Review* 61:47-66.

Kingston, Paul W. 1990. Illusions and Ignorance about the Family-Responsive Workplace. *Journal of Family Issues* 11:438-54.

Lehigh, Scott. 1995. Social Insecurity. *Boston Globe*, 20 Aug.

Lipsky, Michael and Stephen R. Smith. 1989-90. Nonprofit Organizations, Government, and the Welfare State. *Political Science Quarterly* 104:625-48.

Mirvis, Philip H. 1992. The Quality of Employment in the Nonprofit Sector: An Update on Employee Attitudes in Nonprofits Versus Business and Government. *Nonprofit Management and Leadership* 3:23-41.

Onyx, Jenny and Madi Maclean. 1996. Careers in the Third Sector. *Nonprofit Management and Leadership* 6:331-45.

Osterman, Paul. 1995. Work/Family Programs and the Employment Relationship. *Administrative Science Quarterly* 40:681-700.

Parsons, Talcott. 1952. *The Social System*. Glencoe, IL: Free Press.

Preston, Anne E. 1989. The Nonprofit Worker in a For-Profit World. *Journal of Labor Economics* 7:438-63.

———. 1990. Changing Labor Market Patterns in the Nonprofit and For-Profit Sectors: Implications for Nonprofit Management. *Nonprofit Management and Leadership* 1:15-28.

Pynes, Joan E. 1997. The Anticipated Growth of Nonprofit Unionism. *Nonprofit Management and Leadership* 7:355-71.

Salamon, Lester S. and Helmut K. Anheier. 1997. The Civil Society Sector. *Society* 34:60-65.

Seccombe, Karen and Cheryl Amey. 1995. Playing by the Rules and Losing: Health Insurance and the Working Poor. *Journal of Health and Social Behavior* 36:168-81.

U.S. Bureau of Labor Statistics. 1998. Employee Benefits Survey. Table 3. Other Benefits: Eligibility for Specified Benefits, Full-Time Employees. Http://stats.bls.gov/news.release. ebs3.t03.htm.

U.S. Department of Labor, Women's Bureau. 1997. *What Works! The Working Women Count Honor Roll Report*. Washington, DC: U.S. Department of Labor, Women's Bureau.

ANNALS, *AAPSS*, **562**, March 1999

A New Work-Life Model
for the Twenty-First Century

By ROSALIND C. BARNETT

ABSTRACT: With the coming of the new century, talk of change and new beginnings is everywhere—the new family, the new workforce, the new corporation, the new employee-employer contract. In the midst of all this talk of change, however, policies and practices in the work-life area remain surprisingly the same. No innovative ways of framing the issues have captured the imagination of policymakers; no dramatically new approaches have been embraced to meet the needs of changed constituencies. The author argues that this stagnation is due to well-entrenched but out-of-date assumptions about men and women, work and family. These assumptions have served to severely limit the development of creative approaches to corporate work-family policies. The challenge for the new century is to break the hold of these assumptions and find fresh approaches to work-life issues. The aim of this article is to articulate one such fresh approach.

Rosalind C. Barnett is a senior scientist and resident scholar in the Women's Studies Program at Brandeis University and a senior scholar in residence at the Murray Research Center at Radcliffe College. Her research focuses on job stress and work-family relations with special emphasis on the interaction of work and family experiences in exacerbating or mitigating the stress-illness relationship. She has published over 80 articles and chapters and six books, the most recent of which, She Works/He Works *(1996), received a national Books for a Better Life Award.*

THE goal of this article is to develop a new model of work-life issues that reflects today's complexities and can guide corporate policies and programs as we move into the next century. Before we look to the future, however, we need to see where we are now and ask how we got here. Given the importance of work-life issues for the continued success of corporate America and its workforce, this retrospective overview and evaluation of the work-life models that have been driving corporate policies is timely.

In this article, I argue that extant work-life models reflect dated and inaccurate understandings about women, men, and the complex realities of work-life matters. The staggeringly rapid changes in the demographics of the labor force, in family patterns, in male and female sex roles, and in career expectations have far outpaced workplace responses. The most dramatic shift in workforce demographics is the marked decrease of the sole-breadwinner family and increase of the dual-earner family. Indeed, some estimates indicate that the sole-breadwinner family now represents less than 5 percent of the workforce. Thus corporate policies, no matter how well intentioned, are bound to miss their mark, grounded as most are in the 1950s vision of the family. As a result of the failure to keep pace, workplace policies and programs designed to meet the needs of the new workforce look remarkably similar to policies and programs that were in place 25 years ago.

Drawing on the research literature, I trace the evolution in thinking about work-life relationships and identify three primary stages that prompted the following models of work-family interaction workplace responses: the emergence of work and family issues at the workplace (the separate-spheres model); toward work-life (the overlapping-spheres model); and the family work-life integration (the work-integration model). Although outdated, these models continue to frame workplace practices. I propose a new model—the work-life systems model—that better captures the realities of today's workforce. This model reflects workers' experiences as they craft a new lifestyle that integrates work, family, and community, while taking into account such previously ignored factors as positive aspects of work-life integration, the quality of family life, and the nature of work. My hope is that this new model will generate innovative corporate responses that are more likely to meet the needs of the workforce of the twenty-first century.

STAGE 1: THE EMERGENCE
OF WORK AND FAMILY ISSUES
AT THE WORKPLACE

Demographic shifts

The phrase "work-family" emerged in the 1980s, a time when married women's labor force participation experienced a steep increase and when the spheres of work and family were more clearly separated than they are today. This increase in women's labor force participation represented the culmination of a long trend that had begun in the 1920s.

Indeed, the massive movement of women into the labor force has been described as "one of the most significant social and economic trends in modern U.S. history" (Hayghe 1997, 41). By the 1970s, the 50-year reign of the Ozzie-and-Harriet family was proclaimed to be definitely over (Coontz 1997, 57).

Understandably, corporations were exhorted to respond to workers' nonworkplace needs. Although framed as workers' needs, the real message was that employed women with children, not employees in general, were under stress trying to manage their family demands or, more accurately, their child-rearing demands, while meeting their workplace obligations. Something had to be done to help.

Seen from the perspective of the 1990s, the early decision to operationalize work-family issues as women's issues rather than as employees' issues was quite unfortunate and haunts us today. That decision created a disconnect between the way work-family issues are discussed explicitly and the way they are treated implicitly. As we shall see, the distinction between rhetoric and practice has been a mainstay in the area of work-family.

Then, as now, most adult men were in the labor force. Then, unlike now, most had stay-at-home wives. It is important to note, however, that, even at its high point in the 1950s, "less than 60 percent of American children spent their youth in an Ozzie-and-Harriet type family" (Coontz 1997, 56). Although the majority of women were in the labor force, their participation rates varied

by marital and parental status. Single women were far more likely to be employed than were married women, and married women with infants were less likely to be employed than married women with school-age or older children.

Prevailing values and attitudes

The prevailing sex role attitudes at the time were more traditional than they are today. Briefly, there was general consensus that women's primary social roles were as wife and mother, whereas men's primary role was as breadwinner. There was also a pervasive belief that multiple roles were bad for women; married women with children who took on the added role of employee were thought to be inevitably exhausted, highly vulnerable to stress-related problems, and unable to manage adequately the various demands of their complicated and energy-depleting lives. As a result, these women were short-changing their children and husbands and putting them at risk for emotional problems. Finally, there was widespread agreement that the mother-child bond was special and unique and that fathers were not suited for child care or housework. These traditional sex role attitudes—prevalent in the 1950s, 1960s, and 1970s—are, sadly, finding new strength from conservative elements in the present, despite strong evidence that undermines their validity.

These attitudes led inevitably to concern about employed women's ability to meet their work and family obligations. It was (and often still is) assumed that conflict and tension would arise as married women with young children entered the workforce and attempted this difficult balancing act. This view pitted women's individual preferences and priorities against negative implications for their husbands and children. Women had to make difficult choices—did a woman deprive her family to have a career, or did she shortchange her career to care for her family? From this viewpoint, role conflict, the assumed inevitable outcome for married employed mothers, was the result of individual choice rather than a consequence of a particular set of assumptions about women and their concretization in corporate policies and practices.

The separate-spheres model

Corporate responses to work-family issues reflected the demographic and attitudinal realities of the time. Even though Rosabeth Kanter's work (1977) had made many decision makers aware that the spheres of work and family were not separate and, indeed, that there was spillover between them, these understandings were not incorporated into policies. Once again, rhetoric and practice were at odds. In practice, the two worlds of work and family were conceptualized as totally separate and in competition (see Figure 1).

Assumptions

The separate-spheres model assumes that

— work and family are separate spheres with clear boundaries;

FIGURE 1
THE SEPARATE-SPHERES MODEL

— each sphere has it own pressing demands;
— there is an inevitable struggle between these competing demands;
— managing the demands of the two spheres is a woman's issue; and
— inability to keep work free of family intrusions reflects inadequate boundaries and inappropriate priorities.

Moreover, the focus on incompatible role demands was coupled with a notion that the quantity of human energy is fixed and limited. This notion is often referred to as the scarcity hypothesis (Barnett, Marshall, and Singer 1992; Marks 1977; Sieber 1974). Accordingly, the more roles a woman occupied, the greater the demands on her energy and the more depleted her reserves. Thus, employed married women with children were assumed to be less resilient than men and, therefore, at higher risk for such stress-related illnesses as depression and anxiety. In addition, the scarcity model of energy is consistent with the then- (and still-) dominant management fixation on face time as a reflection of employee commitment and productivity. In the face-time framework, because it is believed that nonwork demands deplete employees' energy reserves, the best way to get the most out of employees is to keep them working long hours.

The separate-spheres model was reinforced by the then-dominant corporate culture that explicitly required family matters to be left at the workplace door. To be taken seriously on the job, women would have to conform to the traditional one-dimensional view of men as worker drones. This bifurcated model is still, unfortunately, a part of the corporate landscape. Similarly, the traditional sex role assumptions underlying this model still have a hold on our thinking.

Workplace responses

Against this attitudinal and demographic background, corporations crafted specific work-family aims and policies. The primary aim was to help women employees better manage the boundary between work and family (that is, young children) so that they could be more productive workers (Schein 1990). The primary specific policies were parental leave, flextime, on-site child care, and child care referral services.

Many corporations have these policies on their books, but, in practice, asking for these benefits is often taken as an admission of inadequacy—a sign that women are unable to manage their work and family demands. Moreover, many women felt accurately that these benefits came with strings attached: women who took advantage of them were seen as less committed and less desirable. Their opportunities at the workplace were often curtailed, and their long-term career plans,

jeopardized. Thus the informal corporate culture was often more critical in shaping employee behavior than the formal policies were.

Although these policies and practices did alleviate certain kinds of stress, they did not and could not address the fundamental problems because the underlying assumptions were wrong. Research on multiple roles and stress has provided ample evidence that challenges these old assumptions. For example, we now know that (1) men, not just women, need and want to respond to nonwork obligations; (2) for women and men, combining roles is often energizing, not depleting, especially when the roles are experienced as more rewarding than problematic; (3) the nature of the job itself, not the interface, is often the major source of stress; and (4) work and family are not separable spheres—what happens in one affects what happens in the other (Barnett, Marshall, and Singer 1992; Bolger et al. 1990; Repetti 1989; Stroh, Brett, and Reilly 1992; Thoits 1992).

These findings, as well as dramatic changes in the demographics of the workforce, have prompted a new view of work-family.

STAGE 2: TOWARD WORK-LIFE

Demographic shifts

The demographics of the workforce have undergone a sea change in the past 20 years and have spurred new views of work-life. Four trends are especially noteworthy: (1) the continuing increase of dual-earner couples; (2) an increase in the percentage of mothers with young children in the workforce; (3) a growing similarity in the labor force patterns of women and men; and (4) a proliferation of new family forms.

In 1999, it is generally agreed that the days of the sole-breadwinner dad and the stay-at-home mom are numbered. The new American family is the dual-earner couple; between 1975 and 1993, the number of two-paycheck families in America swelled from 43 percent to 63 percent of all families, making them the solid majority today (Holcomb 1998, 69). Moreover, every indication is that these numbers are unlikely to decrease.

The largest increase in married women's labor force participation rate has been among young wives, 25-34 years of age (Oppenheimer 1994), with most of the increase among mothers. According to Coontz (1997), since 1970, "mothers—especially mothers of young children—[have become] the fastest growing group of female workers" (56). For example, between 1970 and 1990, among married women with preschool children in the home, the proportion in the labor force nearly doubled, jumping from 30 percent to 50 percent. Between 1976 and 1996, the participation rate for mothers whose youngest child was school-age (6 to 17 years old) rose 22 percentage points, to 77 percent, while the participation rate for mothers of preschoolers posted a 24-point gain, rising to 62 percent (Hayghe 1997, 42). Moreover, by 1990, 53 percent of women 18 to 44 years old who had given birth within the last 12 months were in the labor force. Only 14 years earlier, in 1976, the proportion of women with children under age 1 who were in the labor force was only 31 percent. By 1996, that figure had risen to 55 percent.

In addition, large numbers of women now work full-time, full-year, and women are no longer staying out of the labor force for extended periods of time after the birth of a child. Gone are the days when women worked before marriage and then after their children were grown. Gone also is the tendency of women to work part-time, part-year. Now women, like men, are working full-time and continuously over their adult years (Coontz 1997). Indeed, women's labor force patterns are now indistinguishable from men's.

Moreover, the tidy two-part structural distinction between single- and dual-earners has given way to a whole array of family forms that focus simultaneously on structure and on roles—single-parent families, stepfamilies, blended families, gay and lesbian families, each with its own challenges to conventional thinking about work and family. Thus, for example, there are single- and dual-earner gay and straight families.

One concrete reflection of these dramatic changes is a semantic shift: work-family has become work-life.

Prevailing values and attitudes

There has also been a major shift in sex role attitudes—a shift away from traditional, nonegalitarian attitudes and toward a more egalitarian view of male and female roles—and related behaviors (Bond, Galinsky, and Swanberg 1998). This shift, which has enormous implications for work-life policies, is just now making its way into popular awareness. What is the evidence for this shift? The evidence comes from many sources, including my own study of 300 full-time employed dual-earner couples. This study was the first to look systematically at this new American family, and the findings, reported in the book *She Works/He Works* (Barnett and Rivers 1996), defy many widely held beliefs. In presenting this evidence, I draw on the major findings from my own study as well as the findings from several other recent large-scale studies. With respect to sex role attitudes, these data indicate that, in general, women as well as men have the following beliefs:

Belief 1: Men and women have equal responsibility for maintaining the home. Men in dual-earner couples do roughly 45 percent of the housework, as assessed by their own and their wives' reports (Barnett and Shen 1997; Bond, Galinsky, and Swanberg 1998). A high percentage of married men and women, especially well-educated, professional employees, would like to reduce their work hours and spend more time with their families.

Belief 2: Men and women have equal responsibility for breadwinning. Forty-eight percent of married employed women provide half or more of the family income (Families and Work Institute 1995). The qual-ity of work experiences is as strongly associated with women's well-being as with men's (Barnett et al. 1995).

Belief 3: The mother-child bond is no more special than the father-child bond. The quality of family experiences— marriage and parenting—is as strongly tied to men's well-being as to women's. In addition, men whose children are in day care experience levels of separation anxiety that are at least as high as those experienced by women.

Belief 4: Fathers can and should play a major role in child care. Men's relationships with their children are central to men's physical and psychological well-being (Deater-Deckard et al. 1994). When those relationships are troubled, men experience high levels of stress-related problems. Men who do less child care relative to their wives experience high distress, and their wives feel more dissatisfied about their marriages (Ozer et al. in press).

These new demographic and attitudinal shifts have given rise to the overlapping-spheres model (see Figure 2).

The overlapping-spheres model

This model differs markedly from the separate-spheres model in several major ways. First, there is an interdependence between work and life. Second, there is a shift away from the single-minded focus on conflict and problems to an appreciation of the positive effects of operating simultaneously in two spheres.

FIGURE 2
THE OVERLAPPING-SPHERES MODEL

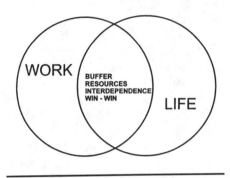

Finally, boundaries are less clear, reducing the temptation to focus solely on interface issues.

Assumptions

The assumptions are also vastly different. Most important are the following:

— Work and life are two spheres that overlap considerably.
— What happens in one sphere has a major effect on what happens in the other sphere.
— There is no implicit conflict between the demands made in the two spheres.
— Positive outcomes are often possible as consequences of functioning simultaneously in the work and family spheres.
— Both men and women have to integrate these two aspects of their lives.

Workplace responses

As more and more men and women share the breadwinning and nurturing aspects of their lives, they look to their employers to recognize and facilitate these new and complex imperatives. From the employer's perspective, it is increasingly necessary to attract both partners in order to keep one. Yet, for the most part, corporate work-life policies have not responded to this need.

The work-life policies and practices associated with this model were the same as those associated with the earlier, separate-spheres model: parental leave, flextime, on-site child care, child care referral services.

Employees who have these options tend to take advantage of them. Unfortunately, many employers do not offer them, again underscoring the gap between rhetoric and policies. Even when companies do offer these options, there is still widespread concern about possible unintended negative consequences. These concerns are heightened at times of downsizing, mergers, and layoffs. Thus, despite high levels of perceived conflict between work, personal, and family life, considerable displeasure with the demands of long work hours, and a strong preference among men and women for substantially reducing their time on the job (Jacobs and Gerson 1997), many employees are reluctant to take advantage of these work-life options.

When the considerable attitudinal and demographic changes are compared with the predominant work-life policies and practices, the most striking conclusion is that everything has changed and nothing has changed.

STAGE 3: THE FAMILY
WORK-LIFE EXPERIENCE

Demographic shifts

Two trends are significant. First, people, particularly highly educated people, are having fewer children and investing more heavily in their partnerships and nonwork activities. Second, the lengthening life span means that more and more workers are thinking beyond their work lives and making commitments to non-work activities that are rewarding today and that may someday be their central concern. Thus, for many employees, the workaholic credo holds little appeal. These demographic shifts are mirrored in recently documented attitudinal changes.

Prevailing values and attitudes

Male as well as female workers express the wish to work substantially fewer hours; would exchange salary increases and promotions for more time off from work; bemoan the scarcity of personal and family time; and express the same level of conflict between work, personal, and family life. With the full participation of women in the labor force, and with the reality that women's economic contribution is critical to the support of the family, new pressures and new rewards have surfaced for today's young adults. Increasingly, men and women are entering marriage with a new contract, one that honors the importance to both of them of their careers. This new contract dramatically affects work-related decisions

FIGURE 3
THE WORK-LIFE INTEGRATION MODEL

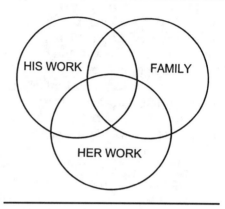

and the traditional gendered division of labor in the home.

Work-life integration model

This new marital contract further complicates the work-life picture. The reality is that in every dual-earner couple, family demands have to be harmonized with the demands of at least two workplaces, each with its own requirements (see Figure 3).

Assumptions

The clear assumption of this model is that a good job benefits both the employee and the spouse, and a bad job impairs the functioning of not only one but two workers. Thus every employer benefits if all employers institute effective work-life policies that support dual-earner couples.

The realization that men and women can successfully occupy numerous work and nonwork roles has been accompanied by a revised model of human energy. The scarcity hypothesis, although still prevalent in popular depictions of harried working women, has been largely supplanted by an alternative model—the expansion hypothesis (Barnett and Baruch 1985). According to this new view, the more roles one occupies, the better are one's chances of gaining important psychological inputs. Rather than focusing on role demands, or outgo, this model focuses on role rewards, or income. Thus, although one expends energy when one assumes additional roles, one experiences a net gain in energy because of the benefits associated with multiple roles. The degree to which there is a positive gain depends, in part, on which roles one occupies and on the quality of those roles—some combinations may be more beneficial than others. The benefits of multiple role involvement include monetary income, heightened self-esteem, the power to delegate onerous role obligations, opportunities for social relationships, and challenge. The failure of many studies to support the scarcity hypothesis (Barnett and Baruch 1985; Hyde, DeLamater, and Hewitt in press) has led to general acceptance of the expansion hypothesis.

Workplace responses

Awareness of these demographic and attitudinal shifts, along with the tightening of the job market, has affected the aim of corporate work-life policies. The singular focus both at the workplace and in work-life policies on the worker and his or her needs has over time given way to the realization that most workers are partnered and that the needs and wishes of the partner also have to be considered. It appears that corporate values are catching up with the values expressed by increasing numbers of employees. Now the expressed aim is to help men as well as women better integrate their work and nonwork lives in order to attract and retain outstanding workers and to optimize their productivity. This aim also reflects the growing realization that men, as well as women, parents as well as nonparents, are multidimensional beings and that men, as well as women, thrive when they are engaged in several roles. Thus corporate policies are needed to aid all employees in integrating the various aspects of their lives.

What new corporate policies have been instituted to reflect this new aim? Unfortunately, there have been almost no new policy initiatives. Currently, the most widely available work-life policies are parental leave, flextime, on-site child care, child care referral services, and elder care referral services.

Thus these massive changes in the nature of the workforce, in sex role attitudes, and in underlying assumptions are not reflected in policies. With the exception of elder care referral services, we have the same policies that marked the separate-spheres era. Once again we see a gap between rhetoric and practice.

Moreover, although there is general consensus about the worthiness of this small subset of policies and programs, surprisingly few of even large, progressive companies make this package available to their employees. In a recent survey (described later in this article) of the top 10 family-friendly companies as assessed by their employees, all 10 had elder care programs, 9 out of 10 had flextime and job sharing as well as unpaid family leave beyond that mandated by the Family and Medical Leave Act, but only 3 out of 10 had on-site or near-site child care and subsidies, allowances, or vouchers for child care (Bankert and Litchfield 1997). Moreover, these benefits are much more prevalent in the large companies that were overrepresented in this survey.

Furthermore, there is no evidence that the penalties of using these benefits have abated. Many employees report "high immediate and long-term costs" of opting for these family-friendly policies (Jacobs and Gerson 1997, 12). In a large-scale study funded by the National Institute of Mental Health (Hyde, Essex, and Horton 1993), 63 percent of the men reported that they did not take parental leave when their babies were born because their supervisors would not like it, and 43 percent said that they feared negative repercussions from coworkers. Once again we see evidence of the wide discrepancy between rhetoric and practice.

Given the seismic shifts that we have discussed, it is clear that policies developed for a simpler time and a different attitudinal climate are no longer adequate. A new vision is required.

MOVING TOWARD STAGE 4:
A WORK-LIFE SYSTEMS
FRAMEWORK

The driving force behind this new model is the growing concern that, despite all the rhetoric about the importance of work-life issues,

corporate policies and practices have not changed in any essential way. Consequently, the gap between the needs of the workforce and the realities of the workplace is widening. This gap is becoming increasingly apparent to policymakers as a result of media attention to these issues. Moreover, current low unemployment means that desirable employees are likely to have choices about where to work and will be better able to maximize their work-life strategies. Thus businesses with more innovative and responsive policies will be increasingly attractive to those very employees they most want to recruit and retain. To develop such policies, businesses need a new model that takes into account the complex lives today's employees lead.

To that end, I propose a new model called the work-life systems model (see Figure 4). It differs from its predecessors in that there are no longer separate spheres, nor are there overlapping spheres. Now the worker—with his or her personal needs—is part of an interactive system.

Assumptions

This systems perspective reflects several new assumptions:

— The operative unit is the worker's work-life system, not the individual worker.
— Decisions are no longer seen as pitting one person's needs against another's; rather, decisions are made to optimize the well-being of the system.
— The better the quality of one's nonwork relationships, the bet-

FIGURE 4
THE WORK-LIFE SYSTEMS FRAMEWORK

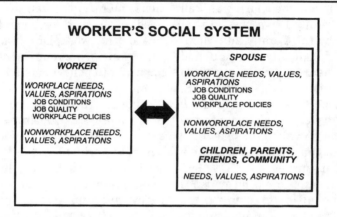

ter is one's health and the higher is one's resilience.
— One's distress is affected by what is happening in the lives of those in one's system (for example, one's partner's job).

This model broadens the set of factors that affect the decision making of workers and their partners as they develop strategies for meeting their various work and nonwork needs. For example, workplace policies and programs are no longer external realities that workers merely respond to; they are, instead, conditions that, along with other conditions, can either facilitate or impede the realization of family-adaptive strategies. To implement this work-life systems approach, businesses would have to introduce a range of new policies, such as alternative career paths and revised criteria for promotion. If, for example, businesses created reduced-hours career options along with clear criteria for performance review and promotion, then employees could arrange their work schedules to meet the changing needs of their work-life system without fear of reprisals. In addition, if performance were evaluated more on output than input (that is, face time), then workers would have more control over when they did their work. These policies would increase workers' control over critical aspects of their lives, leading, in turn, to decreased distress and heightened well-being. Such an approach is consistent with recent research at Xerox and Fleet Bank suggesting that changes in the way work gets done (for example, job redesign) and changes in corporate culture (for example, training for supervisors) may have significant indirect effects on work-life (Bailyn 1993).

Workplace responses:
Recommendations

How can corporations transform these new realities into an approach to work-life issues that is more in tune with the challenges of the new century? What is needed is a paradigm shift; merely reworking current policies will no longer suffice. The following two recommendations reflect such a shift: developing work-life impact assessments as tools for corporate decision makers; and focusing on the importance of how work gets done.

Work-life impact assessments. By taking the needs of workers and their families into account and preparing "family impact statements" (Barnett and Rivers 1997) that analyze the costs to employees' work-life systems of business decisions before they are implemented, businesses could avoid unnecessary costs—psychological and monetary—and show their commitment to helping all employees integrate the various aspects of their lives.

Businesses need to factor work-life issues into their core decisions; they need to consider how these decisions will affect the ability of employees and their families to manage their work and nonwork lives. Should the company relocate? In addition to the economic and strategic considerations that would inform such a decision, businesses also need to determine the quality of the schools and child care facilities in the new community. Are last-minute travel requirements really necessary? Businesses need to consider the potentially demoralizing and depressing effects of ruptured plans that wreak havoc with employees' ability to honor their commitments to families, communities, or educational institutions. Should a firm be

open on Saturdays or Sundays? Businesses need to weigh their gains against the costs of interfering with employees' religious practices. What about holding meetings before regular work hours? Businesses need to take into account that such meetings would occur just when parents are trying to get their children off to school or are meeting other early-morning commitments. Moreover, many child care facilities do not open early enough to permit workers with very young children to attend early-morning meetings. School buses may not arrive in time to allow parents of school-age children to see their children off before leaving for early-morning meetings. If inquiries suggest that employees will have grave difficulties in accommodating to these possible changes, then managers need to add the likely costs of unexplained absences, tardiness, lowered morale, and turnover to their calculations.

This new process for thinking about business decisions would likely reduce costs to the work-life system while achieving needed corporate goals. For example, management might consider strategies for reducing the burden of early-morning meetings on their employees. One strategy might be to provide on-site day care to cover early-morning meetings. Such a plan might ease the burden on some parents with preschool children, but it would do little to assist parents with school-age children or employees who have other early-morning commitments that are important to them. Thus the benefit to management of holding early-morning meetings would have to be considered in light of these costs to their employees.

The importance of the nature of work. Businesses need to focus on the way work gets done rather than on boundary issues. Although problems at the work-family interface persist, they have already received a disproportionate share of attention compared to other problems that may, in fact, be of greater concern to today's employees. Indeed, numerous studies indicate that boundary issues are not the primary concern of working parents (Stroh, Brett, and Reilly 1992). As pointed out previously (Schein 1990), continued attention to these issues may reflect a "corporate convenient" strategy rather than an "employee-centered" strategy. Stated differently, it is relatively painless for companies to adjust workers' hours and provide day care. Other changes—for example, changes in how the work actually gets organized—are far more difficult to implement (Bailyn 1993).

Structural aspects of the workplace such as flexible scheduling and autonomy are crucial for workers' ability to reconcile their work, family, and personal lives and ultimately for their own physical and mental health. Many employees not only desire these job conditions but are willing to trade such other advantages as promotions and are even willing to change their jobs to get them. In a recent analysis, on average, about 25 percent of workers who did not have flexible schedules indicated that they would be willing to change jobs to get flexibility. Among professional women and men with children under age 6, the comparable figure was about 30 percent. The importance of being able to take time off for family reasons was echoed recently in a first-ever survey conducted by *Business Week* magazine and the Center for Work & Family at Boston College (Bankert and Litchfield 1997). Employees of a small group of large (that is, at least 100 employees) and progressive companies were asked about the family-friendly policies at their places of work. Employees were most critical about the need to work long hours and the inability to take time off for family reasons. Fully 62 percent of employees at the top 10 companies agreed that their organization asked too much of them—at the expense of their family time.

Clearly, it is time to move beyond policies that address only the work-family interface. Much more attention needs to be paid to the nature of the work itself and how it impinges on workers' ability to integrate the various aspects of their lives. To address these concerns, changes in deeply rooted cultural beliefs and management practices would have to be implemented. Importantly, management would have to reject traditional notions of masculinity and femininity and move beyond its fixation on face time rather than on productivity and output. To the extent that this new view is implemented, formal policies and informal corporate culture, which have often been at odds, will come together. Leadership will "walk the talk," thereby alleviating a major source of frustration and anxiety for employees.

CONCLUSION

As the new century approaches, the time has come to discard old work-life models and adopt a new model. The work-life systems model proposed in this article replaces worn-out and bankrupt ideas about gender roles with fresh ideas that will enhance women's and men's ability to successfully integrate the various aspects of their complex lives. Moreover, adopting this model encourages businesses to create innovative workplace practices and programs that will at the same time nurture workers and improve corporate functioning. In so doing, this new model will help close the gap between rhetoric and practice, with beneficial results for all.

References

Bailyn, Lotte. 1993. *Breaking the Mold: Women, Men and Time in the New Corporate World*. New York: Free Press.

Bankert, Ellen and Leon Litchfield. 1997. *Business Week's Work and Family Corporate Ranking: An Analysis of the Data: 1996 Summary Report*. Chestnut Hill, MA: Boston College, Center for Work & Family.

Barnett, Rosalind C. and Grace K. Baruch. 1985. Women's Involvement in Multiple Roles and Psychological Distress. *Journal of Personality and Social Psychology* 49:135-45.

Barnett, Rosalind C., Robert T. Brennan, Steven W. Raudenbush, Joseph H. Pleck, and Nancy L. Marshall. 1995. Change in Job and Marital Experiences and Change in Psychological Distress: A Longitudinal Study of Dual-Earner Couples. *Journal of Personality and Social Psychology* 69(5):839-50.

Barnett, Rosalind C., Nancy L. Marshall, and Judith D. Singer. 1992. Job Experiences over Time, Multiple Roles, and Women's Mental Health: A Longitudinal Study. *Journal of Personality and Social Psychology* 62(4):634-44.

Barnett, Rosalind C. and Caryl Rivers. 1996. *She Works/He Works: How Two-Income Families Are Happier, Healthier and Better Off*. San Francisco: HarperCollins.

——. 1997. Flex-ing It in the Workplace. *Boston Globe*, 21 May.

Barnett, Rosalind C. and Yu-Chu Shen. 1997. Gender, High- and Low-Schedule-Control Housework Tasks, and Psychological Distress: A Study of Dual-Earner Couples. *Journal of Family Issues* 18(4):403-28.

Bolger, Niall, Anita DeLongis, Ronald C. Kessler, and Elaine Wethington. 1990. The Microstructure of Daily Role-Related Stress in Married Couples. In *Stress Between Work and Family*, ed. J. Eckenrode and S. Gore. New York: Plenum Press.

Bond, James T., Ellen Galinsky, and Jennifer E. Swanberg. 1998. *The National Study of the Changing Workforce*. New York: Families and Work Institute.

Coontz, Stephanie. 1997. *The Way We Really Are: Coming to Terms with America's Changing Families*. New York: Basic Books.

Deater-Deckard, Kirby, Sandra Scarr, Kathleen McCartney, and Marlene Eisenberg. 1994. Paternal Separation Anxiety: Relationships with Parenting Stress, Child-Rearing Attitudes, and Maternal Anxieties. *Psychological Sciences* 5(6):341-46.

Families and Work Institute. 1995. *Women: The New Providers: Part One*. New York: Louis Harris.

Hayghe, Howard W. 1997. Developments in Women's Labor Force Participation. *Monthly Labor Review* Sept.: 41-46.

Holcomb, B. 1998. *Not Guilty! The Good News About Working Mothers*. New York: Scribner.

Hyde, Janet S., John D. DeLamater, and Erri C. Hewitt. In press. *Sexuality and the Dual-Earner Couple*.

Hyde, Janet S., Marilyn J. Essex, and Francine Horton. 1993. Fathers and Parental Leave. *Journal of Family Issues* 14(4):616-41.

Jacobs, Jerry A. and Kathleen E. Gerson. 1997. *The Endless Day or Flexible Office? Working Hours, Work-Family Conflict, and Gender Equity in the Modern Workplace*. Philadelphia: University of Pennsylvania; New York: New York University.

Kanter, Rosabeth Moss. 1977. *Work and Family in the United States: A Critical Review and Agenda for Research and Policy*. New York: Russell Sage Foundation, Social Science Frontiers.

Marks, Stephen R. 1977. Multiple Roles and Role Strain: Some Notes on Human Energy, Time and Commitment. *American Sociological Review* 42:921-36.

Oppenheimer, Valerie K. 1994. Women's Rising Employment and the Future of the Family in Industrial Societies. *Population and Development Review* 20(2):293-341.

Ozer, Elizabeth M., Rosalind C. Barnett, Robert T. Brennan, and Jocelyn Sperling. In press. Effects of Childcare Involvement: Does Childcare Involvement Increase or Decrease Distress Among Dual-Earner Couples? *Women and Health*.

Repetti, Rena L. 1989. Effects of Daily Workload on Subsequent Behavior During Marital Interaction: The Roles of Social Withdrawal and Spouse Support. *Journal of Personality and Social Psychology* 57(4):651-59.

Schein, Virginia E. 1990, August 12. The Work-Family Conflict Interface: Challenging Corporate Convenient. Paper presented at the Ninety-Eighth Annual Meeting of the American Psychological Association, Boston.

Sieber, S. D. 1974. Toward a Theory of Role Accumulation. *American Sociological Review* 39:567-78.

Stroh, Linda K., Jeanne M. Brett, and Anne H. Reilly. 1992. All the Right Stuff: A Comparison of Female and Male Managers' Career Progression. *Journal of Applied Psychology* 77(3):251-60.

Thoits, Peggy A. 1992. Identity Structures and Psychological Well Being: Gender and Marital Status Comparisons. *Social Psychology Quarterly* 55(3):236-56.

ANNALS, *AAPSS*, **562**, March 1999

Work and Life Strategies of Professionals in Biotechnology Firms

By SUSAN C. EATON and LOTTE BAILYN

ABSTRACT: Career issues of professionals working in the biotechnology industry give insight into work and life strategies of the future. Through in-depth case studies, we explore commonalities and differences between men and women. We examine individual and organizational factors that serve as barriers or enablers to full integration of work and life issues. The structure of the professionals' work itself contributes to new constructions of the employment relation and to the very concept of career in these firms. The old employment contract no longer concerns employment alone (since key workplace decisions have implications for family life, and vice versa), nor is it clearly any longer a contract, but rather an emergent, ever changing interactive set of adaptations. We argue that this requires a new conception of career, which is more fluid, more adaptable to different life stages and needs, and more variable than the traditional conception.

Susan C. Eaton, M.P.A., is a doctoral candidate in organization studies and industrial relations at the Sloan School of Management at the Massachusetts Institute of Technology (MIT). She has also worked as a labor negotiator, a manager, and a consultant.

Lotte Bailyn is the T. Wilson Professor of Management at the Sloan School of Management at MIT, and chair of the MIT faculty. Her most recent book is Breaking the Mold *(1993).*

NOTE: Research cited in this article on the biotechnology industry was conducted under a grant from the Alfred P. Sloan Foundation to the Radcliffe Public Policy Institute at Radcliffe College. The research team includes Françoise Carré, Paula Rayman, Lotte Bailyn, Ann Bookman, Constance Perin, Susan C. Eaton, Sandra Resnick, Wendy Hernandez, and Pamela Joshi.

WORK and especially professional careers are changing today. We focus here on the effect of these changes on individuals' career choices and on their work-family experiences. In particular, we consider how the new employment contract (if such exists), the new workplace (which is likely to be smaller, less stable, and less predictable for many employees), and the changing nature of work itself (particularly knowledge work) affect careers and their integration with personal life. Our article explores these issues in the context of small and medium-sized biotechnology firms, and we present evidence about the ways work-life issues have a dynamic relationship to career choices.

Some authors suggest that the implicit social and employment contract of the last several decades is breaking down and being replaced (if at all) by a much less clear, less mutual, and less binding set of expectations between employers and employees (see, for example, Kochan 1998; Kanter 1990). Other scholars have commented on the fraying of the psychological contract that used to bind employers and employees together (DeMeuse and Tornow 1990; Robinson and Rousseau 1994; Rousseau 1995). Certainly, many previously taken-for-granted expectations about long-term employment with regular upward progression and one primary employer appear to be under serious challenge, even for professionals. In this rapidly changing context, what can one say about the experience of careers in firms that are themselves changing?

Forecasts suggest that small, entrepreneurial firms are likely to be more typical of future workplaces than the old industrial corporations are. Despite the popular image of large companies' domination of the American economy, most people labor in workplaces that are small; fully 51 percent of U.S. employees work in establishments employing fewer than 50 people. Many new, successful U.S. firms employ a high percentage of "knowledge workers" rather than a majority of production, maintenance, and service personnel. The present study is based on such firms of the future—biotechnology firms that epitomize the new networked, entrepreneurial, collaborative, small, and less secure environments where many professionals will work.

As work becomes more knowledge based and professional, careers in the future may look more like the "boundaryless careers" proposed by some recent observers (for example, Arthur and Rousseau 1996). Though reality has not fully caught up with the popular image of the entrepreneurial professional mainly concerned with "employability" (see Herzenberg, Alic, and Wial 1998; Swinnerton and Wial 1995), a recent Harris poll does show that a majority of employees in a nationally representative sample expect to leave their jobs voluntarily within the next five years, and one in six expects to be fired or laid off (Louis Harris and Associates 1997). Our article explores these issues in one industrial sector.

THE BIOTECHNOLOGY INDUSTRY

Biotechnology is a rapidly growing industry in the United States that includes companies that engage in research, development, production, and commercialization of products using rDNA, cell fusion, and novel bioprocessing techniques (U.S. Office of Technology Assessment 1991). The national population of biotechnology firms is about 1300, and they employ 1.5 million people. Most biotechnology firms are small. A biotech firm of 50 to 150 employees is a medium-sized firm in the industry. Most firms are less than 15 years old, and many face difficult challenges in getting products to market in a tightly regulated environment.[1]

These firms rely on a combination of venture capital, initial public offerings of stock, and alliances or contracts to provide working capital for many years. On average, a new drug requires 15 years and more than $304 million (1996 dollars) to be brought from conception to market (Resnick 1997b; DiMasi et al. 1991). Researchers estimate that only 3 of 10 drugs introduced from 1980 to 1984 had returns higher than their average after-tax research and development cost (PHRMA 1997, chap. 2, p. 3).

Most biotech firms are networked in one form or another via partnerships, alliances, formal and informal collaborations and agreements, and so forth (Powell, Koput, and Smith-Doerr 1996). Uncertainty is the watchword of the industry. "Job insecurity goes with the business," one scientist told us. "There is no such thing as a secure job."

THE STUDY AND DATA

Our study is based on two typical firms drawn from the population of 130 biotech firms in one U.S. state. In the firms we studied, professionals make up more than 60 percent of the workforce, including B.S., M.S., and Ph.D. scientists and M.D.'s or D.V.M.'s. Within the professional workforce, half the employees are men and half women, and the firms are highly labor intensive and professional intensive. This article includes data from interviews with 30 professionals, including 27 scientists, 8 of whom are also managers, and 3 business professionals.

Each of the two sites in this study is an independent, publicly traded company, at a middle stage of development, and each currently employs 50-60 employees. Though interesting contrasts exist between these firms, for the purposes of this analysis, we combine interviews and observations from the companies.

The data offered here are based on in-depth case studies and stem from focused interviews, observations, and group discussions. Employees were selected to represent a range of occupations, ages, family statuses, and lengths of service. While not chosen as a representative sample, they include more than 50 percent of the scientific employees in each firm, and they do not appear to be different from the firms' employee population as a whole.[2]

For a profile of the professional employees interviewed, see Table 1. In the sample as a whole, 80 percent, or 24 of the 30, employees have children, and 90 percent are either in

TABLE 1
CHARACTERISTICS OF PROFESSIONAL
EMPLOYEE SAMPLE (N = 30)

	Female	Male	Total
Sex	15	15	30
Highest degree obtained			
Ph.D. or equivalent	7	8	15
Master's degree	3	4	7
B.A. or B.S.	5	3	8
Less than B.A. or B.S.	0	0	0
Position in company			
Manager (scientist)	4	4	8
Scientist*	10	9	19
Administrator	1	2	3
Full- or part-time status			
Full-time	12	15	27
Part-time	3	0	3
Length of service (years)			
Median	8	6	7
Shortest	1	2	1
Longest	11	13	13
Age (estimated in years)			
Median	39	38	39
Youngest	30	28	28
Oldest	57	54	57
Family status			
Single, no children	1	1	2
Single, with children	3	0	3
Married, with children, at-home spouse	0	1	1
Married, with children, partner working part-time	0	5	5
Partner, no children, two full-time jobs/careers	1	1	2
Married, no children, two full-time jobs/careers	0	2	2
Married, with children, two full-time jobs/careers	10	5	15

*Many scientists have at least one employee to manage.

two-career families or are single parents. But important gender differences exist in the potential impact of family status on these scientists. Although 3 women are single mothers, no men are single fathers. Also, the men have more family support from their partners. One man has a non-working spouse, and 5 of the 15 men with children have partners working part-time. None of the 15 women has such support. In contrast, 10 women are married with children and have partners working full-time, compared to only 5 of the men. Of 11 men with children, 6 have the support of a spouse who either does not work or works only part-time. In contrast, all 13 women with children either have no partners or have partners working full-time.

These data suggest that the issues of work and family (including dependent care) are likely to be highly salient to this group, but not equally by gender. The women are almost three times as likely as the men (13 women, compared to 5 men) to be in the high-stress situation of being either single parents or parents with a full-time working partner.

COMING INTO BIOTECHNOLOGY:
CRUCIAL CHOICE POINTS

Why did these professionals come to work in industry, specifically in small or medium-sized entrepreneurial biotechnology firms? Their alternate career options were either in academe, as faculty members or full-time researchers in a nonprofit institution like a university hospital, or in large pharmaceutical firms. All the Ph.D. scientists had completed at least one postdoctoral fellowship assignment at a university before coming to industry, and several had completed two. The master's-level scientists also commonly had university lab experience. The B.S. scientists also often had begun their paid employment in a university lab.

In the university setting, employment contracts are usually explicit, rather than implicit, and tenured professors have nearly complete employment security. But scientists are often required to raise their own research funds, and tenure is not readily available to everyone. Women achieve tenure less frequently than men, particularly in the hard sciences, even accounting for their smaller numbers in junior faculty ranks (Aisenberg and Harrington 1988).

Some professionals were pushed into biotechnology from academe. Among the negative factors in their prior environment were the perceived difficulties of succeeding in a high-pressure academic environment, including securing research funding and getting tenure. The women who left academe felt particularly strongly about the low chances of success in an academic environment, which may explain why biotechnology employs nearly 50 percent women scientists. "It's too tough for a woman to get tenure in academia," said one female Ph.D. biochemist. "I had friends in academe and friends in industry. I didn't want to work 80-hour weeks [in academe] and not get tenure."

Some men also found the academic environment unfriendly. One male Ph.D. scientist concluded in his first year as a postdoc that

going into academia was not a viable choice. . . . You have to be pretty dedicated. . . . You have to bring in grant money, teach, advise, get a lab up and going. You have to put a huge amount of effort in, with little return. In biotech, they seemed to compensate well and do neat things, though you have to give up some independence.

Ironically, biotechnology seemed to present a more structured and stable environment than academia.

Other factors pulling people into biotech included good compensation and potential promotions. Some scientists, especially non-Ph.D.'s, came strictly for financial reasons, combined with opportunity for advancement. One B.S. scientist, now a manager, said, "There had been a layoff [where I worked], and I wanted a company with decent finances. . . . Money was tight, and the health insurance here was better." Another B.S. scientist who had worked in a university medical school research lab for several years said, "It was fun, but they didn't pay very much. . . . I made the change to make some money. I did not like living off grants; you are never sure the next one is there."

Another attraction was that biotech was an industry of small firms. One director said, "The concept of a small company had appeal. At Company X [a large pharmaceutical firm], there was great security, but I didn't feel like I was making a difference." A B.S. senior scientist said, "I got to expand what I was doing, and I kept learning here," which he felt was more likely in a small than in a large firm. Several biotech employees described jobs in large pharmaceutical companies as constraining their intellectual freedom or making them into "just a number."

At least half the scientists, both men and women, said they came to biotech companies because of the "excitement" of being able to do applied science. One Ph.D. employee, now a senior scientist, came because a friend told him the science projects were good. Another Ph.D. scientist said, "I get to keep doing new things. Things are always changing in this industry. . . . I want to enjoy coming in every day. I want work that is challenging, not boring."

Personal, family, or lifestyle reasons also attracted these employees to these jobs. "I wanted to come to the east coast, closer to home," said a male Ph.D. chemist. A biological immunologist had a lot of "social friends" in the area and did not want to leave her dance group. A Ph.D. biochemist decided to go into biotech because his wife had an academic job offer in the local area, his own academic offer was out of state, and they wanted to stay together in the area.

A mixture of reasons, therefore, attracts these scientists to the industry: the work itself, the extrinsic rewards, their personal lives. Interestingly, the perceived uncertainty seems to be not much greater than that in academia, particularly not for women. Finally, both men and women find the small size of these firms appealing.[3] These reasons suggest several possibilities for developing workplaces that are more responsive to the careers and work-life preferences of tomorrow's employees.

STAYING IN BIOTECH: CURRENT MOTIVATIONS

Once people are employed in the biotech industry, similar reasons keep them there. For roughly half the scientists (43 percent), the work of science itself keeps them employed in the industry. They speak of the excitement and the freedom of working in their scientific areas. "I understood biotech to give you as a scientist more independence, less organizational structure, and a little more freedom," said one woman director.

For the other half, the chance for advancement or promotion is a primary reason they stay where they are, including the opportunity to explore new skills, such as management. For a subgroup of female scientists, family concerns and the flexibility offered in their company keep them committed. Each of several women working part-time said that the opportunity to work part-time was the key reason she was staying at the firm and that her commitment to her job had increased as a result. These women also spoke of working more productively for the hours they were at work than when they worked full-time.

Slightly more than half the scientists (57 percent) spoke of the chance for advancement as a factor in retaining them in the firm. Nonetheless, a few scientists expressed frustration with their own lack of advancement and worried about the limitations or trade-offs of working in industry, particularly when business needs conflicted with their scientific interests. "I often want to explore things that come up in my research," said one male Ph.D. senior scientist.

"Sometimes I stop doing the project, but mostly, I follow the course needed for business."

CAREERS AND INTERNAL MOBILITY

Careers within biotechnology firms via promotion and internal mobility do not follow the linear upward, formalized career pattern of internal labor markets in larger, more traditional firms in the past (Doeringer and Piore [1971] 1985; Becker 1964). In these smaller firms, limited formal hierarchy exists, aside from the distinction between directors and nondirectors—which itself can evaporate when projects change. As the research changes and as the firm grows or shrinks, department names and codes change, and scientists move around from one to another. A number of scientists were unsure of their precise current job titles or grades at the time of their interviews.[4]

Yet nearly all the scientists interviewed have been promoted since their arrival at the firms, though men appear to have done slightly better than women, perhaps because of the greater burden of work and family that most of the women carry. Of those who have been promoted furthest and fastest, two single men without children and three fathers with home support have done the best, moving to higher-level jobs much faster than women who are parents without such support or women working part-time. One male scientist with a full-time working spouse and two children has also been promoted, but his wife's job is secretarial and she handles most of their home responsibilities.

Academic degrees, though important, are not wholly determinative of status (unlike most university settings). Though Ph.D. scientists begin at higher rates of pay and generally supervise employees with bachelor's degrees, a few B.S. and M.S. scientists also are considered full scientific-grade members. The scientific jobs are not only for Ph.D.'s but can be earned by those with bachelor's or master's degrees who perform well over the years.

Most Ph.D. scientists were hired at the level of senior or staff scientist, and most of them have advanced during their first two to three years to senior scientist 2 or its equivalent. Three women and three men have also become managers, but the men have been promoted to higher positions than the women in five out of six cases. Two Ph.D. men were hired at senior scientist 2 and have stayed there for several years. Three men and one woman hired as managers have been promoted to higher-level management during their first four years on the job, while one woman manager at a similar level has not been promoted in that time.

The non-Ph.D. scientists have advanced even further, as a group, though their careers are slightly more idiosyncratic. One B.S. scientist became an associate director. Though he does not manage a group, he is recognized as the source of many creative ideas by everyone in the firm. His career path, however, is defined by most as "unique." Two male B.S. research associates have advanced through the ranks to scientist. One B.S. employee who entered as a temporary quality analyst was made permanent and was promoted to research associate 2 in his seven years with the company. Two women B.S. associate scientists have become senior scientists 1.

These mobility patterns suggest that internal labor markets in some form are alive and well in small firms, even with limited room for mobility at the top. While advancement does not follow a single track, a single set of job titles, or even a predictable degree-based order, more than 50 percent of the professionals interviewed had achieved promotions over an average tenure of five to seven years. This finding is surprising in the insecure environments of the biopharmaceutical companies but perhaps not so surprising when we realize that promotions are one of the few means to reward employees in this setting. Giving them bonuses is difficult in tight financial times; giving them stock options is of limited value when the stock is hovering at a low value; and interesting travel and time off are both limited by the rigorous time requirements of the work.

In summary, careers in biotechnology are not linear, but they do provide opportunity for growth and movement up a shifting hierarchy of job titles and responsibility. This seems to occur in part because of vacancies left by departing managers or senior staff. While degrees and training count in initial job grade and in work assignments, they are not definitive in determining who can be a scientist or who can become a manager; if someone with a bachelor's degree has creative ideas and good scientific skills, that person can become a project manager or associate director. A paradoxical effect of this pattern may be that it ties professionals more closely to the firm, especially those without doctoral or medical degrees.

FAMILY STATUS
AND LIFE STAGE

The prevailing view of careers assumes that professionals are acting as individuals, making maximizing choices. Yet nearly all people are embedded in relationships outside of work. How do professional employees at various life stages seek to integrate work and nonwork (or family) concerns in these biotechnology settings? How do companies respond to employees' dilemmas?

Neither is easy. The industry's insecurity and required long hours combine to create barriers to full engagement with both work and family for many scientists in this study, particularly mothers, who have less support at home than fathers. Some couples reluctantly postpone starting a family because of their job uncertainty and/or work demands on the partners. Commuting marriages mean that two employees see their spouses only weekly or monthly.

The women were more explicit in voicing the difficulties and stresses of these integration issues. One woman explained that she was thinking of an alternate career, one that would be more flexible. She wants to work and knows she would have "no trouble getting a job [in biotechnology]." But, she says, the work is not as challenging as it used to be. It's not the focus of my life and I do not want it to be. I would prefer to have a job with better hours, more like school hours. For instance, when the nursery wants parents to participate, I can never do it. I have to be at work. I do not want my daughter to go to kindergarten and then after-school care every day, and rarely see me except for a couple hours every night!

Another woman, a Ph.D. scientist and mother of an 18-month-old, said that since she became a parent, "my days are more defined in terms of time. I have to be slightly more organized. Before the baby, I used to work till 6 or 6:30 at night. Now I take work home if there is a real push, but I leave at 5 to pick my son up at day care."

BARRIERS TO FULL
INTEGRATION OF
WORK AND FAMILY

One barrier to full integration is a long commute to the workplace, which seems most often to result from a spouse's job or career, a preference for public schools in a specific community, or from a feeling of uncertainty. One scientist said he had a "horrible commute, at least 40 minutes each way, and more in traffic." When asked why he did not consider moving (since his wife's job location was not an issue), he said, "With the kind of situation we're in, the company's [lack of] stability . . . it would make no sense to move. Who knows what will happen?"

A second barrier to full engagement with work and family is the individualistic way that flexible arrangements are frequently negotiated. Even in a company where the chief executive office and human resource director have promoted flexibility, the actual decision on alternative scheduling is usually up to the person's immediate manager, usually a senior director or vice president. In one company, requests for part-time hours are rejected flatly. In another, two women scientists have worked out satisfactory part-time arrangements with their director. At the same company, however, a new mother was denied her request to return to work three days a week by a different manager and was officially terminated when she was unwilling to return full-time. The company did rehire her part-time for a limited period as a consultant, but without benefits or permanent status. Since each person must arrange her own exceptions to the standard schedule, a barrier is created by concerns about precedent and by individual supervisors' personalities and beliefs; these can limit fruitful experimentation.

Here is one example where traditional assumptions about what is a normal schedule may not match the actual needs either of the job or the employee. When one person who had experimented with a four-day, full-time schedule was asked why she was not permitted to continue it, she replied that her manager told her, "I want you on site. I do not want to deal with your job. I can only rely on you if you are here." She explained that she could be available on the fifth day via computer, telephone, or fax, but that was not sufficient for him, even though she described herself as having "100 percent autonomy" and rarely seeing her manager. In his interview, he agreed that he was a "hands-off" manager but said he "preferred" to have her there for five days (cf. Bailyn 1993, chaps. 5 and 6, for related examples and a fuller argument).

The specific work organization patterns and demands in biotech can themselves be a barrier to full integration, if no one with authority is attending to these issues. "I have no predictability," said one Ph.D. director. "I could be in the lab [at 5 p.m.] and get caught up and not be able to leave. We are understaffed now, so I am in the lab a lot. I am writing memos, reports, and making phone calls. I have multiple projects and project meetings. I have minimal secretarial support." This successful woman felt she had been forced to make terrible choices to succeed in her work. "I gave up a lot of family time to get work done," she said. "To get ahead, you have to make a decision. And I have moved further ahead than women who did not make the same decision. But I am not sure I should have done it." She found that when she tried working fewer hours for a period, to spend more time with a seriously ill parent, "it took several months to get back the same level of authority and respect" that she had had before.

Another female Ph.D. scientist explains how poor work organization of projects exacerbates this problem.

There is always a crisis, something that needs to be resolved "right now." Once when my daughter was two months old, I worked 21 straight days. I was trying to breast-feed, and it was impossible. I do not usually work 80 hour weeks, but when there are crises, I do. Management is not shy about asking people to put their personal lives on hold.

Thus family status and life stage concerns interact with firm status in shaping employees' careers in ways that are hard to predict in advance. For example, half the scientists in this study joined the companies at least seven years ago, when both companies were smaller than they are now, and then larger for a time. Since then, many scientists have become parents of small children, so their personal needs have changed. One scientist noted that he has spent more time with his younger children, because he realized what he missed with the older ones. Another male Ph.D. scientist noted that "stability is becoming more important to me; having a child did that. And we are building a new house." Thus he needs to spend more time at home than he did before.

COMPANY RESPONSES

Company responses to professional employees' efforts to integrate the work and nonwork portions of their lives both enable and frustrate work-personal life integration. Positive company responses usually come from a flexible or creative supervisor who is willing to bend the rules or traditions to provide support that employees need to integrate their work and family lives. In the absence of a sympathetic supervisor, company statements or policies concerning family-friendly practices have not resulted in major changes in traditional cultural assumptions (such as the importance of face time, or employees' physical presence).

We observed that technology can assist people in integration efforts. One positive company response has been to provide equipment such as special modems or computer programs so that a few employees can monitor experiments from home (especially over weekends) or analyze data without coming into the office. One manager used his cell phone to minimize disruptive interruptions during nights and weekends.

Part-time schedules negotiated at one of the companies have proved satisfactory to both employees and their supervisors. One employee works 20 hours weekly during two days, working one long day during the week and coming in to work one weekend day. This allows her to monitor cell cultures and experiments at odd hours so that others do not have to check them then, and it enables other family members to care for her children when she is working. Another woman works 30 hours weekly, the minimum for benefit eligibility, but would prefer to work fewer if she could still have the right to health insurance. The part-time employees and their managers are pleased with the amount of work they are doing on these schedules. The women say they are more productive as part-timers because they focus on what they have to get done in more limited time. Yet one company has a policy against part-time work, and the second requires a case-by-case negotiation that is not always successful. Moreover, female scientists (since only women work

part-time here) find themselves feeling grateful for this opportunity, rather than seeing their schedules as contributing effectively to both their work and home obligations.

Working at home is a solution that might help more employees, especially for work such as writing reports. Some portion of biotechnology work cannot be done at home, because it is lab based or due to Food and Drug Administration regulations or confidentiality concerns. But some scientists estimate that up to half their work could be done elsewhere, particularly report writing, data analysis, and reading. Despite this, one human resource director explained that "only the top eight people in the company are allowed to work at home. Below that, it is not permitted." Working at home will not solve all problems. To the extent that supervisors actually require 80-hour weeks, little relief can be expected. But most frontline managers did not expect such long hours from employees.

In biotechnology, as in many other industries, productivity and effectiveness are not necessarily linked directly to hours worked. This creates potential for the future development of more flexible careers. One thoughtful manager, a female Ph.D. scientist, said, "People have very different work styles. Some people work full out and can get more done in seven hours than some other people who work ten hours a day." One is not necessarily a better worker than the other, she said, but "most people's work is not set up where number of [assay] plates done per day is important as a measure or a real indicator of productivity." She thinks that "slower people tend to be good at more analytical kind of work, compared with faster people who are more data-churning people. So the trick is to try to get people to do things they are the best at. You can't make everybody into one thing." When asked how she managed people's work, she said, "I try to deal with content, not time. . . . Most people probably can do their jobs in a 40-hour week." However, she was worried that the chief executive officer would "probably die" if he found out what she had said about 40 hours. "But I just don't believe that more hours is more productivity. If you expect 60 hours a week of people, I find that they burn out. Once they burn out, they can't do much of anything well." A number of employees explained that their flexibility was important to their decisions to stay with the firms, even in hard times.

In summary, we found that work and family integration is an active issue for scientists and managers in biotechnology firms. Company responses in two firms varied from generally unresponsive to relatively flexible, as long as negotiations were individually conducted with direct supervisors. Lacking to date are understandings of professional scientific or managerial careers for men or women that incorporate long-term flexibility in both work and home commitments. Our evidence suggests that such understandings are both possible and desirable for long-term retention and development of professional staff in small and medium-sized biotechnology firms.

CONCLUSIONS AND IMPLICATIONS

What we present here is a work in progress. Ongoing research will include more levels of employees, spouse or partner interviews, and more firms. Still, we can draw some initial conclusions. The old implicit employment contract, which concerns only work, needs rethinking. Key workplace decisions and developments have implications for family life, and vice versa. A new conception of a career is needed that is more fluid, allowing for change over time. It may require a new definition of security. To the scientists and managers we interviewed, fairly insecure firms may seem secure enough as long as their own skills are developing, their home and work lives can be integrated, and their ability to maintain and expand professional networks is enhanced. Promotions and opportunities for mobility provided reasons for them to stay with firms, even if they could make more money by changing jobs; personal reasons and friendships also helped tie them to companies. So neither the old employment contract of staying with a single firm nor the new one of firm-hopping seems to accurately reflect these professionals' realities.

A new concept of career may need to involve a different understanding of flexibility. Ad hoc work-family flexibility leads to a culture where a series of individual successes and failures occurs, rather than a culture that creates innovative opportunities to integrate important realms of life. We propose that policies and practices need to be both more universal (not limited to the top 10 persons in a firm, for instance, but open to all employees), more collectively negotiated at the level of the firm or the work group (for example, not based on a particular supervisor's relationship to a single employee), and more adapted to the individual (allowing for change and growth over time). Life stages make an immense difference in what kinds of flexibility matter to employees at all levels of the firm, and fully understanding this will require future research with employees at all stages of their life course. Firms, too, have their life cycles, and these can also be unpredictable. Universality, collective negotiation, and adaptability of work-life practices are essential in moderating potential harmful effects of this inevitable instability.

If work and jobs are seen as more fluid and changeable, then perhaps the employment contract is not really a contract but something that resembles an emergent, ever changing set of adaptations by both employees and employers. The watchword for this new concept of career is flexibility. Employees, of course, may mean one thing by "flexibility" (such as the ability to adjust their hours to deal with personal needs and concerns), while employers mean another (such as employees' being available when and where they are needed to get the work done). Such different definitions need to be reconciled in ways that do not put individual employees or one gender at risk. Both sides must see flexible arrangements as fair and productive. Employers can and do expect extra effort from employees at crucial times in a project,

but employees should also be able to expect understanding from employers when they need flexibility or ongoing nonstandard arrangements. Work organization needs to be able to encompass both sets of needs.

In thinking about workplaces of the future, we need to remember that the structure of work is evolving both faster and with more variations than are possible to observe and record in any single research project. The assumptions about yesterday's workplaces, which were more rule bound, more stable, and less quickly changing, are still dominating the thoughts of both employees and employers and perhaps even researchers! New characteristics of organizations like the ones described here will have profound impacts on the nature of work, on whatever employment contract(s) develop, on career choices, and on work-life experiences.

In summary, we examined here how the structure of work itself contributes to the opportunities and barriers regarding work and family integration and to the entire concept of career in these potential workplaces of the future. Future firms could be more responsive if they designed their work-life practices and policies, in part, around the inherent meaning of work to their employees, building on the intrinsic value that most people place on the work they do. Company practices that retain valued professionals will be structured in ways that are most meaningful to them. Gender patterns in family status and the kind of support available still matter profoundly for employees in their day-to-day lives and in their careers, and firms can offset this social inequity if they so choose. Company policies concerning work structure can also promote or constrain participation in family and community life. We argue that thoughtful managers can choose to enhance both (and still have fully engaged employees), rather than diminishing them through rigid work practices.

We suggest that career paths evolve over a person's lifetime and are made more complex and interdependent through a series of choices involving not only the individual but also his or her family members. Any new employment understanding, whether contractual or not, will need to incorporate this present reality.

Notes

1. Some of the industry characteristics in this section are drawn from work done by Sandra Resnick. See Resnick 1996, 1997a.

2. Clearly, the scientists interviewed constitute a sample with potential selection bias, in the sense that those who found the uncertainty intolerable might never have come to work in the industry or might have left, thereby leaving the population. We have interviewed five professionals who left the firms, and their decisions seem to have been made for a combination of reasons including work-family considerations, concern about the future of the company, and traditional career advancement concerns. One moved to a larger biotech firm; one moved to a small but growing and wealthier biotech firm; one is at home with a new baby; and two left the industry for jobs with less uncertainty.

3. Some research also suggests that small firms provide a more flexible work environment (MacDermid and Williams 1997; MacDermid et al. 1994).

4. A typical hierarchy of job grades and titles starts with research assistant, then research associate (1 and 2), then senior research associate, then sometimes associate scientist (1, 2, and so forth), then staff scientist

or scientist (1, 2, and so forth), then senior scientist (1, 2, and so forth), then associate director, then director. Project managers usually fall between the scientist and associate director level, though they may also be directors or associate directors.

References

Aisenberg, Nadya and Mona Harrington. 1988. *Women of Academe: Outsiders in the Sacred Grove*. Amherst: University of Massachusetts Press.

Arthur, M. B. and D. M. Rousseau, eds. 1996. *The Boundaryless Career*. New York: Oxford University Press.

Bailyn, Lotte. 1993. *Breaking the Mold: Women, Men, and Time in the New Corporate World*. New York: Free Press.

Becker, Gary. 1964. *Human Capital: A Theoretical and Empirical Analysis with Special Reference to Education*. New York: National Bureau of Economic Research.

DeMeuse, Kenneth P. and Walter W. Tornow. 1990. The Tie That Binds—Has Become Very, Very Frayed. *Human Resource Planning* 13(2):203-13.

DiMasi, Joseph A., Ronald W. Hansen, Henry G. Grabowski, and Louis Lasagna. 1991. Cost of Innovation in the Pharmaceutical Industry. *Journal of Health Economics* 10:107-42.

Doeringer, Peter B. and Michael Piore. [1971] 1985. *Internal Labor Markets and Manpower Analysis*. Lexington, MA: D. C. Heath.

Herzenberg, Stephen A., John A. Alic, and Howard Wial. 1998. *New Rules for a New Economy: Achieving Postindustrial Prosperity*. Ithaca, NY: Cornell University Press.

Kanter, Rosabeth Moss. 1990. *When Giants Learn to Dance: Mastering the Challenge of Strategy, Management, and Careers in the 1990s*. New York: Simon & Schuster.

Kochan, Thomas A. 1998. Back to Basics: Creating the Analytical Foundation for the Next Industrial Relations System. Paper presented at the 50th Anniversary Meeting of the Industrial Relations Research Association, Chicago, Jan.

Louis Harris and Associates, Inc. 1997. Harris Survey at Work. Summary. Louis Harris and Associates, New York.

MacDermid, Shelley M. and Margaret L. Williams. 1997. A Within-Industry Comparison of Employed Mothers' Experiences in Small and Large Workplaces. *Journal of Family Issues* 18(5):545-67.

MacDermid, Shelley M., Margaret L. Williams, Stephen Marks, and Gabriela Heilbrun. 1994. Is Small Beautiful? Influence of Workplace Size on Work-Family Tension. *Family Relations* 43(2):159-67.

PHRMA Facts and Figures. 1997. http://www.phrma.org.

Powell, Walter, Kenneth W. Koput, and Laurel Smith-Doerr. 1996. Interorganizational Collaboration and the Locus of Innovation: Networks of Learning in Biotechnology. *Administrative Science Quarterly* 41:116-45.

Resnick, Sandra. 1996. Appendix to the Proposal: Biotechnology Industry Information. In *Opportunities for Work and Family Integration for Professionals: A Study in Small and Medium-Sized Biotechnology Firms*, ed. Paula Rayman and Françoise Carré. Cambridge, MA: Radcliffe Public Policy Institute.

————. 1997a. Background Information on the Biotechnology Industry Profiles. Radcliffe Public Policy Institute. Memorandum.

————. 1997b. Interview of Peg Hewitt. Center for the Study of Drug Development, Tufts University, Medford, MA.

Robinson, Sandra L. and Denise M. Rousseau. 1994. Violating the Psychological Contract: Not the Exception but the Norm. *Journal of Organizational Behavior* 15:245-59.

Rousseau, Denise M. 1995. *Psychological Contracts in Organizations: Understanding Written and Unwritten Agreements*. Thousand Oaks, CA: Sage.

Swinnerton, Kenneth A. and Howard Wial. 1995. Is Job Stability Declining in the U.S. Economy? *Industrial and Labor Relations Review* 48(2):293-304.

U.S. Office of Technology Assessment. 1991. *Biotechnology in a Global Economy*. Washington, DC: Government Printing Office.

ANNALS, *AAPSS*, **562**, March 1999

Lower-Wage Workers and the New Realities of Work and Family

By SUSAN J. LAMBERT

ABSTRACT: Changes in both social policy and business conditions make this a critical as well as an opportune time to extend a work-family perspective to lower-wage workers and to organizations in the community that, in addition to the workplace, affect the well-being of low-income families. Drawing on literature from the fields of work and family, public policy, and organizational sociology, the author reviews what current research tells us about the special challenges that confront lower-wage workers as they combine work and family responsibilities. Integrating knowledge from these fields leads to concerns about current welfare-to-work efforts and opens up new avenues for improving the prospects of lower-wage workers and their families.

Susan Lambert is an associate professor in the School of Social Service Administration at the University of Chicago. Her areas of expertise include the relationship between work and family life, the effects of family-responsive policies in the workplace, and the changing nature of internal labor markets. Her current research investigates how community agencies and employers structure opportunity for lower-wage workers.

NOTE: The issues presented in this article draw on and extend an analysis initially presented in Susan Lambert and Evelyn Brodkin, Lower-Wage Workers and the New Realities of Work and Family (Proposal to the Ford Foundation, June 1998). These and related issues are also the subject of investigation of Brodkin's companion project titled Work and Welfare in Everyday Life, supported by the National Science Foundation and the Soros Foundation.

TO date, the field of work and family has focused its attention on the experiences and needs of the workers most valued in today's labor market, notably, managerial, technical, and professional workers. It has paid little attention to the special challenges that lower-wage workers face when combining parenting with paid work, to the supports they might find particularly useful in balancing the demands of work and home, or to changes that might help them avoid conflicts between multiple responsibilities.

Moreover, except for research specifying the need for government-supported child care and mandated parental leave, the field of work and family has focused narrowly on the workplace as the source of workers' problems and as the target of intervention. There is growing recognition, however, that communities as well as workplaces need to be family-friendly if workers are to manage work and family responsibilities in a way that supports family well-being. Nowhere is this more apparent than in the lives of lower-income families. Community organizations, both public and private, play a central role in the lives of lower-wage workers, affecting their ability to manage and find employment as well as to care for their children. For example, low-income families often rely on public agencies for medical care and supplemental income and on private agencies for education, job placement, and child care. What happens in the workplace is only one piece of the puzzle of understanding the conditions that affect the well-being of lower-income families and, really, all families.

This is both a critical and an opportune time to extend a work-family perspective to lower-wage workers and to organizations in the community that, in addition to the workplace, affect the lives and life chances of low-income families. It is a critical time to look at lower-wage jobs from a work-family perspective because recent changes in labor market conditions and in social welfare policy have increased pressures on single mothers to accept employment in lower-wage jobs. As will be described, existing research suggests that the occupational conditions associated with lower-wage jobs—few benefits, limited flexibility, routine job tasks, and instability—can undermine personal and family well-being.

It is an opportune time to build knowledge concerning practices that can help lower-wage workers meet their work and family responsibilities because of new initiatives in both the public and private sectors. There is unprecedented interest in improving the structure and nature of lower-level work as a result of the difficulties that businesses are encountering in recruiting and retaining workers for these positions. For example, several companies that must fill vast numbers of lower-level positions (such as Burger King, Marriott, McDonald's, Lands' End) are establishing special programs and policies to improve recruitment and retention in these jobs, offering flexible work hours, bonuses for retention, award programs, and special child care supports. At the same time, welfare reform is spawning new programs and practices not only in the workplace but also in welfare offices and nonprofit agencies. Model programs are being implemented that specify formal relationships between employers and service providers in providing training and counseling to women moving from welfare to work.

Whether the impetus behind these new efforts is recruiting entry-level workers or moving families off welfare, they present innovations that have the potential to help lower-income families in novel and valuable ways. These new efforts, however, are likely to vary in the extent to which they provide supports for meeting work responsibilities as compared to parental responsibilities and thus merit close scrutiny.

Drawing on literature not only from the field of work and family but also from public policy and organizational sociology, I review in this article what current research tells us about the special challenges that confront low-income workers as they combine work and family responsibilities. These literatures provide nuanced, sometimes contradictory, views of the prospects of lower-wage workers in the job market and at home. Their integration leads to concerns about current welfare-to-work efforts as well as new avenues for improving the well-being of lower-wage workers and their families.

VANTAGE POINTS ON LOWER-WAGE WORKERS

Scholars in the field of work and family and those who examine welfare policy treat their subjects of inquiry as though they were distinct, that is, one group looks at workers and the other at welfare recipients. Yet we know that low-wage workers move in and out of the workforce and on and off welfare (Bane and Ellwood 1983; Spalter-Roth and Hartmann 1994). Welfare reform has blurred the distinctions even further as more and more of those receiving welfare are required to also hold a job. The fact that child care is viewed as a work support within the realm of welfare policy, yet is included under the rubric of "family-responsive policies" in the work and family field, is one example of the difference in perspectives offered by these two lines of inquiry. In the following, I summarize the contributions these two fields currently make to our understanding of the challenges lower-wage workers face as they struggle to balance work and family responsibilities.

The field of work and family: Occupational conditions affecting work-life balance

The most important contribution of the literature on work and family is that it maintains a focus on the well-being of workers and their families when considering the merits of occupational arrangements. In doing so, the field has developed important knowledge on the job conditions essential to achieving a good balance between work and family life, notably having some flexibility over work hours, using a variety of skills, and participating in decision making (see Barling 1990; Crouter 1984; Glass and Camarigg 1992; Googins and Burden 1987; Jackson 1993; Katz and Piotrkowski 1983; Lerner 1994; Schein 1995). It also tells us how important both informal supports such as having a supportive supervisor (see Greenberger et al. 1989; Shinn et al. 1989) and more formal supports such as family-responsive policies (see Families and Work Institute 1993; Lambert 1997) are to maintaining the well-being of workers as they combine work and family roles.

But because most of the research in this field has focused on middle-income and often middle- and upper-level workers, we still do not know much about the specific job conditions of lower-level workers and supports they find in the workplace. It is not that researchers in the field of work and family have been insensitive to the needs of lower-level workers. Many go to great lengths to lament that workers in the greatest need of workplace supports are the least likely to get them and speculate that if middle-income workers have problems managing their work and family responsibilities, then lower-income workers must be in dire straits (see Galinsky 1988; Galinsky, Hughes, and David 1990). But only a few studies in this field have focused squarely on the experiences of lower-level workers, probably because a major motivation has been to convince business leaders that work-family supports make good business sense and business leaders care most about workers at the core of their enterprise.

Because lower-wage workers have not been the focus of inquiry, it is unclear the extent to which the lessons learned about essential occupational conditions generalize to these

workers. Studies that have included a broad spectrum of workers provide some indication that lower-wage workers differ from higher-wage workers in the kinds of supports they prefer. For example, research indicates that lower-wage workers and higher-wage workers find different types of child care supports helpful, with lower-wage workers preferring care in their community rather than at their work site (Berkeley Planning Associates 1989; Goff, Mount, and Jamison 1990; Kossek 1991). My study of Fel-Pro demonstrated that family supports (for child care, elder care, personal counseling, and so forth) were more important to lower-level workers than to white-collar workers and managers in terms of promoting both their work performance and well-being (Lambert 1995, 1998). This contrasts with common assumptions that workplace supports are more important to white-collar workers and professionals, who are assumed to experience greater job stress.

Even if the same job conditions are integral to the well-being of workers in all types of jobs, certain job conditions—such as flexibility, challenge, and participation—are likely to look different at the bottom of the organizational hierarchy. For example, Swanberg's study (1997) of a large hotel chain found that even a little flexibility—being able to be a few minutes late for work—went a long way toward helping cleaning personnel arrange for child care. Existing measures of flexibility often do not capture such fine distinctions. In sum, the literature on work and family draws attention to the fact that the effects of jobs extend beyond the workplace, into workers' personal lives. The field has taken giant strides in identifying basic job conditions that shape the balance that workers achieve between work and family life and has made a good case for the necessity of formal and informal supports that can help workers manage their family responsibilities. But, at this point, the field has provided relatively little information on the specific occupational conditions and work-family stresses confronted by lower-wage workers as they combine work with family responsibilities.

The literature on public welfare

Although the policy literature provides more information on lower-wage jobs than is true of the literature on work and family, one actually learns more about lower-wage workers than about lower-wage work. Most studies take a supply-side approach, investigating the characteristics of welfare recipients in terms of their human capital and such "barriers" to employment as having young children. Numerous studies (see Burtless 1995; Harris 1996; Holzer 1996) indicate that the educational attainment of women on welfare remains low; a generous estimate is that about half have not completed high school. Moreover, many have preschool children; in 1991, about 45 percent had children under age 6 (Burtless 1996).

After documenting the "weak labor market preparation" of women on welfare, researchers coming from a supply-side perspective then look to see what kinds of jobs might be available to workers with such low qualifications. This question leads them to focus on jobs requiring few or no skills. Because work is of interest only to the extent it can keep or get families off welfare, we learn little about job characteristics other than compensation that may foster or hinder worker and family well-being. What we do learn is quite dismal.

The fact that most low-skilled jobs do not pay enough to pull a family out of poverty even when workers work full-time year-round has been well known for some time (Blank 1995; Holzer 1996). But the public's understanding, as reflected in recent welfare legislation, is that at least there are enough of these low-paying jobs to go around, that people can work and earn at least something if they want to. Recent studies indicate, however, that low-skilled, lower-wage jobs are in fact scarce when compared to the number of workers seeking them. For example, one study (Kleppner and Theodore 1997) estimates that, in Illinois, there are 25 job seekers for every job that pays at least poverty wages; 72 job seekers for every job that pays at least 150 percent of the poverty line; and 114 workers for every job that pays at least a "livable wage." Similarly, Holzer (1996) concludes from national data that "at any given time there is not a sufficient number of jobs available for all unemployed workers" (29).

Scholars who adopt a supply-side analysis of the problems facing low-skilled workers end up concluding that because there is a shortage of jobs for less educated workers and because the industrial base is shifting away from the manufacturing sector toward the service and technology sectors, there must be an increase in the number of jobs requiring higher or different skills. Thus, in the end, they come full circle, back toward focusing on the characteristics of those in need of jobs, suggesting ways to increase job seekers' human capital and thus their earning potential.

A demand-side look. The problem with supply-side analyses is that they are inconsistent with information on larger changes in the economy. Overall, men are doing less well in the economy than they did a decade ago, and women are doing a little better. In 1992, females working full-time earned 75 percent of what their male counterparts earned, up from 62 percent in the 1980s; but this is largely because men's wages are losing ground, not because women's wages are growing (Blank 1995). Moreover, although on average women have made some wage gains, women in the bottom quarter of the wage distribution have seen their hourly wages fall since 1979 (Blank 1995; Holzer 1996). If there are all those great jobs out there, then why do we see these disturbing trends?

In one of the few demand-side investigations of changes in the U.S. labor market to look beyond issues of compensation, Tilly (1996) marshals evidence on seven dimensions of employment to raise concerns about the plummeting quality of U.S. jobs:

1. Wages. The real hourly wages of production and nonsupervisory workers in private industries fell by 13 percent between 1973 and 1995, and earnings inequality widened by race and level of education so that low-wage workers experienced even greater wage losses.

2. Benefits. The percentage of workers covered by employee-provided health insurance dropped from 63 percent to 56 percent between 1979 and 1993; the percentage of workers for whom their employer paid the full premium decreased 28 percent to 17 percent.

3. Due process. Unions have been the leaders in ensuring due process for terminating employment. Only 17 percent of the workforce is covered by union contracts, as compared to over 30 percent in the 1950s.

4. Hours flexibility. Since 1970, the growth in part-time employment has been largely involuntary; most part-time workers would prefer to work more hours. From an evaluation of a welfare-to-work program in Chicago, Berg, Olson, and Conrad (1991) found that the overwhelming percentage of participants reported that their work days and hours varied from week to week and that they had little choice of when they worked.

5. Permanence. There are fewer opportunities for long-duration jobs, and permanent layoffs are more common today than in past decades. The lack of job permanence affects those at both ends of the occupational spectrum, from managers who have been downsized to lower-level workers pressed into temporary work arrangements.

6. Mobility. Downward mobility has become more common. One-third of workers experienced at least a 5 percent decrease in earnings during

the 1980s; one-fifth did so during the 1970s. Hourly wages particularly have been declining for both men and women.

7. Control over the work process. The one ray of hope is that an increasing proportion of companies are moving toward what are called high-performance work systems, which depend on worker input and loyalty for success and allow workers greater autonomy and input. For example, among *Fortune* 1000 firms, 28 percent had self-managed teams in 1987; by 1991, 47 percent had them.

A demand-side perspective leads us to ask, Given these job characteristics, who should hold these jobs? rather than the supply-side question of, Given these workers, what kind of jobs can they get? When we look at the diminishing quality of jobs in general, I doubt few would conclude that single mothers with young children are best suited for jobs at the lower-end of the occupational spectrum. Since many pay below the poverty line, these jobs should not be a family's sole source of income; since hours fluctuate so much, people with young children may have the most difficulty meeting basic job responsibilities. As Harris (1996) concludes from her study documenting the lack of wage growth and high rates of return to public aid among welfare recipients, "work among poor women should be viewed as the problem rather than the solution" (424). What is actually occurring in the economy is that an increasing proportion of jobs can be considered "lousy" (Burtless 1990). As Kossek et al. (1997) warn, the occupational characteris-

tics encountered by low-skilled workers today may be tomorrow's reality for the majority of Americans. Thus, a demand-side perspective suggests that increasing the education and skills of workers currently disadvantaged in the economy will not be enough to ensure their well-being and that of their family. If there are not enough lousy jobs to go around, there certainly are not enough good ones.

Other contributions of the policy literature. By beginning with a focus on low-income families, the policy literature highlights the fact that family well-being is affected by multiple institutions, not just the workplace. Recent changes in welfare legislation mean that workers in both welfare offices and nonprofit agencies are playing an increasingly important role in linking disadvantaged women to jobs. Caseworkers in both types of social service agencies are being asked to serve as liaisons to employers hiring women on welfare; to help their clients find training, jobs, child care, and transportation; and to support and monitor the work efforts of the women after they have moved into a job.

Prior work on the implementation of welfare policy indicates that "street-level workers" in both public and private agencies have considerable discretion in carrying out basic job tasks (Brodkin 1986, 1997). Caseworkers in welfare offices and nonprofit agencies may function more as employer agents, recruiting and screening prospective employees for firms or enforcing the employer's terms for employment through the use of welfare sanctions. Alternatively, they may develop into employee agents, marketing clients to employers, troubleshooting when difficulties arise on the job, and intervening to support workers when personal or family problems arise. Such differences have important implications for the ability of disadvantaged workers to balance work and family demands.

Moreover, qualitative research in the area of policy studies sheds light on the importance of supports from family and friends in helping lower-wage workers meet the demands of their job. From interviews with women in low-wage jobs, Henly (forthcoming) finds that women depend greatly on their informal social networks for child care and transportation, relying on relatives and neighbors who themselves often have few resources. The supports provided by these resource-poor networks can be seen as supplements for employers as much as for workers because they help employers minimize their labor costs and maximize their hours of operation.

Summary. The policy literature paints a dismal picture of the job prospects for many Americans, especially those with poor education and responsibilities for young children. The misfit between the characteristics that enable workers to balance work and family responsibilities featured in the literature on work and family and the realities of lower-wage jobs is quite apparent. The policy literature puts a great deal of faith in preparing workers for jobs. Certainly, workers—and society—

would benefit from a better educational system, one with more equitable outcomes, and from efforts to train more workers for good jobs in the economy. Nonetheless, the troubling reality remains that there is an increasing proportion of jobs that do not pay a living wage or provide health insurance, that offer few protections to workers, and that provide limited opportunities for advancement, regardless of the job holders' qualifications. Unless these trends are reversed, a growing proportion of workers will require support from public agencies, nonprofit organizations, and from family and friends if they are to stand any chance of meeting the needs of their family and the requirements of their employer.

ANOTHER POSSIBILITY: INTERNAL LABOR MARKETS

The policy literature treats declines in the availability and quality of jobs as though they are the result of forces outside employers' control. Researchers lament how globalization has meant a loss of low-skilled jobs to foreign soils, how advances in technology mean that workers need greater conceptual skills, and how the growing service sector now requires additional "people" or "soft" skills (see Burtless 1995; Holzer 1996). Some even imply that the poor design of lower-wage jobs is a response to the poor preparation and education of many job candidates. For example, Burtless (1995) states that "improving the job skills of unskilled workers can eventually reduce the number of very poorly paid jobs, but only in the very long run after employers have modified a large percentage of jobs to reflect the higher average level of worker skills" (102).

Opening up this chicken-and-egg question for scrutiny is essential to developing alternative strategies for developing interventions that foster the well-being of disadvantaged workers and their families. Tilly (1996) points out that other countries have experienced comparable rates of globalization and technological revolution and have not downgraded their jobs to the same extent. Bielby (1992) observes that "a large body of recent scholarship shows that the technical requirements of work and efforts by employers to economize on transaction costs fail to account adequately for variation across firms in the structure of their employment relation" (648). Jacobs (1994) goes so far as to argue that when jobs require little from workers, that is exactly what an employer gets. When workers have no reason to believe they will be retained when the going gets rough, when they have few prospects for skill development or wage increases, the result is "an unreliable, poorly disciplined work force with inferior skills" (206).

This opposing perspective comes out of theory on and investigations of internal labor markets. Internal labor markets can be defined as the ways in which firms structure opportunity for workers. Firms with strong internal labor markets have ports of entry primarily at lower levels of the hierarchy, with established ladders for moving up in the organization. They also have formal mechanisms for handling employee grievances, personnel procedures, and seniority-based compensation packages that usually include employee benefits.

An abundance of literature on the so-called new employment contract indicates that strong firm-level internal labor markets are being dismantled. Again and again, we hear that workers can no longer expect to stay with a single company for their working life, that workers' prospects depend on whether they have generalizable skills of value in the external labor market and not whether they have specialized, firm-specific skills of value in an internal labor market (Kalleberg, Knoke, and Marsden 1995). Scholars are scurrying to find the mechanisms by which opportunity is now structured in the external labor market, pointing to the possibility that organizational networks are functioning as quasi-internal labor markets (Kariya and Rosenbaum 1995).

One point that comes through clearly in this literature is that there is a great deal of variation in employment arrangements. The sociology of internal labor markets rose in response to economists' conceptualizations of a segmented labor market composed of a primary sector where education and experience lead to higher wages and a secondary sector where wages are low regardless of how much human capital workers have. The segmented labor market approach led to the codification of different sectors of the economy (industrial versus service) as being part of either the primary or secondary labor market. Sociologists took issue with this view, garnering evidence that firms within these different sectors vary greatly in terms of their employment arrangements, some providing benefits and opportunities for advancement and some not (see Althauser 1989; Baron, Davis-Blake, and Bielby 1986; Doeringer and Piore 1971; Sorensen 1983). This gave birth to the notion of firm-level labor markets.

The waters have been muddied further as scholars note that employment arrangements vary even within firms, with some jobs leading to higher pay and promotions and other jobs not (Bills 1987; Finlay 1983; Jacobs 1994; Ospina 1996; Parcel and Sickmeier 1988; Stewman and Konda 1983). Recent research suggests that employers bundle different jobs differently (Hunter 1998; Kalleberg et al. 1996; MacDuffie 1995; Osterman 1994). Jobs that pay well are also likely to provide flexibility and autonomy, and workers holding them are more likely to be covered by formal personnel policies and benefit plans; bad jobs are likely to be bad in a number of different ways. Evidence suggests that variation in within-firm employment arrangements may be increasing; noncore jobs are being outsourced or filled with contingent workers, while the career ladders and compensation packages of those holding core jobs are being strengthened and extended (Pfeffer and Cohen 1984; Jacobs 1994).

The fact that there is so much variation in employment arrangements has important implications for understanding the realities faced by lower-wage workers today. Policy analysts tend to treat a job as a job as a job; that is, they note job titles and basic occupational categories when evaluating the outcomes of welfare-to-work efforts. But as Baron, Davis-Blake, and Bielby (1986) point out, "Much theory and research has ignored the obvious but essential fact that jobs exist in their own subenvironments, just as firms and industries do" (170). Internal labor market theory predicts that jobs with the same title may be very different depending on the larger organizational context. For example, two organizations may have secretarial positions that look alike in terms of basic job responsibilities and design, but the day-to-day realities of these positions may be very different, depending on the organization's retention practices and promotion patterns. Such differences are likely to account for variations in the ability of workers in seemingly similar jobs to maintain employment in the face of often overwhelming personal responsibilities.

Perhaps the most important lesson from the literature on internal labor markets is that there is a great deal of choice in how employers bundle jobs. As Dobbin et al. (1993) indicate,

Organizational analysts have come to the conclusion that common management practices do not arise through spontaneous combustion in thousands of different locations at once; rather they are socially constructed by networks of managers who are attentive to signals and incentives that emanate from the state, the legal system, and the wider political culture. (396)

A recent study by Hunter (1998) is especially helpful in identifying factors that affect employers' choice of arrangements for lower-level workers. Hunter compared the job of nursing assistant across nursing homes in Massachusetts. He hypothesized and found that the quality of this job varied a great deal across nursing homes in terms of compensation, job protection, and opportunity for advancement. A good proportion of the variation in employment conditions could be accounted for by how the nursing home positioned itself in the market and by the professional affiliations and training of upper managers. Specifically, the job of nursing assistant was bundled well when the nursing home tried to differentiate itself in the market as a choice provider and when the managers went through standardized training and were active in professional associations in the nursing home industry.

Hunter's study and others indicating that employment arrangements are as much strategic as they are market driven are important because they open up new avenues for improving lower-wage jobs. When firms position themselves as providing a superior product or a superior service, jobs are more likely to be designed well because such jobs require a higher level of worker performance than is true of the same jobs in firms with a more general, less differentiated niche (Arthur 1992; Davis-Blake and Uzzi 1993; Kochan and Osterman 1994; Osterman 1994). Thus, encouraging U.S. business to emphasize quality over quantity is likely to benefit workers as well as consumers. Moreover, targeted education and training programs that present good job design and comprehensive compensation packages as standard practice for the design of lower-level jobs might go a long way toward improving the prospects and lives of lower-wage workers and their families. As Bills (1987) reminds us, "The underlying imperatives typically held to affect internal labor markets are inevitably filtered through managerial beliefs" (202). Which workers are seen as core to the enterprise and which are not is not simply a result of the imperatives of technology. It is easy to see how lower-level workers who are closest to the product and customer can be viewed as essential to profitability and organizational success (Jacobs 1994), but this is rarely the case.

NEW AVENUES

Integrating the insights provided by knowledge on work and family, welfare policy, and internal labor markets suggests new avenues for supporting lower-wage workers as they combine work and family responsibilities. In this final section, I summarize possible new directions for both practice and research.

Suggestions for practice

One new direction would be to emphasize workplace development as much as workforce development. Current public policy is focused squarely on workforce development, that is, on increasing the human capital of women who collect welfare so they can fit into existing lower-level jobs. What is needed is a balanced focus on workforce development (preparing people for jobs) and workplace development (designing jobs for people). The declining quality of U.S. jobs suggests that increasing job skills will not be enough to ensure the well-being of families most at risk in the current economy. Attention also needs to be given to improving the basic characteristics of lower-level jobs and the internal labor markets in which they are embedded. One avenue for accomplishing this is to train supervisors and managers in the standard practice of designing jobs well.

A second new direction would be to focus on the intersection of public sector and private sector institutions. New public-private partnerships between employers and service providers provide a unique opportunity to integrate workplace development with workforce development. For example, Marriott's Pathways to Independence program has received wide acclaim from both public sector and private sector leaders for its attention to the special needs and circumstances of women moving from welfare to work (Milbank 1996). This program gives joint attention to employers' concerns, workers' skills and needs, and welfare regulations. It provides an example of how the efforts of community organizations and employers can be coordinated to support worker-recipients. Such partnerships can provide a forum for dialogue between the public and private sectors as well as a foundation on which to launch interventions that improve the conditions of lower-level jobs that make it difficult

for workers to balance work and family responsibilities.

Third, support should be given to firms that emphasize quality rather than cost containment. Firms that try to differentiate themselves in terms of having a superior product or service tend to bundle their jobs better than those with more generic marketing strategies that rely on cost-containment strategies for profitability. When cost containment is the primary way to profits, the result is not only shoddy products and service but also shoddy jobs.

In high-performance work systems such as total quality management, workers are viewed as assets rather than as expenses to be contained. Currently, the federal government plays a role in supporting total quality management by giving the Malcolm Baldrige Award to companies that are outstanding examples of this particular work system. One key component of the evaluation for this award is how human resource policies support and encourage worker participation and compensate workers for their contributions to the larger organization. The quality of employment arrangements is viewed as critical to organizational success. Providing incentives for the adoption of high-performance work systems across industries and firms may do more to further the well-being of lower-level workers than interventions targeted at individual workers; Kochan and Osterman (1994) make some interesting recommendations on how this can be accomplished.

A final suggestion for practice is to train caseworkers in the new realities of work in America. Case-workers involved in welfare-to-work efforts need to have a good understanding of the nature and structure of lower-level jobs if they are to help disadvantaged women make progress in the labor market. They have to know how to recognize the difference between jobs that lead somewhere and those that lead nowhere. Some jobs have high external mobility, some have high rates of internal mobility, and some have no clear path anywhere. Jobs without a clear path up or out lead to what Bridges and Villemez (1991) refer to as "rational shopping behavior," where workers quit their present job to try out a new one because there is no other way to explore alternative employment possibilities. In these jobs, high turnover results from the structural characteristics of the job, not from the inadequacies of jobholders. Case-workers need to be aware that bad job habits can be structurally induced and would likely occur regardless of the worker-recipient's qualifications or motivations.

Suggestions for future research

One avenue for new research is to investigate the well-being of families as they move off welfare. The success of welfare reform is being evaluated on the basis of how many families are moved off welfare, not out of poverty. A study of welfare recipients by Harris (1993) reveals that education and training provide a quicker route off welfare than does work experience but that this occurs because education and training help women secure jobs with more hours, not higher wages. Thus, in some circumstances,

increased labor force participation, even when accompanied by higher earnings, may undermine the well-being of disadvantaged families. Researchers in the field of work and family have the unique perspective and right theoretical expertise to address the issue of how different types of welfare-to-work efforts affect the well-being of single mothers and their children.

A second avenue is to study the special needs and circumstances of lower-wage workers and their families. Research is needed that focuses exclusively on lower-level jobs so that subtle distinctions in the design and implementation of lower-wage work can be identified. Small differences in job design may make a big difference in the ability of lower-wage workers to balance their work and family roles. Moreover, we need to know more about the special needs of lower-wage workers, who often head households on their own. Currently, we know many lower-wage workers prefer different supports than higher-wage workers do, but we lack information on the full range of supports they may find useful, both in the workplace and in their community.

A final avenue for new research is to investigate new initiatives to recruit and retain lower-level workers. Such initiatives vary in terms of their specific components, including, for example, mentoring programs that provide both technical and emotional support to lower-level workers, efforts to restructure entry-level positions to provide greater variety and flexibility, and provision of training and education so that workers can be quickly promoted into higher-paid jobs. Some of the employers implementing new policies and programs aimed at recruiting and retaining lower-level workers are involved in formal relationships with social service agencies to hire women on welfare; some are not. It is likely that because welfare recipients are often viewed as having limited work motivation, practices developed as a part of welfare-to-work programs focus mostly on helping workers meet work responsibilities rather than family responsibilities. On the other hand, efforts developed independently of welfare reform may focus more on providing family or personal supports or on improving the design of lower-level jobs because often the impetus for change is to become an employer of choice. Investigating the nature and focus of the practices implemented under these different circumstances could provide useful information on the prospects of lower-level workers under varying policy and workplace conditions. Moreover, an investigation of independent, private sector initiatives might uncover supports for workers' personal and family lives that can be adopted by welfare-to-work programs.

References

Althauser, Robert. 1989. Internal Labor Markets. *Annual Review of Sociology* 15:143-61.

Arthur, Jeffrey. 1992. The Link Between Business Strategy and Industrial Relations Systems in American Steel Minimills. *Industrial and Labor Relations Review* 45:488-506.

Bane, Mary Jo and David Ellwood. 1983. *The Dynamics of Dependence: The Routes to Self-Sufficiency*. Report prepared for Assistant Secretary for Planning and Evaluation, Office of Income Security Policy, Department of Health and Human Services, Washington, DC.

Barling, Julian. 1990. *Employment, Stress and Family Functioning*. New York: John Wiley.

Baron, James, Alison Davis-Blake, and William Bielby. 1986. The Structure of Opportunity: How Promotion Ladders Vary Within and Among Organizations. *Administrative Science Quarterly* 31:248-73.

Berg, Linnea, Lyn Olson, and Aimee Conrad. 1991. Causes and Implications of Rapid Job Loss Among Participants in a Welfare to Work Program. Paper presented at the annual research conference of the Association for Public Policy and Management, Bethesda, MD.

Berkeley Planning Associates. 1989. *Employer-Supported Child Care: Measuring and Understanding Its Impacts on the Workplace*. Report prepared for the Department of Labor, Office of Strategic Planning and Policy Development, Washington, DC.

Bielby, William. 1992. Organizations, Stratification, and the American Occupational Structure. *Contemporary Sociology* 21:647-49.

Bills, David. 1987. Costs, Commitment, and Rewards: Factors Influencing the Design and Implementation of Internal Labor Markets. *Administrative Science Quarterly* 31:202-21.

Blank, Rebecca. 1995. Outlook for the U.S. Labor Market and Prospects for Low-Wage Entry Jobs. In *The Work Alternative: Welfare Reform and the Realities of the Job Market*, ed. D. Nightingale and R. Haveman. Washington, DC: Urban Institute Press.

Bridges, William and Wayne Villemez. 1991. Employment Relations and the Labor Market: Integrating Institutional and Market Perspectives. *American Sociological Review* 56:748-64.

Brodkin, Evelyn. 1986. *The False Promise of Administrative Reform: Implementing Quality Control in Welfare.* Philadelphia: Temple University Press.

———. 1997. Inside the Welfare Contract: Discretion and Accountability in State Welfare Administration. *Social Service Review* 71:1-33.

Burtless, Gary, ed. 1990. *A Future of Lousy Jobs? The Changing Structure of U.S. Wages.* Washington, DC: Brookings Institution.

———. 1995. Employment Prospects of Welfare Recipients. In *The Work Alternative: Welfare Reform and the Realities of the Job Market,* ed. D. Nightingale and R. Haveman. Washington, DC: Urban Institute Press.

———. 1996. The Transition from Welfare to Work: Policies to Reduce Public Dependency. In *Families, Poverty, and Welfare Reform,* ed. L. Joseph. Chicago: University of Chicago, Center for Urban Research and Policy Studies.

Crouter, Ann. 1984. Participative Work as an Influence on Human Development. *Journal of Applied Developmental Psychology* 5:71-90.

Davis-Blake, Alison and Brian Uzzi. 1993. Determinants of Employment Externalization: A Study of Temporary Workers and Independent Contractors. *Adminsitrative Science Quarterly* 38:195-223.

Dobbin, Frank, John Sutton, John Meyer, and Richard Scott. 1993. Equal Opportunity Law and the Construction of Internal Labor Markets. *American Journal of Sociology* 99:396-427.

Doeringer, Peter and Michael Piore. 1971. *Internal Labor Markets and Manpower Analysis.* Lexington, MA: D. C. Heath.

Families and Work Institute. 1993. *An Evaluation of Johnson & Johnson's Work-Family Initiative.* New York: Families and Work Institute.

Finlay, William. 1983. One Occupation, Two Labor Markets: The Case of Longshore Crane Operators. *American Sociological Review* 48:306-15.

Galinsky, Ellen. 1988. Business Competitive Policies and Family Life: The Promises and Potential Pitfalls of Emerging Trends. Paper presented at the Women and Labor Conference, sponsored by the Labor Education Center, Institute of Management and Labor Relations, Rutgers University, New Brunswick, NJ.

Galinsky, Ellen, Diane Hughes, and Judy David. 1990. Trends in Corporate Family-Supportive Policies. *Marriage and Family Review* 15:75-94.

Glass, Jennifer and Valerie Camarigg. 1992. Gender, Parenthood, and Job-Family Compatibility. *American Sociological Review* 98:131-51.

Goff, Stephen, Michael Mount, and Rosemary Jamison. 1990. Employer Supported Child Care, Work/Family Conflict, and Absenteeism: A Field Study. *Personnel Psychology* 43:793-809.

Googins, Bradley and Diane Burden. 1987. Vulnerability of Working Parents: Balancing Work and Home Roles. *Social Work* July-Aug.:295-99.

Greenberger, Ellen, Wendy Goldberg, Sharon Hamill, Robin O'Neil, and Constance Payne. 1989. Contributions of a Supportive Work Environment to Parents' Well-Being and Orientation to Work. *American Journal of Community Psychology* 17:755-83.

Harris, Kathleen. 1993. Work and Welfare Among Single Mothers in Poverty. *American Journal of Sociology* 99:317-52.

———. 1996. Life After Welfare: Women, Work and Repeat Dependency. *American Sociological Review* 61:407-26.

Henly, Julia. Forthcoming. Barriers to Finding and Maintaining Jobs: The Perspective of Workers and Employers in the Low-Wage Labor Market. In *Hard Labor: Poor Women and Work in the Post-Welfare Era*, ed. J. Handler and L. White. Armonk, NY: M. E. Sharpe.

Holzer, Harry. 1996. *What Employers Want: Job Prospects of Less-Educated Workers*. New York: Russell Sage Foundation.

Hunter, Larry. 1998. Customer Differentiation, Institutional Fields, and the Quality of Entry Level Service Jobs. Working paper, University of Pennsylvania, Philadelphia.

Jackson, Amelia. 1993. Black, Single, Working Mothers in Poverty: Preferences for Employment, Well-Being, and Perceptions of Preschool-Age Children. *Social Work* 38:26-34.

Jacobs, David. 1994. Organizational Theory and Dualism: Some Sociological Determinants of Spot and Internal Labor Markets. *Research in Social Stratification and Mobility* 13:203-35.

Kalleberg, Arne, David Knoke, and Peter Marsden. 1995. Interorganizational Networks and the Changing Employment Contract. Paper presented at the International Social Network Conference, London.

Kalleberg, Arne L., Peter V. Marsden, David Knoke, and Joe L. Spaeth. 1996. Formalizing the Employment Relation. In *Organizations in America: Analyzing Their Structures and Human Resource Practices*, ed. A. L. Kalleberg, D. Knoke, P. V. Marsden, and J. L. Spaeth. Thousand Oaks, CA: Sage.

Kariya, Takehiko and James Rosenbaum. 1995. Institutional Linkages Between Education and Work as Quasi-Internal Labor Markets. *Research in Social Stratification and Mobility* 14:99-134.

Katz, M. and C. Piotrkowski. 1983. Correlates of Family Role Strain Among Employed Black Women. *Family Relations* 32:331-39.

Kleppner, Paul and Nikolas Theodore. 1997. *Work After Welfare: Is Illinois' Booming Economy Creating Enough Jobs?* DeKalb: Northern Illinois University, Office of Social Policy Research.

Kochan, Thomas and Paul Osterman. 1994. *The Mutual Gains Enterprise: Forging a Winning Partnership Among Labor, Management and Government*. Boston: Harvard Business School Press.

Kossek, Ellen. 1991. *Child Care Challenges for Employers*. Horsham, PA: LRP Press.

Kossek, Ellen, Melissa Huber-Yoder, Dominic Castellino, and Jacqueline Lerner. 1997. The Working Poor: Locked Out of Careers and the Organizational Mainstream. *Academy of Management Executive* 11:76-92.

Lambert, Susan. 1995. An Investigation of Workers' Use and Appreciation of Supportive Workplace Policies. In *Best Papers 1995: Proceedings of the Academy of Management*, ed. Dorothy Perrin Moore. Madison, WI: Omni Press.

———. 1997. Expanding Theories of Occupational Structure: Examining the Relationship Between Employer Responsiveness and Worker Well-Being. In *The Integration of Social Work and Social Science*, ed. D. Tucker, R. Sarri, and C. Garvin. New York: Greenwood Press.

———. 1998. Workers' Use of Supportive Workplace Policies: Variations by Race and Class-Related Characteristics. In *Workforce Diversity*, ed. A. Daly. Washington, DC: NASW Press.

Lerner, J. 1994. *Working Women and Their Families*. Thousand Oaks, CA: Sage.

MacDuffie, John Paul. 1995. Human Resource Bundles and Manufacturing Performance: Organizational Logic and Flexible Production Systems in the World Auto Industry. *Industrial and Labor Relations Review* 48:197-221.

Milbank, Dana. 1996. Marriott Is Training People on Welfare. *Wall Street Journal*, 31 Oct.

Ospina, Sonia. 1996. *Illusions of Opportunity*. Ithaca, NY: Cornell University Press.

Osterman, Paul. 1994. How Common Is Workplace Transformation and Who Adopts It? *Industrial and Labor Relations Review* 47:173-88.

Parcel, Toby and Marie Sickmeier. 1988. One Firm, Two Labor Markets: The Case of McDonald's in the Fast-Food Industry. *Sociological Quarterly* 29:29-46.

Pfeffer, Jeffrey and Yinon Cohen. 1984. Determinants of Internal Labor Markets in Organizations. *Administrative Science Quarterly* 29:550-72.

Schein, Virginia. 1995. *Working from the Margins: Voices of Mothers in Poverty*. Ithaca, NY: Cornell University Press.

Shinn, M., N. Wong, P. Simko, and B. Ortiz-Torres. 1989. Promoting the Well-Being of Working Parents: Coping, Social Support, and Flexible Job Schedules. *American Journal of Community Psychology* 17:31-55.

Sorensen, Aage. 1983. Sociological Research on the Labor Market: Conceptual and Methodological Issues. *Work and Occupations* 10:261-87.

Spalter-Roth, Roberta and Heidi Hartmann. 1994. Dependence on Men, the Market, or the State: The Rhetoric and Reality of Welfare Reform. *Journal of Applied Social Sciences* 18:55-70.

Stewman, Shelby and Suresh Konda. 1983. Careers and Organizational Labor Markets: Demographic Models of Organizational Behavior. *American Journal of Sociology* 88:637-85.

Swanberg, Jennifer. 1997. Work and Family Issues Among Lower-Level Workers. Ph.D. diss., Brandeis University, Waltham, MA.

Tilly, Chris. 1996. *The Good, the Bad, and the Ugly: Good and Bad Jobs in the United States at the Millennium*. New York: Russell Sage Foundation.

ANNALS, *AAPSS*, **562**, March 1999

Creating a Research and Public Policy Agenda for Work, Family, and Community

By PAULA M. RAYMAN and ANN BOOKMAN

ABSTRACT: In the last decades, there has been considerable effort from researchers and public policymakers to set an agenda for the United States on work, family, and community issues. There has been movement in both research and public policy to connect work and family perspectives, and, more recently, community contexts have been recognized as well. However, current research and public policy models have been limited by a number of deficiencies that prevent them from developing and implementing an agenda that has the capacity to move our nation forward to meet the challenges that lie ahead. In addition, there is little direct connection between the findings from current research and the content of new public policies. This article will review existing work, family, and community research and public policy in terms of prevailing strengths and deficiencies and then set forth possibilities for a future agenda.

Paula M. Rayman, director of the Radcliffe Public Policy Institute, is a nationally recognized scholar on the economy and work organization. She is a member of the faculty at the Harvard Graduate School of Education and is the editor of the Temple University Press series Labor and Social Change. Her numerous published works include The Equity Equation *(1996).*

Ann Bookman is a member of the faculty at the College of the Holy Cross and director of the Center for Interdisciplinary and Special Studies. From 1993 to 1996, she served as policy and research director of the Women's Bureau at the U.S. Department of Labor. She was also executive director of the bipartisan Family and Medical Leave Commission and principal author of A Workable Balance, *the commission's report to Congress.*

IN the 1890s, a snapshot of the United States would have revealed that the survival of about half of American families rested on an agrarian economy. Rapid migration to the cities was occurring, and the industrial revolution was beckoning farmers, new immigrants, former sharecroppers, and unmarried women into the factories. It was a turbulent moment, full of chaos and crisis but also promise and expectation.

In the 1990s, we again face a turn of the century, again in turbulent times. A current snapshot of our nation would reveal only 3 percent of the workforce employed in agriculture, with the majority of American workers employed in the service or high-technology sectors of the economy. Today 71.8 percent of all women are employed in the labor force, and the majority of women with pre–school-age children work outside the home.

During the turn of the last century, different stakeholders in the nation's social and economic welfare produced an amazing array of innovative policies and programs to address the challenges they faced. Business and labor leaders, government and community representatives, women and men, people from different faiths, races, and ethnicities pulled together to launch new ventures that would provide the basis for a strong emerging industrial society: public school education, immigrant aid societies, women's rights groups, labor and business organizations, and public policies that covered occupational health and safety, a shorter workweek, and voting rights.

As we face the twenty-first century, there is a great need to pay attention to the connections between economic and social policies and the nation's social capital: How do current economic forces, particularly the organization of work, affect the well-being of contemporary families and their communities? What new public policies and community initiatives are now required to ensure a better quality of life for all in America in the years ahead?

To respond to these key questions, new research is necessary to identify what current work-family-community policies and programs offer the best hope for the future, which need to be altered, and which demand further investment. A central problem we face in thoughtfully responding to these questions is that there is often a schism between the research and policy forums in our nation. We need to develop an integrated research and policy agenda, with each informing the other, so that new solutions can readily emerge. Moreover, within the separate arenas of work-family research and policy, there are also schisms: for example, economists who research work-productivity issues rarely speak to those doing research on family and community welfare; those shaping policies on technological impacts on work rarely converse with those shaping policy on parental involvement in children's education.

The present article, which offers a rationale for an integrated research-policy agenda on work, family, and community, will begin with an overview of the current status of related research and policy arenas. Best practices in both the research and policy fields will be highlighted. The final section of the article will be a call for change in how academics conduct research and how government responds to work-family issues.

OVERVIEW OF RESEARCH

The overview perspectives will be in two parts, the first focusing on work organization and the connections between work and family, the second, on family life.

Research on work and family connections

In 1977, Rosabeth Moss Kanter provided the first full-scale review of work and family interactions in her monograph, *Work and Family in the United States*. In it she raised the question of how work organizations could better take into account the interface between the personal lives of people and their work. But the research on which such a response would have to rest—the careful description and understanding of this interface—has only just begun.

Since the industrial revolution, work life and family life have been seen as distinct areas, each with a set of researchers. On the work side of the equation, Cappelli (1995) notes, "the United States lacks systemic, longitudinal data on work organizational practices, let alone employment arrangements" (573). The literature that informs the topic of work is multifaceted, and only when considered as a whole does it begin to provide the building blocks for a comprehensive view of the issue.

The empirical literature largely flows from the neoclassical economic perspective. It tends to highlight quantitative changes in types of employment, factors that affect firm adjustment, and measurements of labor force skill levels, supply and demand factors, and costs and benefits of labor cutbacks or labor retention.

Research from the institutional perspective examines labor allocation decisions within firms and the institutional mechanisms through which employers and workers maintain the employment relationship (Doeringer and Piore 1971). Research has tended to view the growth of alternative arrangements and changes in job stability as a manifestation of changes in employer practices and the structure of internal labor markets (Berger and Piore 1980; Carré 1992; Doeringer et al. 1991). Some economists have argued that the "mix" of different kinds of work-life arrangements within firms is changing (Osterman 1982, 1988). Others have focused on the sectorial shifts of job loss and job creation (Bluestone and Harrison 1982).

The research on this subject by economists has almost exclusively been concerned with quantitative and continuous change in employment and to a much lesser extent with qualitative and discontinuous employment patterns. Most recently, there has been special attention to the emergence of nonstandard work arrangements (Carré 1992; Ferber and Waldfogel 1996; Steinberg 1997). Researchers in this field have noted the complexity of the literature due to the heterogeneous nature of the workforce employed in alternative arrangements. Under debate are issues of choice over the employment situation on the employee side and the pressing need for flexibility on the employer side. The factors influencing this shift from traditional work practices to nonstandard ones are difficult to discern because they vary by sector and firm size. However, this new area of investigation has much potential meaning for the work-family research agenda due to the consequences of such a shift for individual workers, their families, and communities. For example, the gender and racial distribution of workers employed in alternative arrangements varies significantly. Women account for two-thirds of the part-time workforce and 53 percent of temporary agency workers. Over 60 percent of women working for a temp firm have at least one child under 18. Only 45 percent of temporary firm workers have health insurance coverage.

The literature on how work affects family outcomes spans the economic, sociological, psychological, business, and management fields. However, compared to the previously mentioned research, this is not considered hard research by most economists. Researchers have developed a variety of measures of employment and workplace practices that influence family outcomes. Some authors look at work solely in terms of employment, such as the effects of labor force participation on wives. Other studies develop more detailed measures of workplace demands and practices such as specific job tasks, work schedules, job security, and the presence and utilization of work-

family programs (Applebaum and Batt 1994; Googins, Griffin, and Casey 1994; Galinsky, Bond, and Friedman 1993; Pleck 1993; Voydanoff 1990). Still other research examines the relationship between broad economic indicators and family life, such as the consequences of unemployment and economic insecurity (Leana and Feldman 1992; Conger et al. 1990; Brenner and Mooney 1983; Rayman and Bluestone 1982). These studies have shown that the greater the amount of economic insecurity, the more volatility for individuals, their families, and the negative rippling effects on local communities.

In the last five years, there has been innovative research on the impact of workplace design on individual and family well-being and community involvement. The 1997 National Study of the Changing Workforce (Bond, Galinsky, and Swanberg 1998) found that employees with more supportive workplaces are more likely than other workers to have high levels of job satisfaction, greater loyalty to firms, less stress, and more energy for meeting off-the-job activities. The Ford Foundation report Relinking Life and Work (Rapoport and Bailyn 1996) explored the possibilities of pursuing a dual agenda in the workplace that considers enhancing productivity and employees' needs at the same time. Through case studies, this report documents that a corporate culture that creates difficulties in work-family integration also leads to unproductive work practices. In 1998, the Radcliffe-Fleet report continued documentation of the possibilities of a "win-win" strategy of integrating increases in work productivity with benefits for individual health and family life (Radcliffe Public Policy Institute 1997). For example, by organizing work design so that there was more focus on specific loan tasks, underwriters were able to work more efficiently, get home earlier, and experience fewer sleep problems. The latter, in turn, led to more family time, less stress at home and at work, and more focused attention and better communication at work.

This new cluster of studies is creating new ways of thinking about the interface of work organization and family and, importantly, creating new methodologies for assessing and implementing win-win practices. However, as most studies have been conducted at large, mostly professional work sites, the universality of the findings is limited, and more research in different kinds of workplaces needs to be launched. Moreover, great challenges remain in devising accurate productivity measures in the nonmanufacturing sectors of the economy. The research on work-life issues and the dual agenda of making life better both at home and at work has been undertaken primarily without input from economists, and, concurrently, most economists have not paid attention to this area of research. For the field to move forward, more interdisciplinary thinking will be necessary.

Research on family life

Social scientific study of the family began to develop in the second half of the nineteenth century. Anthropologists such as Lewis Henry Morgan, known for his study of Iroquois kinship terms, were among the first to study how family structure and kinship relations vary by culture and in different historical periods. Morgan and his peers brought a strong evolutionary bias to their study of the family, arguing that the family has passed through different stages of development and become more efficient and adaptive to its environment over successive generations (Morgan 1877). Some evolutionists, like Friedrich Engels, studied the preindustrial family and debated whether matriarchal or patriarchal family structures shaped the origins of the family (Engels 1902). These debates were never decisively resolved and, in fact, are still a subject of some controversy (Gough 1972; Sacks 1974; Leacock 1981).

Research on the family in the first half of the twentieth century has been called the period of "emerging science" (Bahr, Wang, and Zhang 1991; Christensen 1964). Social Darwinism was fading, and there was increasing emphasis on objectivity and rigorous methodology. Although studies from that period had different foci, such as marriage, fertility, and child socialization, they had a common set of questions concerning the impact of industrialization and urbanization on the "traditional family," by which they meant the extended family. Many studies documented a weakening of communal and familial solidarity in the face of dramatic economic change. They argued that traditional family was disintegrating, leaving the isolated nuclear family, which they claimed was an inferior familial structure (Byington 1910; Thomas and Znaniecki

1918; Lynd and Lynd 1929). While this has been largely refuted by contemporary social historians, it was a very influential perspective at the time, both as public ideology and social scientific truth.

In the period after World War II, the sociologist Talcott Parsons became very influential in the study of the American family. His theories emphasized specialization and differentiation of roles. He argued that public institutions, such as schools and factories, were taking over many of the traditional economic and educational roles of the family and that the small nuclear family units that remained were now free to "specialize," that is, to deal with child rearing and to provide emotional sustenance and security to family members (Parsons and Bales 1969).

Many social scientific studies of the 1940s, 1950s, and 1960s were internally focused, investigating the inner workings of the family and looking at issues such as intrafamilial role conflict, sources of marital satisfaction, and factors affecting the socialization of children. Studies focused on interaction and communication between family members, and the unit of analysis tended to be the individual or the single nuclear family household (Baldwin 1948; Lasko 1954; Ferreira and Winter 1965). Some researchers adopted a conceptual framework organized around developmental stages or a life cycle approach. While this is a model based on change over time and an intrinsic sense of dynamism in individual growth and family relations, it is not a model that was able to mesh the changing world around the family with the changes internal to family members and households. Except for a few studies, such as the sociological classic *Middletown* (Lynd and Lynd 1929), research on family life showed a stark lack of attention to the interface between family and community or family and workplace.

This began to change in the late 1970s and further developed in the 1980s with the growth of a new school of social historians who were keenly interested in the historical development of the American family in relation to other social institutions. Their work was based on the assumption that families still had an important economic function, even if the locus of work had shifted, and that communal ties and organizations were central in shaping the ways that families raised their young and survived in a variety of institutional contexts (Cott and Pleck 1979; Tilly and Scott 1978; Coontz 1988; Gordon 1988; Mintz and Kellogg 1988). Sociologists, anthropologists, and historians began to look at the specific interface between work and family (Kessler-Harris 1982; Sacks and Remy 1984; Bose, Feldberg, and Sokoloff 1987; Gerstel and Gross 1987; Dornbusch and Strober 1988; Hochschild and Machung 1989), and some probed the implications of this interface for community issues (Hayden 1984; Pappas 1989). In-depth studies emerged in the 1970s and 1980s that examined the experiences of specific types of families in their workplace and community contexts, including working-class immigrant families (Rubin 1976; Lamphere

1987; Zavella 1987) and African American families (Ladner 1972; Stack 1974; Gutman 1976; Willie 1976; Jones 1985). This integrative approach has reached full flower in the 1990s with a number of excellent studies that not only show the interconnections between work, family, and community but also call for a fundamental rethinking of how families spend their time and their resources and what families need for both survival and growth (Schor 1992; Berry 1993; Bailyn 1993; Rubin 1994; Hochschild 1997).

While the last two decades of writing from historians, sociologists, and anthropologists has richly described the interface between work, family, and community, the reality they have documented has only begun to penetrate the world of public policymaking. Why is this the case? Some have blamed the arcane language and inability to communicate that characterizes much academic writing. Others have blamed the bureaucratic, anti-intellectual nature of the civil service at the federal, state, and local levels. Still others point the finger at the insensitivity of many politicians—be they elected policymakers on Capitol Hill or the politically appointed policymakers that come and go with each successive administration—to anything but special interest groups and their own constituents. Clearly, there is enough blame to spread around many sectors. It is important, however, to examine how the research and policymaking functions of government are actually structured if we are to mount any serious realignment between the worlds of research and policy.

THE PARAMETERS OF POLICYMAKING: STRUCTURAL CONSTRAINTS AND SUBSTANTIVE DEBATES

Policymaking does not happen in a vacuum. There are a host of factors that shape both policy development and substantive policy outcomes. We need to understand how policymaking institutions are organized and to analyze the ideas underlying current policy debates.

The structure of policymaking

Just as the academic disciplines are often fragmented in their approach to work, family, and community, so, too, are government agencies. The structure of the executive branch agencies at the federal level provides a case in point. For example, the Departments of Labor, Commerce, and the Treasury, as well as the Small Business Administration, all deal with important issues of economic policy that deeply affect the ability of working families to prepare themselves for work, support their families, remain marketable in a rapidly changing workplace, and eventually retire. Yet there is rarely any substantive interaction between these agencies. There is an unchallenged assumption that the policy issues affecting workers and labor organizations will be dealt with by the Labor Department, while the policies of concern to business will be handled by the other three.

There is a similar division of labor on policy issues affecting families and children. Policy issues related to children's education are handled largely by the Department of

Education, while the Department of Health and Human Services leads efforts around child care policy and a wide variety of health policy issues. Policy issues affecting communities are largely delegated to Housing and Urban Development, particularly for poor inner-city communities, and the Environmental Protection Agency. It makes little sense to develop employment policy for business separate from the concerns of labor, and no sense to develop any kind of employment policy without considering the families on whom businesses depend and the communities in which they are located. Clearly, this division of labor at the federal level makes the development of public policies that promote the integration of work, family, and community very difficult.

In addition to their Washington, D.C., offices, each executive branch agency has field offices in one of 10 designated federal regions. While, clearly, field offices help to enhance the effectiveness and responsiveness of federal agencies to local conditions, the downside is that the fragmented structure of data gathering and policymaking at the federal level becomes replicated at the state and local levels. In fact, many state governments organize their own gubernatorial cabinets and state government agencies along the lines of the federal model, once again impeding an interdisciplinary and cross-agency approach to policy development.

The debates underlying policymaking

While a history of specific public policies affecting workplaces, families, and communities is beyond the scope of this article, it is important to review some of the general debates that have shaped policymaking over the last quarter century. Each year hundreds of bills are introduced on the floor of the U.S. Congress, yet very few become law. This may be attributed in part to partisan turf wars and bickering, and/or to budgetary constraints. But, on a deeper level, our elected representatives are reflecting a pervasive ambivalence that lies within the electorate itself about the efficacy of using public policy to address the nation's problems. The legacy of American individualism has created a suspicion of government policy as the instrument of change, and the result is a seemingly unending series of debates that never seem to move toward a viable compromise. What is the nature of these general debates, and how do they affect the policy arenas of employment; children and families; and community?

In the arena of workplace and employment policy, there are four fundamental debates that regularly recur. First, there is a debate about the place of regulation in a free-market economy and basic philosophical differences about whether government has any right or any role to intervene in the affairs of the private sector. The extremes of no regulation and a centrally planned, state-run economy are not at issue. Rather the debate concerns how much regulation, under what conditions, and with what exceptions. It is striking that some proposed federal mandates that would greatly benefit working families, such as the Family and

Medical Leave Act or the Plant Shut-down Notification legislation, were either stalled for many years or never enacted. Other federal interventions that have greatly benefited business, such as the Chrysler Corporation and savings and loan bailout bills, were enacted swiftly and at great expense to the taxpayers.

A second debate centers on whether state mandates are preferable to federal mandates when the free market is being subjected to regulation. Again, looking at the case of the Family and Medical Leave Act, during the years that it took for the proposed bill to become a federal law, many states introduced and passed comparable legislation at the state level. These state statutes allowed local lawmakers to specify which employers were covered and which were excluded, which employees could take leave and for how long, in a way that would not be adverse to local economic conditions. Ultimately, the federal bill was less generous to working families than those passed by the states because of an overriding fear of such mandates on the part of the business community.

A third area of debate concerns the relationship of U.S. products and markets to international products and markets. Issues of job security, wage rates, and labor standards, all of key concern to working families, are often lost in the battles between protectionists and free traders. In some ways, these battles are a replay of the regulation debate but taken to the global level.

The fourth debate on employment policy concerns the issue of workforce development and whether the government has a role to play in ensuring that all U.S. workers have opportunities for lifelong learning to retain their marketability. Although no one would dispute the need for the U.S. companies to remain highly competitive, there is a lack of consensus about public investments in human capital. Some see workers as assets to be developed, while others view them as costs to be cut. These differences extend beyond training and education programs to debates about the scope of employee benefits and the basic nature of the employer-employee relationship.

Turning to the issues of child and family policy, the general debates are equally sharp and often have an added moral or religious dimension that makes differences appear irreconcilable. The basic debate has been about whether the government has any role in family matters. Many believe the family is a private sphere that should remain outside the reach of any type of public policy, while others argue that certain types of programs and services that support children and families are worthy of public investment and that it is appropriate for the government to step in, especially when families cannot take care of their own children. It is ironic that those who seem most opposed to government's involvement in family life are the first to blame the family, along with changes in gender roles, marriage, and parenting, for many economic and social ills.

A related debate centers on the issue of family structure. For some there is only one valid and valued type of family structure, while others believe that diverse types of families—two-parent and single-parent, heterosexual and homosexual—can equally well raise children and provide stability and support for young and old alike. This process of valuing and devaluing extends to issues of race, ethnicity, and class. And those who champion a "government keep its hands off the family" position in principle are often the first to propose punitive policies toward poor families and families of color. Recent proposals on welfare reform that appeared to be in favor of laudable goals such as "personal responsibility" in fact reflected a deep distrust of the ability of some families—especially those headed by poor women and women of color—to accept any responsibility. These proposals looked to government to punish such families when they "failed."

Perhaps nowhere is there a more profound lack of consensus than on gender roles and the place of women in both the workplace and the family. This issue remains at the core of most child and family policy debates. Whether the policy proposal addresses reproductive choice, child care, or sexual harassment, we remain in a national fog about who women are and the diversity of their aspirations and their realities. Women work, as breadwinners and as homemakers. They are parents, alone and with partners. They are caregivers and the consumers of caregiving services. But we cannot seem to decide for policy purposes how to value their many economic and familial contributions to our society.

Finally, in the area of community, there are certainly some shared values regarding the desirability of safe, clean, stable communities in which businesses can prosper and families can live. But what is required to create the conditions for such communities to develop and how will they be sustained over time? Again we see debates that have had a major policy impact center around whether government has a legitimate role to play in creating and sustaining communities. Some minimize the role of government, believing that volunteer efforts and charitable contributions can ensure vital communities—the famous "thousand points of light" model. Others envision a role for government, preferably in partnership with other sectors, in creating multiple models of community suited to the cultural diversity of families and the varied needs of large and small businesses.

At the heart of this debate are questions about the efficacy of public investment in community-based programs and services, such as child care centers, senior centers, and safe houses for victims of domestic violence. There is division about creating an infrastructure that connects one community to another, particularly the inner city to the suburbs. There are additional debates about strengthening the regulation of both industry and natural resources in order to keep the air and water in our communities clean. These issues divide our policymakers and create policy stalemates that are sorely in need of resolution.

ATTEMPTS AT INTEGRATION: EFFORTS TO LINK RESEARCH AND POLICY

The idea that we need a more dynamic and interactive relationship between researchers and public policymakers is certainly not new. There have been a number of efforts to bring together researchers and policymakers on behalf of working families that have met with limited success. In this section of the article, we will review a few examples of such efforts from the last three decades, each spearheaded by a different sector, and attempt to understand both what they have achieved and what their limitations have been, with an eye to forging a stronger relationship in the future.

A federal government initiative: The White House Conference on Families

During the Carter administration (1976-80), there was an ambitious initiative designed to address issues facing American families that culminated in the 1979 White House Conference on Families (WHCF). This effort, first proposed by Jimmy Carter during the 1976 presidential campaign, was much more than a single conference. It included 500 hearings and forums at the state and community level. It also included the National Research Forum on Families in Washington, D.C., which brought together scholars from diverse disciplines. Finally, 2000 delegates were selected from a diverse cross-section of American families to hammer out a set of policy recommendations. The delegates worked in a series of 20 issue groups covering such topics as work and family, economic pressures, family violence, education, health, housing, child care, community institutions, and the media, to name a few. Three final conferences were held on the East Coast, in the Midwest, and on the West Coast to work out a policy agenda. Those recommendations that won the support of delegates at all three conferences included a call for "family-oriented personnel policies" such as flextime, better leave policies, shared and part-time jobs; new efforts to prevent alcohol and drug abuse; changes to the tax code such as eliminating the marriage tax penalty; reform of social security; promotion and support of a variety of child care choices; and so on (Listening to America's Families 1980).

After this extensive process of developing policy proposals that included input from researchers as well as business leaders, labor leaders, community services providers, and families themselves, a period of implementation and advocacy was planned and funded as part of the formal WHCF activities. There was a recognition from the inception of this effort that staff and planning would be needed to transform the recommendations into reality. The six-month implementation period included several elements. There was an emphasis on communicating the recommendations to the public through the cooperation of multiple media outlets. The recommendations were analyzed to determine where change efforts should be focused, that is, whether the public sector, the private sector, or the voluntary sector would be the major venues of change. All federal agencies, for example, were charged with reviewing the recommendations and generating short-term and long-term strategies for change. There was also attention given to mobilizing interested community-based constituencies and establishing long-term vehicles for implementation. Particularly noteworthy in this regard was the establishment of the Office for Families by President Carter, which was to oversee the implementation of recommendations from the WHCF. The Office for Families was given a broad mandate including policy analysis, technical assistance, advocacy, research, and funding to support activities at the state and local levels.

The WHCF, which made a concerted effort to link academic researchers with business, labor, community, and religious leaders, was impressive in many regards. The conference helped to increase public awareness about the consequences of public policy choices for American families, yet little of what was proposed by conference delegates and speakers became policy. Clearly, the election of Ronald Reagan in November of 1980 signaled a very different approach to family values and family policy from that pursued by the Carter administration. In 1981, a period of significant budget cuts to many family support programs began, and an era of "new federalism" shifted much of the responsibility for family well-being from the federal government to the states. In an analysis of state legislative activity on family

policy issues in the years following the WHCF, it has been argued that the political culture of each state has a defining influence over what bills are proposed and become policy (Zimmerman 1992). States with a "moralistic" political culture, in which government was viewed as an "instrument for promoting the general welfare" (85), enacted policies with a distributive and redistributive orientation. In states with a "traditionalist" political culture, where "the role of government [was] limited to maintaining the existing order and encouraging traditional patterns," the policies enacted were less distributive and more regulatory in nature (86).

Whether one tries to evaluate the effectiveness of the WHCF at the federal or state level, the key issue at that time did not revolve around the ability to infuse policy development with social science data but, rather, around the seismic changes to the social and political landscape represented by the Reagan presidency and the ascendancy of conservative grassroots organizations with a narrow definition of the family and a negative view of the government's role in promoting family well-being. There was a receptivity to the findings and expertise of researchers on the part of policymakers working with the Carter administration that all but disappeared during the Reagan years. The decision to hold the National Research Forum on Family Issues early in the process leading up to the regional meetings and to utilize academics to construct a "factual framework" and write a specially commissioned series of research papers (Listening to America's Families 1980, 157) that contextualized all subsequent policy discussions was testimony to the seriousness with which the planners tried to integrate research data and policy development. Ultimately, however, the macrolevel sociopolitical changes that occurred while Reagan was president overshadowed these efforts.

An academic research initiative:
  The Bush Center Project
  on Infant Care Leave

Another initiative that sought to link researchers and policymakers was a project conceived in 1983 by the Bush Center in Child Development and Social Policy at Yale University. This project was designed to look at "the impact on families and children of the lack of leave time and support for parenting in the early years of life" (Zigler and Frank 1988, xvii). In order to do this, an advisory committee was formed that included prominent scholars in the fields of child development, pediatrics, law, and social policy, as well as representatives from business, labor, and the federal government. The project staff was mandated with conducting original research and collecting existing data on the subject of parental leave for infant care both in the United States and in other countries with relevant private sector and public policies. The advisory committee was charged with critiquing the research and generating a set of national policy recommendations.

After two years of study, discussion, and debate, from 1983 to 1985, the committee concluded that "the infant care leave problem in the United States is of a magnitude and an urgency such as to require immediate national attention" (Zigler and Frank 1988, 350). Based on an extensive review of existing policy options and a thorough assessment of the sometimes competing needs of infants, parents, and employers, the advisory committee recommended that the United States adopt a national infant care leave policy in which all workers, regardless of firm size, length of service, or other factors, would be entitled to a six-month job-guaranteed leave of absence from their job to care for their infant. It was further recommended that these leaves be paid at 75 percent of the salary of the parent for up to three months and that the second three months of leave be provided on an unpaid basis. This recommendation was deemed essential to creating the foundation upon which to build a healthy, durable parent-child relationship. The committee further stated that benefits be continued for the family throughout the leave period and that a combination of employer-employee contributions be used to finance the recommended level of income replacement.

When the advisory committee completed its work, a coalition of grassroots women's, civil rights, and children's advocacy organizations was already preparing the first national legislation on parental leave, the Family and Medical Leave Act. When the Family and Medical Leave Act was first introduced in Congress in 1986, the work of the Bush Center advisory committee provided much important data and background information relevant to the drafting of the bill. However, the Reagan administration was philosophically opposed to the idea of government mandates and any kind of interference in the affairs of the private sector. Thus the specific provisions of the first bill were quite a long way from what the Bush Center advisory committee had formulated. Immediately, there were compromises made about the length of the proposed leave and which employees and employers would be covered, in an effort to build as broad a bipartisan coalition of supporters as possible. The recommendation concerning the provision of wage replacement was virtually ignored. Again, deep policy debates and divisions between lawmakers impeded the realization of sound policy proposals with extensive social scientific backing. It was not until a Democratic administration had control of both the White House and the Congress that this set of policy proposals became the public policy of the Unites States, and the Family and Medical Leave Act was enacted in 1993.

A philanthropic sector initiative:
  The Carnegie Corporation's
  task force

From 1990 to 1993, the Carnegie Corporation of New York convened a task force to study the first three years of life and to make recommendations for the development of public policies that could foster the healthy growth and development of our nation's youngest citizens. This effort brought together an impressive array of researchers, practitioners, and policymakers. The research component of the project was significant for placing a spotlight on new scientific findings regarding the importance of the first three years of life for optimal brain development. The results of the research by the task force were compiled in the report *Starting Points: Meeting the Needs of Our Youngest Children* (1994). The report documented a "quiet crisis" occurring in the United States and characterized conditions faced by children from the prenatal period to age 3 as being marred by increasing rates of poverty; changing family and employment patterns affecting caregiving for young children; inadequate child care arrangements, especially for infants and toddlers; and discouraging trends regarding health and family violence.

Based on this reality, the task force made policy recommendations in four key areas, four key starting points to "move our nation toward the goal of giving all children the early experience they need to reach their full potential and ensuring that no child falls through the cracks" (*Starting Points* 1994, 6). The report fully documented the changing nature of the workplace and its impact on young children and their parents. To meet the new realities faced by working families, the task force recommended promoting responsible parenthood; guaranteeing quality child care choices; ensuring good health and protective services; and mobilizing communities to support young children and families.

When *Starting Points* was released in Washington, D.C., in 1994, there was a concerted attempt to build bridges between the multiple sectors that the task force envisioned working together on behalf of young children. The First Lady spoke about the importance of the report's findings, along with cabinet secretaries from the Departments of Health and Human Services, Justice, and Education, business leaders, and leaders of local community-based agencies. The Carnegie Corporation also set up a special grant program to encourage local communities to take the findings of the report and attempt to change reality at the grassroots level. In 1996, the corporation made awards to 14 cities and states across the country that showed particular promise in building community-based multisector partnerships to promote the healthy development of children and their families. When the grants come to an end, it will be important to evaluate the long-term sustainability of these partnership efforts.

Even with an administration in the White House sympathetic to the findings of this report, there has been little dramatic increase in federal funding for programs to support children from zero to 3 years of age. Probably the most significant accomplishment of the *Starting Points* task force was its ability to focus national attention on brain development research, an effort that was carried forward by such initiatives as the April 1997 White House conference on brain research and the "I Am Your Child" public education campaign. In the past when research findings have shaped policy development, the impetus has come largely from the social sciences. In this instance, the ability of the task force to translate data from the hard sciences into terminology accessible to the lay person and then translate the implications of these findings into public policy was a breakthrough.

LESSONS LEARNED

The three initiatives just described provide useful models for linking research and policy. The primary accomplishment seems to have been in the area of increasing public awareness about the new challenges facing working families. Yet, in each instance, there has been little to show in terms of new public policies. The most targeted effort, the Yale Bush Center's recommendations around parental leave, took eight years to become law, and the law that was passed was a very diluted version of what the experts had suggested. Instead of a universal six-month leave with some pay, we have a law that covers only 55 percent of the workforce for 12 weeks of unpaid leave. The WHCF took a much more comprehensive approach, but a great deal of what was proposed 20 years ago is still being debated today and has not become public policy. Why is this the case?

One reason could be the social location of the institution playing the leadership role in the initiative. Yet in the three examples discussed, it does not seem to make a great deal of difference in terms of policy impact whether the recommendations come from the government, the academy, or the philanthropic sector. Another reason could be that research on workplace, family, and community needs has not been adequately integrated into policy development. But this also has not been the case in the three examples profiled. The WHCF had a special research forum in which scholars from diverse disciplines contributed their expertise, and scientific research has certainly been central to policy initiatives originating in the academy and the philanthropic sector. Each of the efforts discussed developed a persuasive set of policy proposals, yet each faced obstacles in the actual implementation of their agenda: all three efforts faced insufficient capacity in both national and community-based organizations to carry out the policy agenda developed. The WHCF was also hampered because the work of the conference became located inside a single federal agency and became highly bureaucratic, and a change in administration halted the development of key political leadership and new programmatic initiatives.

Looking further for the causes of the lack of progress on the policy front, it could be argued that there is a lack of national consensus about what the proper role of government is in supporting working families. We as a nation are not divided only about what public policies we need but also about whether new public policies are the best path toward a solution for the problems of integrating work, family, and community. This lack of consensus among the citizens is, not surprisingly, reflected in deep partisan divisions between our elected representatives at all levels of government. Perhaps we need research to address the issue of whether and how public policies can really make a

difference in helping working families to integrate their work, caregiving, and communal responsibilities before an integrated research and policy agenda can be developed.

BUILDING A SUCCESSFUL RESEARCH AND POLICY AGENDA

In order for there to be a coherent agenda for work, family, and community integration in the United States for the twenty-first century, a successful strategy must develop along three dimensions: an interdisciplinary research agenda that promotes thinking out of the box; a public policy agenda that connects grassroots organizations with active national networks; and leadership from academics and public officials to work together with business, labor, and civic leaders to take risks and create models for change. Linking all three dimensions is needed. Indeed, in order for us to build a successful agenda, we will carefully have to develop a national consensus of where we want to go in order to ensure quality of work and family life. We also will need a strong commitment to a strategic, long-term plan of how to get from here to there. Building this consensus will require a new way of thinking about how the institutions of work, family, and community are connected so that they enhance each other.

An economy that is viable and vibrant requires the unleashing of innovation and creativity from all of our nation's people. This is especially true for a future economy that will increasingly rest on a workforce that is knowledge based and has a high capacity for communication and flexibility. Correspondingly, the future of democracy depends upon the ability of citizens to contribute to and feel part of the larger community. The well-being of future society depends upon parents' having the time to provide the necessary care and attention to their children and for people to have time to properly care for the elderly and disabled.

Innovation and creativity emerge from working smart (that is, efficiently using knowledge and skills), not long. Feeling part of the larger community emerges from spending time on community activities. Parental involvement in the education of our nation's children, and caregivers' involvement with a variety of dependents, require flexible schedules. In our society, as it is currently organized, there is no time for people to attempt a successful integration of work and family and community. Thus we are in a position to fail to meet the economic, political, and social challenges that lie ahead.

The place to begin is with the question, What do we need in order to create a national consensus for an integrated work, family, and community agenda? The following points are offered to indicate some of the key ingredients that are necessary, with the understanding that this listing is just the beginning stage of a longer national conversation.

1. *Public and private funders should invest in research that both is interdisciplinary and links the academy with the community.* The problems we face are interdisciplinary, so the solution must be—we need to link social sciences and hard sciences and build bridges between different social scientific disciplines. Theory builders and researchers need to be in dialogue with people who face diverse dilemmas in the integration of work, family, and community. Research questions must reflect the different class, racial, and gender constructions of family and community life.

2. *Mechanisms for policy formation should be created that promote cross-agency collaboration.* Just as academics must reach across disciplinary boundaries, policymakers must reach across rigid bureaucratic structures and systematically link their efforts. Moreover, the government needs to be strongly committed to citizens' concerns. Efforts to reinvent government to date have substituted a market mentality and language for a genuine dialogue between citizens and government. For example, citizens cannot be reduced to mere customers.

3. *We must learn from historical examples and best practices.* As described in this article, the WHCF in 1979 convened people from grassroots organizations and national groups and linked academics with policymakers. The WHCF made much headway in providing steps toward an integrated agenda for America and in many ways was both a success and a story of hope.

4. *Leadership on the national and community levels must be developed that transcends partisan politics.* As the foregoing illustrates, we need effective and consistent leadership that supersedes narrow political

interests and changes in administrations and is committed to building a vision for an integrated agenda. Only with such leadership from multiple sectors, which draws upon the best and the brightest from business, labor, the academy, religious, and political and civic organizations, can we expect an agenda to be realized.

5. *Grassroots organizations must be linked with national groups.* Leadership development needs to be connected to the building of grassroots efforts and then connected to national groups. A successful example of this process happened in the 1980s with the work of a California-based grassroots group, the Child Care Employees Project. This organization was launched to give national attention to the fact that child care workers in our country are grossly underpaid and undervalued. Through two decades of research, such as the National Child Care Staffing Study, and significant grassroots action, most notably the Worthy Wage Campaign, these issues reached national visibility at the White House Conference on Child Care in October 1997 and were a part of the president's $21.8 billion child care investment proposal. While this effort suffered when the resources for the proposal were tied to the fortunes of the recently failed tobacco bill, it underscores the promise of efforts that originate at the grassroots level and the challenge of translating grassroots campaigns into national public policy.

These five ingredients are essential but not sufficient to achieve an integrated research and policy agenda for America's working families. There are other factors that will be identified as the cross-sector discussion unfolds. For example, in building a national consensus on work, family, and community, we will need to overcome the powerful sense of cynicism that currently pervades people's perceptions of public policy and public policymakers. A successful national conversation will also acknowledge deep differences between the American people on specific work and family issues. However, much common ground already exists regarding a yearning for a better quality of life that reduces the stresses of economic insecurities and lack of time for family life. For now, our conversation begins with a focus on raising the stakes involved in continuing to do business as usual and establishing a new way of thinking about the significant societal issues we face concerning work, family, and community.

References

Applebaum, Eileen and Rosemary Batt. 1994. *The New American Workplace: Transforming Work Systems in the United States.* Ithaca, NY: ILR Press.

Bahr, Stephen J., Gabe Wang, and Jie Zhang. 1991. Early Family Research. In *Family Research: A Sixty-Year Review,* ed. Stephen J. Bahr. New York: Lexington Books.

Bailyn, Lotte. 1993. *Breaking the Mold: Women, Men, and the New Corporate World.* New York: Free Press.

Baldwin, A. L. 1948. Socialization and the Parent-Child Relationship. *Child Development* 19(3):127-36.

Berger, Suzanne and Michael J. Piore. 1980. *Dualism and Discontinuity in Industrial Societies.* New York: Cambridge University Press.

Berry, Mary Frances. 1993. *The Politics of Parenthood: Childcare, Women's Rights, and the Myth of the Good Mother*. New York: Viking Penguin.

Bluestone, Barry and Bennett Harrison. 1982. *The Deindustrialization of America: Plant Closings, Community Abandonment, and the Dismantling of Basic Industry*. New York: Basic Books.

Bond, J. T., E. Galinsky, and J. E. Swanberg. 1998. *The 1997 National Study of the Changing Workforce*. New York: Families and Work Institute.

Bose, Christine, Roslyn Feldberg, and Natalie Sokoloff, eds. 1987. *Hidden Aspects of Women's Work*. New York: Praeger.

Brenner, H. M. and A. Mooney. 1983. Unemployment and Health in the Context of Economic Change. *Social Science and Medicine* 17(16):1125-38.

Byington, M. F. 1910. *Homestead: The Household of a Mill Town*. Philadelphia: Russell Sage Foundation, Press of William F. Fell.

Cappelli, P. 1995. Rethinking Employment. *British Journal of Industrial Relations* 33(Dec.):563-602.

Carré, Françoise. 1992. Temporary Employment in the Eighties. In *New Policies for the Part-Time and Contingent Workforce*, ed. V. L. duRivage. Armonk, NY: M. E. Sharpe.

Christensen, H. T. 1964. Development of the Family Field of Study. In *Handbook of Marriage and the Family*, ed. H. T. Christensen. Chicago: Rand McNally.

Conger, R. D., G. H. Elder, F. O. Lorenz, R. L. Simons, L. B. Wheelock, S. Huck, and J. N. Melby. 1990. Linking Economic Hardship to Marital Quality and Instability. *Journal of Marriage and the Family* 52:643-56.

Coontz, Stephanie. 1988. *The Special Origins of Private Life: A History of American Families 1600-1900*. London: Verso.

Cott, Nancy F. and Elizabeth H. Pleck, eds. 1979. *A Heritage of Her Own: Toward a New Social History of American Women*. New York: Simon & Schuster.

Doeringer, Peter B., K. Christensen, P. M. Flynn, D. T. Hall, H. C. Katz, J. H. Keefe, C. J. Ruhm, A. M. Sum, and M. Useem. 1991. *Turbulence in the American Workplace*. New York: Oxford University Press.

Doeringer, Peter B. and Michael J. Piore. 1971. *Internal Labor Markets and Manpower Analysis*. Armonk, NY: M. E. Sharpe.

Dornbusch, Sanford M. and Myra Strober, eds. 1988. *Feminism, Children, and the New Families*. New York: Guilford Press.

Engels, Friedrich. 1902. *The Origins of the Family, Private Property, and the State*. Chicago: Charles K. Kerr.

Ferber, Marianne and Jane Waldfogel. 1996. *"Contingent" Work: Blessing and/or Curse*. Cambridge, MA: Radcliffe Public Policy Institute.

Ferreira, A. and W. Winter. 1965. Family Interaction and Decision Making. *Archives of General Psychiatry* 13:214-23.

Galinsky, Ellen, James T. Bond, and Dana E. Friedman. 1993. *The Changing Workforce: Highlights of the National Study*. New York: Families and Work Institute.

Gerstel, Naomi and Harriet Gross, eds. 1987. *Families and Work*. Philadelphia: Temple University Press.

Googins, Bradley K., M. L. Griffin, and J. C. Casey. 1994. *Balancing Job and Homelife: Changes over Time in a Corporation*. Boston: Boston University, Center for Work and Family.

Gordon, Linda. 1988. *Heroes of Their Own Lives: The Politics and History of Family Violence, 1880-1960*. New York: Viking.

Gough, Kathleen. 1972. An Anthropologist Looks at Engels. In *Woman in a Man-Made World: A Socioeconomic*

Handbook, ed. Nona Glazer and Helen Youngelson Waehrer. Chicago: Rand McNally.

Gutman, Herbert G. 1976. *The Black Family in Slavery and Freedom, 1750-1925*. New York: Pantheon.

Hayden, Delores. 1984. *Redesigning the American Dream: The Future of Housing, Work, and Family Life*. New York: Norton.

Hochschild, Arlie Russell. 1997. *The Time Bind: When Work Becomes Home and Home Becomes Work*. New York: Henry Holt.

Hochschild, Arlie and Ann Machung. 1989. *Second Shift: Working Parents and the Revolution at Home*. New York: Viking Penguin.

Jones, Jacqueline. 1985. *Labor of Love, Labor of Sorrow: Black Women, Work, and the Family from Slavery to the Present*. New York: Basic Books.

Kanter, Rosabeth M. 1977. *Work and Family in the United States: A Critical Review and Agenda for Research and Policy*. New York: Russell Sage Foundation.

Kessler-Harris, Alice. 1982. *Out to Work: A History of Wage Earning Women in the United States*. New York: Oxford University Press.

Ladner, Joyce. 1972. *Tomorrow's Tomorrow: The Black Woman*. New York: Harper & Row.

Lamphere, Louise. 1987. *From Working Daughters to Working Mothers: Immigrant Women in a New England Industrial Community*. Ithaca, NY: Cornell University Press.

Lasko, J. K. 1954. Parent Behavior Toward First and Second Children. *Genetic Psychology Monographs* 49:97-137.

Leacock, Eleanor Burke, ed. 1981. *Myths of Male Dominance: Collected Articles on Women Cross-Culturally*. New York: Monthly Review Press.

Leana, Carrie R. and Daniel C. Feldman. 1992. *Coping with Loss: How Individuals, Organizations, and Communities Respond to Layoffs*. New York: Lexington Books.

Listening to America's Families: Action for the 80s. 1980. The report to the president, Congress, and the nation of the White House Conference on Families.

Lynd, R. S. and H. M. Lynd. 1929. *Middletown: A Study in American Culture*. New York: Harcourt, Brace, & World.

Mintz, Steven and Susan Kellogg. 1988. *Domestic Revolutions: A Social History of American Family Life*. New York: Free Press.

Morgan, Lewis Henry. 1877. *Ancient Society*. London: Macmillan.

Osterman, Paul. 1982. Employment Structures Within Firms. *British Journal of Industrial Relations* 20(Nov.):349-61.

———. 1988. *Employment Futures: Reorganization, Dislocation, and Public Policy*. New York: Oxford University Press.

Pappas, Gregory. 1989. *The Magic City: Unemployment in a Working Class Community*. Ithaca, NY: Cornell University Press.

Parsons, Talcott and R. F. Bales. 1969. *Family, Socialization, and Interaction Process*. Glencoe, IL: Free Press.

Pleck, Joseph H. 1993. Are Family-Supportive Employer Policies Relevant to Men? In *Men, Work, and Family*, ed. J. C. Hood. Newbury Park, CA: Sage.

Radcliffe Public Policy Institute. 1997. *The Radcliffe-Fleet Project Report*. Cambridge, MA: Radcliffe Public Policy Institute.

Rapoport, Rhona and Lotte Bailyn. 1996. Relinking Life and Work: Toward a Better Future. A report to the Ford Foundation.

Rayman, Paula M. and Barry Bluestone. 1982. *Out of Work: The Consequences of Unemployment in the Hartford Aircraft Industry*. Chestnut Hill, MA:

Boston College, Social Welfare Research Institute.

Rubin, Lillian. 1976. *Worlds of Pain: Life in a Working Class Community*. New York: Basic Books.

Rubin, Lillian B. 1994. *Families on the Fault Line: America's Working Class Speaks About the Family, the Economy, Race, and Ethnicity*. New York: Harper Collins.

Sacks, Karen. 1974. Engels Revisited: Women, the Organization of Production, and Private Property. In *Women, Culture, and Society*, ed. Michelle Z. Rosaldo and Louise Lamphere. Stanford, CA: Stanford University Press.

Sacks, Karen and Dorothy Remy, eds. 1984. *My Troubles Are Going to Have Trouble with Me: Everyday Trials and Triumphs of Women Workers*. New Brunswick, NJ: Rutgers University Press.

Schor, Juliet. 1992. *The Overworked American: The Unexpected Decline of Leisure*. New York: Basic Books.

Stack, Carol B. 1974. *All Our Kin: Strategies for Survival in a Black Community*. New York: Harper & Row.

Starting Points: Meeting the Needs of Our Youngest Children. 1994. New York: Carnegie Corporation of New York.

Steinberg, Bruce. 1997. *Temporary Help Services: 1996 Performance Review*. Alexandria, VA: National Association of Temporary and Staffing Services.

Thomas, W. T. and F. Znaniecki. 1918. *The Polish Peasant in Europe and America*. Chicago: University of Chicago Press.

Tilly, Louise A. and Joan W. Scott. 1978. *Women, Work, and Family*. New York: Holt, Rinehart, & Winston.

Voydanoff, Patricia. 1990. Economic Distress and Family Relations: A Review of the Eighties. *Journal of Marriage and the Family* 52:1099-1155.

Willie, Charles. 1976. *A New Look at Black Families*. Bayside, NY: General Hall.

Zavella, Patricia. 1987. *Women's Work and Chicano Families: Cannery Workers of the Santa Clara Valley*. Ithaca, NY: Cornell University Press.

Zigler, Edward F. and Meryl Frank. 1988. *The Parental Leave Crisis: Toward a National Policy*. New Haven, CT: Yale University Press.

Zimmerman, Shirley. 1992. *Family Policies and Family Well-Being: The Role of Political Culture*. Newbury Park, CA: Sage.

Book Department

INTERNATIONAL RELATIONS AND POLITICS

GLASER, JAMES M. 1996. *Race, Campaign Politics, and the Realignment in the South.* Pp. xv, 229. New Haven, CT: Yale University Press. $28.50.

Although V. O. Key's *Southern Politics in State and Nation* became a classic work by underscoring the centrality of race in southern politics, the social, economic, and political history of the South made such a conclusion obvious. In *Race, Campaign Politics, and the Realignment in the South*, James Glaser builds on Key's thesis by examining the emergence of the Republican Party in the South in general and in Mississippi, Alabama, Texas, and Virginia in particular. While the Democratic Party has traditionally used race to mobilize southern white support, profound changes in the South in the past 30 years have significantly altered not only the political landscape of the region but also the strategies adopted by both political parties. The dismantling of social, political, legal, and economic structures that effectively excluded meaningful participation of blacks in political life contributed to the infusion of blacks into the electorate. The growing influence of blacks in the political process and in the Democratic Party facilitated the expansion of the Republican Party in the South. Furthermore, economic development in the region gave rise to a large urban and suburban middle class, which became the base of support for the Republican Party. Industrialization and the infusion of northern investment in the South helped to further integrate that region into the rest of the United States, thereby creating new political and economic power centers and necessitating the development of new political strategies. But the racial dichotomy, which often reinforces the widespread perception that economic and social progress enjoyed by Americans of African ancestry comes at the expense of Americans of European ancestry, continues to dominate southern politics.

Instead of relying primarily on public opinion data or electoral data, Glaser emphasizes that participant observation and interviews with various political figures and ordinary voters often yield more accurate information. Downplaying the usefulness of quantitative studies of southern voters, Glaser believes that understanding southern politics comes from knowing about the context in which mass political decisions are made. His detailed analysis of political campaigns in Mississippi and elsewhere clearly demonstrates the usefulness of this methodology, especially when compared to quantitative approaches. His personal observations enrich his description of strategies that Democratic and Republican candidates for Congress have used and their intentions in using them. A central thesis of the book, that Republican progress has been impeded and that the Democratic party's fate was not sealed by the civil rights movement and the political changes it engendered, is strongly supported by the careful analysis that emanates partly from interviews and observation.

Maintaining that issues of race are never far from the minds of southern campaign managers, Glaser stresses that the racial composition of a congressional district determines which strategies will be most effective, how a candidate's time will be spent, which media are to be employed, and which issues will be highlighted. As more whites have left the Democratic Party, largely in response to rising black political influence in it, Republican candidates have emphasized racial issues in an effort to solidify their base. This is particularly the case in areas where growing black electoral power has triggered a white backlash. But Glaser argues that because outright racist appeals are no longer socially acceptable, southern Republicans often camouflage their racial messages as conservatism. For example, when blacks raised questions about flying the Confederate flag, Republicans claimed that the controversy was a "heritage issue." Many southern whites who oppose social and economic equality for blacks now label themselves conservatives in an attempt to appear neutral on racial issues.

Democrats, on the other hand, try to maintain an alliance composed of an increasing number of blacks and a declining white base. While the percentage of black voters identifying themselves as Democrats ranged from 76 to 96 percent during the 1980s, the percentage of blacks identifying themselves as Republicans has remained small, not rising above 12 percent of black voters. Consequently, the Democratic Party has become more responsive to black concerns while the Republican Party has opposed them. Faced with difficulties inherent in maintaining their racial coalitions, Democrats have generally refused to respond to racial issues raised by Republicans. Instead, they attempt to convey two different messages, one to blacks and the other to whites. It is here where Glaser's explanation of Democratic strategies appears weakest. He contends that because of racial segregation, Democratic politicians can reach black voters without having white voters hear their message. But this is virtually impossible in a media-saturated society.

In areas where redistricting has weakened previously predominantly black or white districts, black-white coalitions are likely to emerge. Mike Espy, before becoming secretary of agriculture in the first Clinton administration, exemplifies this approach. By focusing on issues, such as the catfish industry, that transcended racial boundaries, Congressman Espy was able to gain both white and black support. Other Democrats, however, have concentrated on gaining black support and have largely ignored white minorities in their districts. But as issues of class and race intersect and become more complex, a strategy of building biracial and multiracial coalitions is likely to be the most effective.

Although the Republicans have been successful at the presidential level, they have experienced less lower-level electoral success. Glaser gives several reasons for this, chief among them being that it takes time to build a political party. Many southerners are reluctant to run as Republicans for lower-level offices. Furthermore, Democrats, who controlled the electoral machinery throughout the South, better understood campaign strategy and were more capable of building biracial coalitions, something Republicans will have to do to gain dominance.

Despite his detailed analysis of elections at the grassroots level and his nuanced approach demonstrating the complexities of political campaigns in an environment in which race continues to be a significant consideration, Glaser's neglect of the broader national political environment leads him to conclude, erroneously, that many of the political behaviors discussed in his book are almost unique to the South. While race continues to matter, viewing political contests primarily through a racial prism reinforces many of the problems that Glaser believes should be avoided. This problem is underscored by the fact that the author repeatedly reminds the reader that race is always a factor in southern congressional campaigns.

Although the book is well written, its scholarly approach makes it less accessible to a general audience. Nonetheless, this book is likely to be of interest to those who are concerned about race relations in general and voting behavior in particular in the South.

RICHARD J. PAYNE

Illinois State University
Normal

RINEHART, JAMES F. 1997. *Revolution and the Millennium: China, Mexico, and Iran*. Pp. 208. Westport, CT: Praeger. $59.95.

James F. Rinehart's book is an important exploration and analysis of the role of millenarian belief systems in revolutionary movements in three social contexts: China, Iran, and the Indian communities component of the Mexican Revolution. Rinehart identifies the "millenarian paradigm" as "a terrible vision of the present world as an evil one ruled by demonic forces that have to be destroyed through a cleansing violence so that a new age of perfection may be ushered in." The existence of this paradigm within various religious traditions provides a potential mobilizing impetus for mass participation in revolutionary movements in a society characterized by dire social conditions, particularly if such conditions are perceived to have their origin in the incursions and activities of a foreign power.

Beyond its capacity to mobilize the multitude for participation in mass movements, Rinehart argues that a second important revolution-facilitating function of millenarianism lies in its conception that "the forces of justice and righteousness were led by divinely inspired leaders who derived their charismatic powers from the needs and chiliastic yearnings of the people. Millenarianism, thus, acted as a doctrinal platform to elevate a prophet to revolutionary leadership."

Finally, Rinehart proposes that millenarian-like revolutionary movements accomplish social therapy by purging troubled societies of past "burdens of humiliation, frustration, and indignation" and by helping its members establish new positive identities to replace those previously "lost or destroyed" by societal disasters such as political subjugation, economic exploitation, and cultural subversion by another society.

Rinehart has made a significant contribution to our understanding of revolutionary processes in certain societies. But occasionally he may have conceptually imposed too much orderliness on religious millenarian belief systems where the reality was perhaps more chaotic or, as he suggests at times, "vague." For example, he periodically observes that religious millenarianism tends to be backward looking, aspiring to recapture a lost "golden age." But this notion seems to conflict with the repeatedly cited millenarian theme of a supernaturally empowered messiah who would (presumably for the first time) create a new "perfect society." Indeed, Rinehart asserts that the religious millenarian theme of the possibility of the perfection of human society has been a key contribution to modern revolutionary visions.

It might also have been useful for Rinehart to explicitly assess the ability of revolutionary ideologies derived from or influenced by religious millenarianism to accomplish what appears to be the crucial function of providing a unifying motivational theme capable of binding otherwise diverse classes or social groups together in a coordinated revolutionary effort. This was achieved in China and Iran. But the uniqueness of the Mexican Indian millenarian tradition to only one of several major population groups likely prevented it from transforming into a general ideology of the Mexican Revolution and probably contributed to the relative defeat of the goals of this sector of the Mexican Revolution.

On the whole, however, Rinehart has enhanced our comprehension of cultural, psychological, and mobilizing factors involved in revolution.

JAMES DeFRONZO

University of Connecticut
Storrs

ROBINS, ROBERT S. and JERROLD M. POST. 1997. *Political Paranoia: The Psychopolitics of Hatred*. Pp. x, 366. New Haven, CT: Yale University Press. $30.00.

In this psychiatric tour de force, Robert Robins and Jerrold Post boldly claim to demonstrate that "behind every destructive mass movement of this, history's bloodiest century, are the dark forces of political paranoia." What is the basis of the claim, the nature of the demonstration?

The starting assumption is that the concept of paranoia must be expanded beyond its original meaning: an individual psychiatric disorder characterized especially by extreme suspiciousness, along with centrality ("all focuses on me"), grandiosity, fear of loss of autonomy, projection, and delusional thinking. Because it centers on power relationships, paranoia is "the quintessential political disease." The roots of paranoia are both sociobiological and psychological. Suspicion of and aggressiveness toward outsiders, fear and distrust of enemies, the primitive ego defenses of denial, distortion, and delusional projection—these are deeply ingrained traits essential to human survival. "But where is the boundary between adaptive suspicion in the service of detecting deception and pathological paranoia?" the authors ask. Indeed, that is the continuing question as the discussion moves from the characterization of clinical paranoia to observations on the paranoia of groups, cultures, mass movements, and their leading figures.

Drawing the line between psychopathology and normality in political struggles is difficult because severely disturbed people are unlikely to be effective and the social context may or may not be receptive to paranoid messages. What is requisite is a political culture marked by "the paranoid style," meaning that there is a prevalent worldview ("mentality") that sees in all history and politics a hostile conspiracy. The paranoid message in such a context draws on traditional beliefs and images to identify the threatening enemies—as in the scapegoating of witches, Jews, "rich" peasants, and other demonized elements in a population. Entire societies may be paranoid. The cultures of Russia, the Arab Middle East, Israel, Mexico, Vietnam, China, and Malaysia are described as inclined toward paranoid thinking. Whether subsocietal or societal, the paranoia of groups is founded on "the need for enemies." Group identity is consolidated by mobilizing against real or imagined threats and may be most enduring where a traditional enemy also endures, as in the Balkans, Cyprus, and the Middle East.

Like individuals, paranoid groups may experience overwhelming stress and apocalyptic disintegration. Examples are the Jonestown mass suicide, the destruction of the Branch Davidians near Waco, and the Aun Supreme Truth cult's attempt to precipitate the final showdown by the deadly 1995 poison gas attack in the Tokyo subway. These cases anticipate a more general discussion of the "defensive aggression" encouraged by the paranoid themes of Judaism, Christianity, Islam, and Sikhism. Each is portrayed as an instance of "a paranoid social system with a powerful governing idea."

Subsequent chapters explore the theorizing and promotion of paranoid messages, covering a wide range of political movements, organizations, and figures, such as the Christian Identity Movement, the Nation of Islam, the John Birch Society, Lyndon LaRouche, anti-abortion militants, the militia movement, and sundry white (for example, David Duke) and black (for example, Louis Farrakhan) racists. More extensive treatments are accorded paranoids who rose to dominate and terrorize nations: Pol Pot, Idi Amin, Joseph Stalin, Adolf Hitler.

Specialists in political violence will find little new in the descriptive contents of this work but will find provocative the myriad highly speculative analytical observations. Despite their claim, Robins and Post do not succeed in demonstrating that collective political violence is best explained as paranoid symptomatology writ large. No specific criteria are provided for differentiating reasonable from pathological suspicion, or normal from pathological interpretations of mandates to defend one's people, nation, or faith. No clear guidance is given for objectively identifying paranoid belief systems, cultures, messages, or leaders. At bottom, the argument founders in making para-

noia so universal and pervasive that exceptions can hardly be imagined, much less specified. In short, the argument is untestable.

AUSTIN TURK

University of California
Riverside

RUTTAN, VERNON W. 1996. *United States Development Assistance Policy: The Domestic Politics of Foreign Economic Aid.* Pp. xxiv, 657. Baltimore, MD: Johns Hopkins University Press. No price.

In *United States Development Assistance Policy,* Vernon Ruttan, a leading development economist, traces the history of U.S. foreign economic assistance from the end of World War II through the early 1990s. His knowledge of the topic is encyclopedic, which is both the strength and weakness of the book.

United States Development Assistance Policy consists of five parts. Part 1 discusses the domestic sources of U.S. foreign assistance policy and the rationales for providing aid. Part 2 reviews the evolution of U.S. policy from its origins in President Truman's Point Four speech through the end of the 1980s. Part 3 discusses bilateral assistance programs, while part 4 examines multilateral assistance programs. Part 5 discusses proposals for reforming foreign economic assistance programs.

Specialists in development policy will find *United States Development Assistance Policy* to be a required reference. Ruttan discusses almost every aspect of U.S. economic assistance programs, and he conveys this information clearly. By the same token, nonspecialists are likely to find his devotion to detail—which goes so far as to include the observation that the first director-general of the International Labor Organization was a leading

French socialist who died suddenly in 1932—overwhelming. This problem is made worse by the book's tendency to stray from the subject of economic assistance to extended discussions of tangential issues such as the role the press played in Vietnam and the wisdom of public officials' lying to the American people.

The great length of *United States Development Assistance Policy* and its painstaking detail might be less off-putting if they served a larger analytical point. But they do not. Ruttan argues in chapter 1 that "foreign assistance policy [is] at least as responsive to the ebb and flow of domestic, political, economic concerns as to changes in the international political and economic environment." He assumes rather than demonstrates this point, however, and one is left wondering if the relative effects of domestic and external forces can ever be disentangled. At the same time, few scholars would dispute his point that domestic politics affect development assistance (and U.S. foreign policy more generally). The more interesting question is which interests matter and when. Ruttan ignores this question, even after spending 500 pages chronicling specific instances of how domestic interests shape U.S. economic assistance programs.

JAMES M. LINDSAY

University of Iowa
Iowa City

STARRETT, GREGORY. 1998. *Putting Islam to Work: Education, Politics, and Religious Transformation in Egypt.* Pp. xvi, 308. Berkeley: University of California Press. $55.00. Paperbound, $22.00.

Sociologists, anthropologists, Middle East area specialists, historians, and political scientists can learn much from this thoughtful and well-written work. Starrett offers insightful analysis of education and other state-sponsored programs as he explains the persistence of Egypt's contemporary Islamic Trend, *al-tayyar al-islami*. More than a movement, this trend has "become one of the most important contexts in which everyday life is lived." Egypt's Islamic Trend is not due essentially to economic despair or political repression (as many observers argue); rather, it is nurtured by the very state that seeks to destroy it. Through education, the state attempts to define the correct path of Islam, thereby asserting a "moral authority of the state" in order to achieve security and political stability. Beyond the school, the state reinforces its Islamic message through television, radio, print media, publishing houses, and an extensive network of state-run mosques.

Ironically but inevitably, as the state continues to preach its own version of Islam in order to repress Islamist movements that oppose it, it adds to the "Islamization of Egyptian public culture" and further legitimizes the Islamic Trend. It thus invites "radical criticism and increases the hunger for religious resources that cannot be met solely by the public sector."

Even as the *'ulama* ("official" learned men of Islam) lose ground to popular sheikhs, the state dispatches them into society to teach the "correct" Islamic way and to fight extremism. The state uses public school teachers in this battle as well. "The Ministry of Education has recently begun requesting in its teacher-education exams an essay on 'The role of the teacher in combating terrorism,'" a.k.a. Islamic extremism.

So why does the government—which is decidedly not a secular one—persist in promoting any version of Islam? Simply put: if you can't beat 'em, join 'em. But Egypt's way is to try to do both: beat and join them. Starrett shows us that by joining them, the government has fueled its own opposition, both militant and mainstream. (Physically beating them does also.) While offering this explanation for the strength of the Islamic Trend and criticizing the government for helping sustain it, Starrett does not suggest any policy alternatives. Perhaps there is none. The government of Egypt cannot destroy the Islamists without paying too high a price in human lives and international support. Nor can it fully join the Islamists without risking a costly societal backlash or rebellion (and international support).

It appears, then, to be stuck with its own two-faced approach: portions of the government sustaining Islam, through education, the media, and popular culture; portions attempting to curb Islam, through suspect elections, the police, and regulatory agencies. Starrett helps us to understand the "functionalization" of religion, or the manipulation of Islam for political purposes, and explains how the government of Egypt is effective at "putting Islam to work." In so doing, the government sustains the trend that seeks its destruction.

DENIS J. SULLIVAN

Northeastern University
Boston
Massachusetts

*AFRICA, ASIA, AND
LATIN AMERICA*

GARCIA, MARIA CRISTINA. 1996. *Havana USA: Cuban Exiles and Cuban Americans in South Florida, 1959-1994*. Pp. xiii, 290. Berkeley: University of California Press. No price.

María Cristina García's *Havana USA* is a clearly written and well-documented account of Cuban migration to the United States during the second half of the twentieth century. The book consists of two parts: "The Immigration" and "The Emigrés." The first part, with chapters titled "Exiles, Not Immigrants: Cuban Immigration to the United States 1959-1973" and "The Mariel Boatlift of 1980: Origins and Consequences," focuses on the first three waves of immigration: 1959-62, 1964-73 (the so-called freedom flights), and from April to October 1980 (the Mariel boatlift). García points out how each wave of Cuban exiles brought to South Florida a broader representation of Cuban society with regard to socioeconomic status, race, ethnicity, and geographic distribution. How Cubans from different migratory waves perceive one another is also discussed, as is why the overwhelming majority of Cuban exiles have chosen to migrate to the United States (as opposed to Spanish-speaking countries). García also explores the reaction of the United States to the Cuban influx, whether on the part of the average citizen, the North American Catholic church, numerous voluntary relief services, or the print media. She highlights how state and federal government agencies, through special aid programs and legislation, responded to the needs of the new immigrants; and how in a period when the Cold War was being waged Cubans on U.S. soil became symbols of anti-Communism who eventually managed to have enormous influence on U.S. foreign policy toward the Castro regime.

The second part of *Havana USA* is made up of three chapters: "Defining an Identity in the United States," "The Evolution of Cuban Exile Politics," and "Cuban Writers and Scholars in Exile." As the different titles suggest, these chapters deal with issues of identity, assimilation, and biculturalism; the diverse and conflicting political views within the Cuban community on U.S. politics toward Cuba; and the role of Cuban exiles in local, county, and state politics. García gives a thorough overview of literary and artistic contributions of the émigré Cuban community. She carefully details how this group of Cubans has helped to shape local media, views on assimilation, and the field of education in South Florida. She continues with her analysis of how Americans perceive the now well-established and successful Cuban community. The same people who welcomed the first group of exiles in 1959, García emphasizes, now question the émigrés' obsession with their homeland and their refusal to assimilate, especially with regard to their constant use of Spanish. García contends that Cuban exiles do not see a contradiction between being American and at the same time wanting to maintain, and pass on to their children, their emotional ties to their homeland, their customs, their traditions, and, above all, their language. Each new wave of immigrants, García explains, has reinforced this attitude. The émigrés' perspective is that they have readily assimilated into the American fabric. As proof, they point to an annual income almost the equal of the national average, extraordinarily high naturalization and voter registration rates, successful entrepreneurship, and powerful political lobbies in Washington.

In her conclusion, García enumerates the ever present concerns of what will happen once there is a change of guard in Cuba. Will older Cuban émigrés, who once called themselves exiles and hoped only for a short sojourn in the United States, return to their homeland? Will their children, born in the United States and a hybrid of the societies in which they were raised, want to move to a country they know only through stories told by their parents and grandparents? Will more Cubans come to the United States looking for better economic opportunities? Will Cubans who stayed on the island and those who left learn to come to terms with each other? Will the strong Cuban community of South Florida be willing to share its power base with new immigrants from Latin America, and will they attain a more harmonious relationship with Miami's African American community?

María Cristina García's book provides a lucid, balanced, and insightful understanding of the Cuban American experience. It is a must-read book for anyone interested in the history of Cuban immigration, for those engaged in the study of identity and assimilation patterns of immigrant groups, and for anyone interested in the history of South Florida.

GLADYS M. VARONA-LACEY

Ithaca College
New York

WILLIAMS, PHILIP J. and KNUT WALTER. 1997. *Militarization and Democratization in El Salvador's Transition to Democracy*. Pp. ix, 244. Pittsburgh, PA: University of Pittsburgh Press. $45.00. Paperbound, $19.95.

The January 1992 peace accord between the government of El Salvador and the FMLN (Farabundo Martí National Liberation Front) leftist rebels ended a protracted civil war that ravaged the small Central American country and, with it, the 65-year military domination of the nation's politics. These developments, in turn, invigorated the process of demilitarization and democratization of the Salvadoran society that was initiated in the 1980s.

The long and turbulent nature of Salvadoran civil-military relations requires detailed historical knowledge as well as sophisticated methodological skills. It took the combined efforts of two social scientists, a political scientist (Williams) and a historian (Walter), to navigate through a complex web of over six decades of social upheaval and peace, coups and countercoups, and militarization and democratization to produce this impressive and well-crafted volume.

Williams and Walter begin with a review of the relevant literature and correctly decide that the concepts of militarization and demilitarization are the most appropriate to the Salvadoran case. In their minds, these two terms not only "presuppose intervention and disengagement, respectively, [but] they imply much more." Militarization and demilitarization define "the sources of the military's power, how it uses its power, and the limits of that power."

The direct involvement of the Salvadoran military commences with the 1931 coup and the countercoup that followed, which came at the heels of an intense competition between the coffee oligarchy and the newly modernized military. Effort for more social justice by the restless but marginalized lower classes complicated the country's political landscape, as did regional conditions and American hegemonic intentions. In time, divisions in Salvadoran society and international developments (including the Cuban Revolution) affected the attitudes and behavior of the military. Ever since then, the Salvadoran armed forces enjoyed a privileged status; political developments in the country were initiated and controlled by the military.

The political crisis of the 1970s and the bloody civil war that followed forced the military to seek a solution to the country's problems by aligning itself with moderate and reform-oriented political groups. In so doing, the Salvadoran military once again initiated a process of demilitarization and democratization. While the army and the civilian-led government sought to defeat the FMLN rebels, parallel negotiations eventually produced the 1992 peace accord. Williams and Walter conclude this excellent volume by analyzing the shrinking role of the army and speculating on the future of Salvadoran civil-military relations.

CONSTANTINE P.
DANOPOULOS

San José State University
California

EUROPE

FRIEND, JULIUS W. 1998. *The Long Presidency: France in the Mitterrand Years, 1981-1995.* Pp. xii, 308. Boulder, CO: Westview Press. $40.00.

In this study of contemporary political history, Julius Friend provides concise yet comprehensive coverage of France during François Mitterrand's 14-year tenure as head of state. The book discusses the most important aspects of the politics of that period, including Mitterrand's transformation of a moribund Socialist Party into an effective means for his ascent to the presidency. In this process, Mitterrand, who never fully believed in socialism, removed from his party most of its traditional ideological content. He also manipulated and used his political associates and often discarded or betrayed them. The book is particularly revealing about Mitterrand's complicated relationships with Rocard, Jospin, and Bérégovoy. A consistent theme that emerges from the treatment of intraparty and interparty relationships in France is that personal ambition has been far more important than programmatic or ideological consistency. Mitterrand's Machiavellian comportment is illustrated by his surviving the scandals that marred his presidency: the use of HIV-contaminated blood for transfusions; money laundering; and dealings with terrorists.

This book constitutes a fair-minded treatment, giving credit or blame where it is due. Major achievements of the period are discussed: the enhancement of civil liberties; the extension of the power of trade unions; the pluralization of the media; the liberalization of citizenship laws; and the preparation of the country for fuller integration in a united Europe. Certain institutional innovations are emphasized: decentralization, the reduction of the number of simultaneously held elective offices, and the orderly transition from Gaullism to post-Gaullism and power sharing ("cohabitation") within the existing constitutional context. The book does not ignore significant policy failures, especially with respect to employment, the nationalization of industries, and school reforms.

Friend is particularly strong on foreign policy. He explores several seemingly permanent themes: France's nuclear nationalism; *francophonie*; the special relationship with Africa (a relationship marked by a combination of old-fashioned imperialism and paternalism); the chronic pro-Arabism and hostility to Israel; competition with Germany; and participation in peacekeeping and humanitarian operations, sprinkled with continuing attempts to assert France's "presence" on the global diplomatic stage. Here, too, Friend does not overlook the country's disappointments. France was unable to prevent the reunification of Germany, the disintegration of Yugoslavia, the de facto destruction of Lebanon as an independent state, or the outbreak of the Persian Gulf war.

Friend's well-informed chronology is coupled with an analysis of Mitterrand's historical record and image—marred by revelations about his Vichy past, his continued friendship with a notorious collaborator, and his reluctance to help prosecute war criminals. Mitterrand shared de Gaulle's artfully constructed national mythology about the Resistance and about the Vichy state as a mere his-torical parenthesis that had nothing to do with the "real" France and no continuity with the ensuing republic.

The book is well documented. Friend makes full use of Mitterrand's own writings and of existing biographies, complemented by personal interviews with numerous politicians.

WILLIAM SAFRAN

University of Colorado
Boulder

LOWRY, BULLITT. 1996. *Armistice 1918*. Pp. xv, 245. Kent, OH: Kent State University Press. $35.00.

For over half a century, those interested in a detailed account of the 1918 armistice with Germany have relied on Harry R. Rudin's book with the same title (New Haven, CT: Yale University Press, 1944). At that time, the archives were still closed. A few works whose authors had access to additional materials had appeared since, but no one had retraced the fundamental issues with the attention to broader context and research in newly opened archives until Bullitt Lowry decided to do so.

On the whole, this book is an extremely carefully and thoughtfully produced piece of research and writing. Examining the now available archival materials in Great Britain, France, and the United States, and utilizing the most recent scholarly literature on the subject, Lowry has provided readers with what is likely to be the definitive account of a major event. Unfortunately, unlike Rudin, Lowry did not (could not?) include the texts of the armistices with all the Central Powers, but he has made a major contribution by tracing the interrelationship of the debates within each of the major powers with current developments at the front and the calls for an armistice by Germany's allies.

Two significant aspects of the discussion come across clearly. First, there are the differences between the French, British, Italians, and Americans as well as the emerging ones between the Italians and the Serbs. Second, there is the general expectation until the very last moment that fighting would be likely to continue for weeks, perhaps months, before Germany signed. While the former point is generally recognized, the latter has disappeared in the light of hindsight.

Lowry shows how Edward House at times did not implement the instructions President Woodrow Wilson provided; he is also sensitive to the extent to which the British, and possibly others, deciphered the exchanges between the two. He also convincingly explains the contemporary views of General John Pershing, who favored an armistice but worried that Wilson might approve one that would be too lenient.

Unfortunately, Lowry is not familiar with Raymond G. O'Connor's *Diplomacy for Victory: FDR and Unconditional Surrender* (New York: Norton, 1971), which demonstrates the great influence of the 1918 armistice, as opposed to a demand for unconditional surrender, on World War II policy. There are also dubious assertions about reparations and the 1919 peace terms that the scholarship of recent decades has discredited. But these are minor matters. What the reader sees is the attempts by an alignment of disparate countries engaged in a struggle for national interest during a bloody conflict all attempting to bring into the ending of that war as much as possible of their aims for the future. This was surely no easy task, and Lowry has traced its accomplishment in exemplary fashion.

GERHARD L. WEINBERG

University of North Carolina
Chapel Hill

TSOUKALIS, LOUKAS. 1997. *The New European Economy Revisited*. Pp. xiii, 306. New York: Oxford University Press. Paperbound, $19.95.

When *The New European Economy* was first published in 1991, it was rightly received as a significant contribution to the literature on European integration. Loukas Tsoukalis first briefly reviewed the history of postwar European integration, emphasizing its revitalization in the 1980s with the European Community's program for the completion of the Single Market by the end of 1992; he then provided a close examination of various aspects of the European political economy. He contended that regional integration was in many respects incompatible with the postwar European commitment to mixed economies organized along national lines and that further trade liberalization resulting from the Single Market program would only make these incompatibilities more apparent.

Subsequent developments have borne out this analysis, meriting a second edition in 1993. The book presently under review revises the narrative still further while adding several new chapters, justifying the addition to the original title ("revisited"). The historical review now includes attention to the negotiation of the Maastricht Treaty and its cool reception by European publics; the analysis of monetary policy has been divided into two chapters, one focusing on exchange-rate stabilization under the European Monetary System and the other on the proposed European monetary union; and a new concluding chapter introduces 10 theses on European integration.

Tsoukalis finds that economic integration, particularly in its latter stages, is necessarily invasive of national sovereignty and that it has generally weakened the power of the state either to (re)allocate resources or to stabilize markets. He provides a pragmatic account of both the policy and the political implications of economic and monetary union, and likewise assesses the European Union's planned expansion into Central Europe. While Tsoukalis's 10 theses provide an excellent point of departure for advanced classroom discussion, it does bear noting that the book presupposes a familiarity with both postwar European history and contemporary policy issues that is probably beyond the reach of most American undergraduates.

In essence, the new concluding chapter distills a political analysis of European economic integration that was more diffuse in previous editions. But it was never the boldness of Tsoukalis's analysis that generated attention; rather, it was the remarkable breadth of his synoptic account of the major features of Europe's political economy. The new chapters renew the topicality of the book and underline its central message: that there are no easy solutions to the inherent conflict between Europe's national political structures and its regional market.

DAVID M. ANDREWS

Scripps College
Claremont
California

UNITED STATES

AMENTA, EDWIN. 1998. *Bold Relief: Institutional Politics and the Origins of Modern American Social Policy*. Pp. xii, 343. Princeton, NJ: Princeton University Press. $39.50.

This exploration of American social policy begins with a stunning table that shows that in 1938 America spent more of its gross domestic product on social programs than did any industrial nation in the world. By the end of the New Deal decade, in other words, America was the world leader in the development of a welfare state. Instead of telling the usual story about America's backward welfare state, Amenta attempts to explain something more complex. In some eras, such as the late nineteenth century and again in the 1930s, America created relatively generous social programs. In other times, such as the 1940s, America's commitment to these programs lagged behind that of other nations. Just as historical sociologists have uncovered a precocious welfare state in the late nineteenth century based on the expansions of Civil War pensions, so Amenta has rediscovered the existence of the Works Progress Administration (WPA). He makes it clear that the work relief programs were the primary vehicles for the expansion of social welfare spending during the 1930s.

Concerned with both historical narrative and sociological explanation, Amenta develops a theory of institutional politics to analyze changes in social policy over time. His chief contribution lies in his attention to the link between democracy and the expansion of social programs. At the beginning of this century, restrictive electoral practices made it difficult for Congress to pass social welfare legislation. The situation changed with the realignment that brought the Democrats to power. Furthermore, this realignment came about not so much by voters' switching parties but by the increased participation of voters who previously had been discouraged or banned from voting.

Eventually, this realignment led to the creation of the Social Security Act and the WPA. In thinking about the contents of such pieces of legislation, Amenta argues that institutions matter. Hence, the existence of a state program to cover the risk of, say, unemployment precluded a federal unemployment insurance program.

What distinguishes Amenta's analysis from that of his colleagues is that it is dynamic in nature. Gains made by a reform-oriented executive branch can be lost, as, in fact, they were during the 1940s. In that decade, the polity again constricted, and congressmen not predisposed toward social spending eliminated the WPA. The situation was different in Great Britain, not so much because of Britain's commitment to a welfare state but, rather, because of political and institutional factors.

Nicely written, with little of the jargon that degrades sociology, this book should help to reorient our thinking on the development of American social policy. We tend to get fixated on individual aspects of social welfare policy. Helping us to see the larger picture, Amenta makes us realize what has been missing.

EDWARD D. BERKOWITZ

George Washington University
Washington, D.C.

CARR, LESLIE G. 1997. *"Color-Blind" Racism*. Pp. ix, 192. Thousand Oaks, CA: Sage. $45.00. Paperbound, $21.95.

Reckonings with the "unfinished business" of the nation's founding typically have been characterized by prolonged and painful challenge to the established order, consequent redirection of the law, and subsequent limiting principles that ameliorate the impact of legal change. Slavery was undone formally by the Thirteenth Amendment but reintroduced in fact by black codes and peonage. Reconstruction's limitations on regressive tendencies were marginalized by, among other things, the separate-but-equal doctrine. This premise was displaced by the desegregation mandate, which eventually was cramped by principles limiting the basis, reach, and duration of constitutional responsibilities. Contemporary insistence upon a color-blind Constitution defines an equal protection guarantee

that is calibrated to defeat overt racial preferences (including affirmative action programs) but not the subtle discrimination and unconscious racism that most commonly affect historically disadvantaged minorities in the post-*Brown* era.

Some might view the repetitious pattern of change and resistance as a quintessential dialectic yielding a normative synthesis of incremental rather than wholesale progress, or as an indication that legal change provides a tempting shortcut but ultimately poor substitute for moral reckoning. Others, such as Leslie Carr, interpret the racial landscape as the preordained sculpting of its material base. Carr possesses an enviably sophisticated grasp of Marxist theory. His use of it as the prism through which to view racial reality, however, trades largely on conclusory observations rather than on amplification of why such doctrine should have the interpretive edge over other perspectives. It is Carr's assertion rather than persuasion, for instance, that challenges a less dogmatic sense that human beings individually and collectively tend to prioritize and rationalize pursuant to what they perceive as their self-interest.

From Carr's perspective, American society is governed by "an inverted constitution" that is created by an "inverted material world" and interpreted by "color-blind conservatives" who "stand in a line of ideologists that reaches back to the dawn of inequality in human societies." Observations like these vie with varying perspectives that typically demand more than the author's say-so as a condition for releasing them. Some view the Constitution as a mere baseline rather than a box, for instance, or would equate color blindness with the desegregation mandate as an exercise in fast-forwarding the law beyond society's moral development. Minus an explanation for bypassing competing interpretations or understandings, the reader may accept Carr's findings as self-evident or sense a somewhat underachieved mission. Compounding any impression of incompleteness is an unusually high rate of technical glitches that range from misspellings (for example, "Jessie" Jackson, "*Plessey*" v. *Ferguson*, "Gunner" Myrdal) to imprecise or ambiguous characterizations of legal doctrine or case law.

The bottom line is that Carr affords some valuable historical insight into racial reality, effectively illuminates the artificiality of race as a cultural concept, challenges the reader to decide whether indifference to competing perspectives or technical editorial quality should influence judgment of the book's substantive merit, and probably will have his work product judged on the basis of whether the reader sings in his or some other choir.

DONALD E. LIVELY

Florida Coastal School of Law
Jacksonville

GERHARDT, MICHAEL J. 1996. *The Federal Impeachment Process: A Constitutional and Historical Analysis.* Pp. xiii, 233. Princeton, NJ: Princeton University Press. $29.95.

Impeachment is in the air again, which means that the air quality cannot be good. Michael Gerhardt's book is thus nothing if not timely. Moreover, Gerhardt had the advantage both of the extensive literature that attended the impeachment proceedings involving President Nixon (who resigned before the full House voted on the articles of impeachment) and of the perspective and information that the passage of time and intervening developments have afforded. The most significant of those developments were the impeachment proceedings against three federal judges in the late 1980s, a Supreme Court decision

sharply limiting if not foreclosing altogether judicial review of impeachment proceedings, and the work of the National Commission on Judicial Discipline and Removal, whose report was issued in 1993.

Although timely, free of the partisan baggage with which some of the Watergate impeachment literature is freighted, and informed by more recent historical scholarship, Gerhardt's book has little that is original or otherwise interesting to the serious scholar and much that will puzzle or bore the intelligent nonspecialist. The best parts of the book for the latter are the material in part 1 on the historical origins of the process (pages 1-21), chapter 9 on the scope of impeachable offenses (pages 103-11), and the first part of chapter 11 on judicial review of impeachments (pages 118-23). A scholar or nonspecialist who continues to read in chapter 11, however, is likely to be put off—as elsewhere in the book—by Gerhardt's undiscriminating catalogues of arguments pro and con, by his inability clearly to convey his meaning, and ultimately by the suspicion that on some points there is simply less there than meets the eye (for example, pages 139-43). In that regard, it should be noted that the text ends on page 178.

Withal, as politicians engage in irresponsible talk about impeaching federal judges for judicial decisions that the politicians (or their constituents) deplore, and the prospect of impeachment proceedings against a president (at the time of writing) confronts us again, it is useful to have Gerhardt's reassurance that in the past, when push has come to shove, our politicians have acted responsibly. That is particularly good news because, as Gerhardt describes, what politicians do in the griffinlike court of impeachment—where senators sit "on Oath or Affirmation" in proceedings that may be presided over by the chief justice of the United States—is unlikely to be reviewable in a court of law. Guess who urged the Court to reach that result on behalf of the United States? Kenneth W. Starr.

STEPHEN B. BURBANK

University of Pennsylvania
Philadelphia

GURSTEIN, ROCHELLE. 1996. *The Repeal of Reticence: A History of America's Cultural and Legal Struggles over Free Speech, Obscenity, Sexual Liberation, and Modern Art*. Pp. ix, 357. New York: Hill & Wang. $27.50.

Impassioned and meticulously documented, *The Repeal of Reticence* argues that under the banner of free speech, the United States has drifted too far toward license. Magazines and movies bombard with images of sex and nudity. Major newspapers race to titillate with details of the sex lives of public figures. Art shocks with depictions of bodily functions and homoerotic activities. Intellectuals worship mass culture and Madonna, while the American Civil Liberties Union rushes to defend high school students who circulate crude, racist booklets that depict a black principal skewered on a dart board with the caption, "What would happen if I shot [principal Timothy] Dawson in the head?"

What has become, Rochelle Gurstein asks, of taste, decorum, and reticence? In a society where everything is known, mystery dissolves, privacy ceases to exist, and love becomes a mere clinical exercise. Taking a position that is decidedly unpopular, Gurstein writes that dogma, intolerance, and speech repression are not key threats today. Rather, it is our lack of reticence or impulse control, and the resulting coarsening of public life.

How did we end up this way? Gurstein reviews America's historical struggles over obscenity, sexual liberation, and art, showing that the "party of exposure"

(pornographers, tabloid newspaper writers, and shock artists) got the upper hand by means of the progressive science of sexology, sensationalistic newspapers, and realistic fiction, all abetted by a legal establishment that relentlessly defended free speech over all other social values. Defenders of the "party of reticence" were laughed at as prudes and hypocrites, dismissed as censors, or accused of assisting in a guilty cover-up.

A fine book with a strong, textured argument, *The Repeal of Reticence* would have been even better had Gurstein addressed the economic side of the party of exposure. Simply put, sex sells, and it is easier to market cheap situation comedies than Dostoyevsky. A $2 billion a year industry, pornography is defended by a vast public relations industry and lawyers. Her book also might have addressed a paradox implicit in our society's attitude toward exposure versus reticence: we both want and shrink from knowledge at the same time. In an age of AIDS, it is vital to know where danger lies, even if the information is distasteful or unromantic.

Still, *The Repeal of Reticence* is a powerful book and a fine read. It is good to see cultural criticism coming from someone unlike Robert Bork—whose bombastic *Slouching Toward Gomorrah* is calculated to offend even the reticent—someone with taste and conviction who does not write out of conservative or fundamentalist principle.

RICHARD DELGADO

University of Colorado
Boulder

KWASNY, MARK V. 1996. *Washington's Partisan War, 1775-1783*. Pp. ix, 425. Kent, OH: Kent State University Press. $35.00.

The myth that citizen-soldiers—symbolized by the Minutemen militia at Lexington and Concord—held primary responsibility for America's success in the Revolution was shattered and then replaced early in this century by an equally forceful argument that made Washington's professional Continental Army the real heroes in the war against Britain. In recent decades, however, the pendulum has started back again as a new group of military historians have provided a more evenhanded treatment of the contributions made by both regular and partisan forces. Mark V. Kwasny's book adds significantly to that new and balanced story.

Students of the American Revolution have long appreciated the violent civil war that raged in the Carolinas between patriot and loyalist partisan bands; most are equally aware of the unorthodox, guerrilla-like tactics employed by the patriot Swamp Fox, Francis Marion, and the infamous loyalist Banastre Tarleton. Yet Kwasny argues that partisan warfare was confined neither to the South nor to these well-known commanders. Such activity—admittedly less brutal—also occurred throughout the war in the states surrounding New York City, and the commander and strategist of those partisan campaigns was none other than George Washington.

Most histories of the war point to Washington's disdain for the militia as a regular fighting force. Clearly, Washington knew from experiences in the French and Indian War that militia units were disorderly, undisciplined, unreliable, and often disobedient, but, according to Kwasny, he also understood some of their positive attributes. As the war progressed, he learned how to use these attributes effectively.

At the start of the war, Washington envisioned an eventual fighting force consisting of two parts: a large, professionally trained regular army used in direct engagements with the enemy, and separate militia units tasked with defending towns and coastal areas from surprise attacks. As Kwasny points out, however, a combination of factors—Congress's inability to give him the regular army he desired, militia failures as defense forces, and the necessity to use combined units in some campaigns—forced Washington to continually adjust his initial policy. Over the course of the war, he learned that militia members were indeed unreliable reinforcements for regulars, lost their enthusiasm waiting for possible attacks, and could not hold areas against sizable British forces without Continental Army support. They could, however, stop Tory recruiting in the countryside, harass and annoy British encampments, act as a forward defense shield, gather intelligence, significantly slow down enemy advances, and fight long and hard once an actual attack occurred.

Based on a thorough examination of the private and public correspondence of major participants as well as congressional and state papers, Kwasny provides a straightforward narrative and convincing analysis of the evolving role of partisan units in the American Revolution while increasing our appreciation of Washington's complex understanding of their usefulness and specialized capabilities.

JOHN G. KOLP

U.S. Naval Academy
Annapolis
Maryland

MANFREDI, CHRISTOPHER P. 1998. *The Supreme Court and Juvenile Justice*. Pp. xvi, 256. Lawrence: University of Kansas. $35.00.

During the latter part of the sixties, the Supreme Court in its *Kent* and *Gault* decisions transformed the traditional juvenile court. The contemporary juvenile court that emerged was a product of not only those decisions but also the political and social ramifications that they produced. This is the important point that Christopher Manfredi repeatedly drives home by uncovering a wide range of background details leading to those important Supreme Court decisions.

The book mainly focuses on the case of Gerald Gault, a juvenile who was sent to Arizona's reform school for making an obscene phone call. The nonadversarial manner in which Gault was quickly adjudicated delinquent paved the way for a sweeping set of decisions that were to guarantee juveniles the right to counsel and other due-process-oriented rights. In describing the Gault case, Manfredi shows us that decision making went beyond the intended best interests of the state and the child.

In addition to *Gault*, Manfredi also considers the *Kent* decision and the subsequent consequences of related cases. The *Kent* decision was the first step on a legal road toward criminalization that the Court could not possibly anticipate. It involved a case of waiver in which judicial discretion was used without any formal hearing of the facts. The *Kent* decision led the Court to the *Gault* decision, with its more sweeping set of reforms. Both decisions changed the composition of juvenile justice by allowing other political and social concerns to address the manner in which juvenile courts are to operate. This is most obviously reflected in the contemporary criminalization of juvenile justice.

The criminalization of juvenile justice has produced a political legislative agenda that could not have possibly been anticipated by the initial *Kent* and *Gault* decisions. Both reforms have led to numerous commission reports that have advocated change in the manner in which juveniles are defined as delinquent or as

offenders. Criminalization has not only increased the eligible population of juveniles ending up in the criminal court; it also has divided populations of juveniles into more diverse legal categories.

Too often our debates about juvenile justice are uninformed by the prior sets of assumptions that have led to the system's current state of being. This book goes a long way toward filling that void by pointing to the particular direction of current and future juvenile justice reforms.

SIMON I. SINGER

State University of New York
Buffalo

REEVES, KEITH. 1998. *Voting Hopes or Fears? White Voters, Black Candidates and Racial Politics in America.* Pp. xv, 177. New York: Oxford University Press. $39.95. Paperbound, $16.95.

This book joins the public debate and dialogue about the electability of minority candidates in majority-white political districts. It brings to the debate and dialogue an empirically based argument and interpretation. Unlike so many tracts and treatises on the subject that are scholarly advocacy and political posturing, this is a brilliant and insightful exposition and discussion. There is nothing like it on the intellectual horizon. It is judicious in its argument, careful in its description and discussion, and meticulous about its quantitative findings. It is a well-reasoned, sophisticatedly written, and substantively based book.

Reeves states his thesis thus: "It is my contention . . . that the paucity of black officeholders from non-majority-black areas is due in significant part to the continued racial animus underlying whites' political thinking and voting behavior." Conventional wisdom says and contends otherwise. In fact, numerous conservatives, both black and white, in and out of academia, on the Supreme Court, in both the print and electronic media, in elected and appointive office as well as on the news and talk shows and magazines, proffer the position that the Voting Rights Act is now a form of affirmative action and has outlived its usefulness. Reeves tests this assumption and argument.

Using methodological pluralism, electoral data from the state of Louisiana, attitudinal data from the 1992 Detroit Area Study, a content analysis of newspaper coverage of biracial campaigns in New York and Seattle, polling data from California's 1982 gubernatorial race, and a carefully controlled experiment affords Reeves the right to conclude that "race-conscious districting—albeit imperfect—is a demonstrably effective action that brings about a level playing field for black office-seekers." However, long before Reeves reaches this conclusion about a remedial course of action, he empirically demonstrates that "black office-seekers who compete in majority-white settings in the main are unable to attract consistent widespread support because race perniciously influences both the tenor of their electoral campaigns and their outcomes." Reeves arrives at his policy recommendations not only by the sheer weight of the data and the current nature of things. Theory and data in this book are supplemented from and superbly contextualized in practice and reality. Serving as an expert witness in the *Hays* v. *Louisiana III* case for the late judge, jurist, and legal scholar A. Leon Higginbotham, Jr., he uncovered the nature, scope, significance, and continuance of racially polarized voting in Louisiana, the South, and America. Overall, I highly recommend this innovative work to laypeople, academicians, and policymakers alike.

HANES WALTON, JR.

University of Michigan
Ann Arbor

RUDY, WILLIS. 1996. *A Campus and a Nation in Crisis: From the American Revolution to Vietnam*. Pp. viii, 263. Madison and Teaneck, NJ: Fairleigh Dickinson University Press. No price.

Willis Rudy offers a useful survey of the reaction on American campuses to war. His book covers five wars and draws on an extensive secondary literature to show that campuses were closely involved with the national war effort during the American Revolution, the Civil War, World War I, World War II, and the Vietnam war. Rudy persuasively argues that campuses generated debate about national involvement in warfare. He contends that in these "crucial periods," "colleges and universities" "played an important part" in determining national decisions. An extensive bibliography allows readers to move directly from the text to promising areas for further research.

As Rudy's thesis statement shows, he paints with a broad brush. No specialist will contest that campuses participated in national debates surrounding wartimes. Still, selection of subject and materials will leave readers who want a more definitive treatment unsatisfied. By selecting certain conflicts and omitting the unpopular Mexican War of 1848 and the Spanish American War of 1898, Rudy leaves the impression that opposition to war is exclusively a twentieth-century phenomenon. His reliance on secondary literature creates an uneven treatment of the reaction to each war. For example, his treatment of World War II ends with

Pearl Harbor and the nation's official entry into that war, while he discusses Vietnam to the time of Richard Nixon's Vietnamization policy and the winding down of American involvement. Further, his story excludes discussion of the many ways in which campuses actually involved themselves in war. For instance, in World War II, some colleges started aviation programs; others tried to maintain enrollments by persuading students that they would serve their country better by completing their college degree and then enlisting.

Rudy's selection of secondary materials creates a story about what happened mainly on the campuses of larger, eastern colleges and universities. His bibliography contains no mention of recent excellent histories of Middlebury College or Wesleyan University, for instance. The story of how historically black colleges and women's colleges involved themselves in wartime debates lies beyond this book's purview. African Americans enter Rudy's story not at all, and women only with relation to the institution of coeducation at northern universities during the Civil War. Rudy thus misses several good stories, such as the campaign of African Americans for a fully integrated military and the termination of Emily Balch in 1919 from Wellesley College for her political and religious opposition to World War I.

Perhaps because Rudy sees no downside to campus engagement with national wartime agendas, he never assesses the cost to scholarship and speech that wartime engagement brought. From the Revolution through Vietnam, those who questioned activists' agendas have suffered, and Rudy's celebration of engagement leads him to ignore or minimize instances when students and administrators trampled on the rights of a minority to express itself.

This book provides general readers with a good read, and students of American higher education with a starting point for more complete and analytical studies.

LOUISE L. STEVENSON

Franklin and Marshall College
Lancaster
Pennsylvania

WILKINS, DAVID E. 1997. *American Indian Sovereignty and the U.S. Supreme Court: The Masking of Justice.* Pp. xv, 403. Austin: University of Texas Press. $40.00. Paperbound, $24.95.

When the Native American Rights Fund, Indian leaders, and other legalists sit down and begin the inevitable challenges to the spurious precedents that have characterized U.S. Supreme Court decisions concerning Native Americans in the nineteenth and twentieth centuries—*Plessy* v. *Ferguson*–like decisions, such as *Lone Wolf* v. *Hitchcock* (1903) and *United States* v. *Kagama* (1886), among others—David Wilkins needs to be at the table, and this book should be required reading for everyone gathered. Indeed, this book should be a part of every constitutional law course and on the reading lists of Native America specialists as well as political scientists; lawyers and law professors; historians, anthropologists, and sociologists; tribal, state, and federal judges; and, perhaps most important, U.S. Supreme Court clerks and U.S. Congress legislative aides.

The primary theme of this book is embraced in the subtitle, *The Masking of Justice.* Wilkins seeks to demythologize the law by closely analyzing 15 Supreme Court decisions. These decisions include very important yet less known cases, from *Johnson* v. *McIntosh* (1823) and the

Cherokee Tobacco case (1871) of the nineteenth century to *Northwestern Bands of Shoshone Indians* v. *United States* (1945) and *County of Yakima* v. *Confederated Tribes and Bands of the Yakima* [subsequent to this case, the "Yakima" Nation officially returned to the original spelling of its people's designation, "Yakama"] *Indian Nation* (1992) of the twentieth century. The cases are discussed with reference to other well-known Supreme Court decisions as well as significant federal and state statutes. Wilkins deciphers case text and logic, places them in their historical setting, and assesses their legal significance. It is an unmasking process that is very effective. Having read this book, one cannot return to these cases and see them in the same light as before.

Just what Wilkins masterfully accomplishes is what he says he will do. He shows that

justices of the Supreme Court, both individually and collectively, have engaged in the manufacturing, redefining, and burying of "principles," "doctrines," and legal "tests" to excuse and legitimize constitutional, treaty, and civil rights violations of tribal nations and, in some cases, of individual Indians. (297)

The legal legacy is an amazing one. There are moot cases that become constitutional watershed decisions; there are wholesale misreadings of legal records; there are gross distortions of history written into law. The litany is not surprising to those scholars who have been working in this field; what is so startling is the comprehensiveness of the abuse of law and justice that has been done and continues to plague our nation's leading legal thinkers. Just as Roger Taney became infamous for presenting fraudulent legal logic in the nineteenth century, so have Antonin Scalia and William Rehnquist authored even greater jurisprudential dementia in more recent decisions.

This is a book about sovereignty and its steady erosion. It is a book about power and its abuse. It is a book about justice and its fleeting nature. Here is a clarion call for the careful examination of Indian legal relationships within the American governmental framework. For treaties to be meaningful and for the founding political and moral principles of the United States to be realized, legal relationships need to be rebuilt based upon a key word or concept stressed by Wilkins, that of consent.

JOHN R. WUNDER

University of Nebraska
Lincoln

WILLIAMS, LOU FALKNER. 1996. *The Great South Carolina Ku Klux Klan Trials, 1871-1872.* Pp. xiii, 197. Athens: University of Georgia Press. $35.00.

Lou Falkner Williams's careful, detailed account of South Carolina's Ku Klux Klan trials provides an excellent case study of the tragic inadequacies of congressional Reconstruction. The story is a familiar one. An "ambiguous national policy" overwhelmed by an "unflinching" resistance from white Southerners, who considered the prospect of racial equality "unthinkable" and the Reconstruction government of South Carolina illegitimate. When white South Carolinians failed to restore white supremacy in the 1870 elections, they instituted a Klan-directed reign of terror that lasted for almost a year and resulted in many deaths, countless whippings, and other inhumane acts. Williams's description of the numerous atrocities perpetrated by the Klan is precise and vivid. It is accompanied by a sensitive explanation of white Southern fears, as well as a compelling presentation of African American aspirations for land, political rights, and education.

The South Carolina up-country was the focus of Klan activity. There the white and black populations were nearly equal and the tax burden on the white farmers particularly severe. In this setting, whites viewed African American demands for equality as a "provocation," and their participation in the militia as unacceptable. The Klan response, Williams explains, "was to a large degree a continuation of the old patrol system" from the days of slavery. The violence it employed was thus a "reaffirmation" of the "value of white male authority" inherent in the peculiar institution.

Congress reacted to the South Carolina outbreak with the passage of the Enforcement Act of 1870 and the Ku Klux Klan Act of 1871. Under their terms, President U. S. Grant suspended habeas corpus in the South Carolina up-country, and federal officials arrested over 600 accused Klansmen. Williams's greatest contribution is her analysis of the complex legal contest that followed. The ultimate intent of the prosecution, Williams demonstrates, was to show that the Fourteenth and Fifteenth Amendments to the Constitution nationalized the Bill of Rights and ensured that all Americans could be protected by their provisions. The court battles in South Carolina thus tested the broad applicability of the Constitution itself. In the end, a number of Klansmen were convicted, and the violence was temporarily halted, but the government lost its constitutional argument and so the "long term goal of changing the social and political structure of South Carolina was a failure." The trials, Williams convincingly concludes, revealed the dilemmas and inconsistencies of a congressional program of Reconstruction in which dedication to black rights was limited by strict constructionist beliefs. Williams's persuasive assessment of the legal strategies and issues of

the Ku Klux Klan trials demonstrates how well they represent in "microcosm" the history of Reconstruction. In the trials, as in Reconstruction as a whole, egalitarian convictions were sacrificed to further "laissez-faire Constitutional principles."

STEPHEN MAIZLISH

University of Texas at Arlington

SOCIOLOGY

BARBALET, J. M. 1998. *Emotion, Social Theory, and Social Structure: A Macrosociological Approach*. Pp. vii, 210. New York: Cambridge University Press. $54.95.

This is an ambitious book, of deep interest to researchers on the emotions and to those concerned with relevant aspects of sociological theory. Contributions to specific studies of social structure are somewhat vaguer, despite the excellent case made for including emotional components in exploring social and political reactions. Without treating the subject systematically, Barbalet raises a number of important issues about interrelationships between advancing capitalism, emotional responses, and both individual and social status concerns that deserve serious attention.

The book rests on deep reading of relevant sociological theory and a considerable body of work on emotion (though the failure to utilize anthropological materials may be regretted). Barbalet correctly notes the importance of emotional factors in early social science literature; the decline associated with an unduly limited view of rationality; and the recent revival of sociological inquiry and relevant theory. The epilogue returns to the relationship between emotions and general sociological formulations, including those of Weber and Marx.

Individual chapters explore particular emotions in relation to social behavior. Thus resentment often fuels class relations. Confidence, an emotion-related category that Barbalet correctly notes as insufficiently explored, brings emotions into the field of business behavior. Shame, and recent reformulations of this emotion along with embarrassment, gain interesting treatment, though in somewhat less direct relationship to conventional categories of social behavior. The role of vengefulness in demands for rights completes the recurrent discussion of the role of emotions in protest. Finally, the role of fear in motivating social reactions, particularly conservative reactions such as those emerging after the French Revolution, rounds out the focus on specific emotions.

The book operates on a fairly general plane, and it depends on available secondary work for illustrative cases. Barbalet handles existing materials with a fine critical sense, advancing his important case for greater consideration of emotions in dealing with social behaviors. There are some fascinating asides, such as a brief discussion of growing demands for individual rights with respect to seeming trivialities in face of increasingly impersonal economic and organizational forces. But the book does suffer from a lack of fuller, less obvious illustrations about how emotions work in class relations, and, indeed, from considerable imprecision about the social classes involved. One cannot use this material, for example, to discuss specific class cultures involving emotions, or relationships between changing social structures and emotional change.

Barbalet disclaims direct contribution to emotions theory, nor does he explain the mission of key emotions. On the whole, however, he subscribes to a basic emotions approach that sees certain reactions inevitably flowing from specific social settings—an approach that con-tributes to, and is reinforced by, a high level of abstraction and a related lack of consistent interest either in cultural comparisons or in historical change.

Yet the basic theoretical points remain well taken, a challenge to scholars dealing with social structures to include serious emotional components and to emotions researchers more consistently to widen their study of impact to include larger structural dimensions. Here, in effect, is a theoretical framework for the more specific investigations the conclusions should inspire.

PETER N. STEARNS

Carnegie Mellon University
Pittsburgh
Pennsylvania

SHIRLEY, DENNIS. 1997. *Community Organizing for Urban School Reform.* Pp. x, 338. Austin: University of Texas Press. $35.00. Paperbound, $17.95.

Dennis Shirley's account of the work of the Texas Industrial Areas Foundation (IAF) is a succinct description of an organization that has found a way to strengthen students' academic performance in traditionally low-achieving public schools. The Texas IAF supports, trains, and encourages the formation of grassroots organizations in low-income, working-class, urban neighborhoods. Students are the beneficiaries of the resulting relationship that is forged between the school and its community. This community of parents, family, neighbors, and friends is empowered to engage authorities and to address the issues that they have identified for improvement or change.

The Texas IAF provides the leadership and organizational skills that result in an empowered community. Its work begins as a facilitator of one-to-one contacts in the community. Next are the house meetings where neighbors come together to identify common problems and to think of ways in which they can be solved. In the third step, the IAF organizers take a more didactic role. They lead training sessions around the identified key issues. They teach parents how to negotiate, mediate, and relate as they develop strategies for addressing school and neighborhood improvement issues.

After the training sessions, the IAF leaders and organizers plan a demonstration such as a Walk for Success to show public support for the targeted improvements. Then comes the public action: a meeting of the community with elected officials who are asked to pledge their support and to commit to regular and careful monitoring of their activities. This combination of one-to-ones, house meetings, rallies, and public meetings builds the social capital that will effect desired changes in the school community.

In case studies of IAF schools and communities, Shirley demonstrates how social capital works. Voluntary associations of parents and friends, who begin as poor, undereducated, disenfranchised nonparticipants in the life of the school and the neighborhood, are transformed into articulate, fully informed advocates for their children and their communities. One reads of parents such as Lili Escobedo, once afraid to speak in public, now an outspoken community leader, and of the Ysleta Elementary School, where steady academic achievement has removed it from the state's "clearly unacceptable" list.

The mission of the Texas IAF is to bring the community "into the heart of the school, and to use the school as a base for the political revitalization of the community." The results of IAF's organizational and leadership activities affirm this mission. The academic environment of children in targeted schools has indeed improved. Parents are engaged. They are empowered politically, socially, and cul-

turally to revitalize the school and the community. Dennis Shirley documents these successes in his highly readable and empowering book.

BARBARA TAYLOR

Lincoln University
Jefferson City
Missouri

ECONOMICS

BIRENBAUM, ARNOLD. 1997. *Managed Care: Made in America.* Pp. xv, 193. Westport, CT: Praeger. $39.95.

In Arnold Birenbaum's *Managed Care*, health care as a market commodity is explored through an analysis of the development of the managed care industry. Birenbaum takes a critical look at the history of managed care (how it works for patients, doctors, and its owners) and outlines arenas in which reform is needed.

Rather than approach managed care from a medical or business perspective, he explores his topic through the lens of social change. He defines changed social relationships: social relationships internal and external to the medical profession, social relationships between consumers and providers, the creation of medical unions, and the social and professional relationships between doctors, hospitals, and specialty services. Never before has health care been addressed as a market commodity rearranging professional dialogue, relationships, and decision making. In addition, Birenbaum tackles the difficult question of medical care as a social good or commodity through a series of discussions describing the contradictions in each of these models.

Birenbaum uses research reports, trends, and anecdotal information to demystify the components of managed care while describing a very complex system of health care delivery. While addressing issues of quality of care, consumer satisfaction, and legislation, he describes the attractiveness of the emerging industry to business.

Birenbaum discusses the private insurance industry's struggles with the development of managed care and its expansion into the Medicaid and Medicare populations. He overlays this with physicians' struggles with loss of autonomy in decision making about individual patient issues, referrals, and practice development.

The balance of power in American health care has historically been in favor of the medical profession, whereas managed care places physicians in a peculiar position as health maintenance organizations (HMOs) pursue profits earned by limiting medical care. Birenbaum's tracking of the shift in power to HMO executives creates a provocative backdrop to understanding capitation, specialty referrals, networks, and continuum of care.

The book outlines the issues for insurance companies: everything from capturing as large a share of the market as possible, to meeting a plethora of state regulations, to meeting shareholders' expectations. It traces the inherent conflict between business, profit making, and service delivery as managed care companies have developed.

Birenbaum provides advocacy guidelines for consumers and a series of questions to ask before joining a plan. He defines a legislative agenda for HMOs, consumers, and the medical profession. He also addresses customer satisfaction, overall quality of care, and the need for public disclosure of fiscal arrangements with physicians.

JUNE CAIRNS

Children, Youth, and
    Family Council
Philadelphia
Pennsylvania

OTHER BOOKS

ARAS, BULENT. 1998. *Palestinian-Israeli Peace Process and Turkey.* Pp. ix, 178. Commack, NY: Nova Science. $49.00.

ARON, RAYMOND. 1998. *Main Currents in Sociological Thought.* Vol. 1. Pp. xxi, 354. New Brunswick, NJ: Transaction. Paperbound, $24.95.

BARBER, BENJAMIN R. 1998. *A Passion for Democracy.* Pp. xii, 293. Princeton, NJ: Princeton University Press. $26.95.

BENDER, THOMAS and CARL E. SCHORSKE, eds. 1998. *American Academic Culture in Transformation: Fifty Years, Four Disciplines.* Pp. xii, 371. Princeton, NJ: Princeton University Press. Paperbound, $16.95.

BENNETT, PAUL R. 1997. *Russian Negotiating Strategy: Analytic Case Studies from SALT and START.* Pp. vii, 163. Commack, NY: Nova Science. $59.00.

COKER, CHRISTOPHER. 1998. *War and the Illiberal Conscience.* Pp. xvi, 240. Boulder, CO: Westview Press. $39.00.

CROISSANT, CYNTHIA. 1998. *Azerbaijan, Oil and Geopolitics.* Pp. vii, 117. Commack, NY: Nova Science. $49.00.

DAVIES, J. CLARENCE and JAN MAZUREK. 1998. *Pollution Control in the United States: Evaluating the System.* Pp. xiii, 319. Washington, DC: Resources for the Future. $48.00. Paperbound, $29.95.

DITTMER, LOWELL, ed. 1998. *Liu Shaoqi and the Chinese Cultural Revolution.* Rev. ed. Pp. xvi, 382. Armonk, NY: M. E. Sharpe. $68.95. Paperbound, $24.95.

DOMINGUEZ, JORGE I., ed. 1998. *International Security and Democracy: Latin America and the Caribbean in the Post-Cold War Era.* Pp. xiv, 346. Pittsburgh, PA: University of Pittsburgh Press. $50.00. Paperbound, $22.95.

FLYVBJERG, BENT. 1998. *Rationality and Power: Democracy in Practice.* Pp. xiii, 290. Chicago: University of Chicago Press. $43.00. Paperbound, $16.95.

GILOTH, ROBERT P., ed. 1998. *Jobs and Economic Development: Strategies and Practice.* Pp. xv, 262. Thousand Oaks, CA: Sage. Paperbound, $24.50.

IDINOPULOS, THOMAS A. 1998. *Weathered by Miracles: A History of Palestine from Bonaparte and Muhammad Ali to Ben-Gurion and the Mufti.* Pp. xiv, 283. Chicago: Ivan R. Dee. $27.50.

JAMES, JEFFREY and HAIDER A. KAHN. 1998. *Technological Systems and Development.* Pp. xii, 141. New York: St. Martin's Press. No price.

LEPGOLD, JOSEPH and THOMAS G. WEISS, eds. 1998. *Collective Conflict Management and Changing World Politics.* Pp. xiii, 245. Albany: State University of New York Press. Paperbound, no price.

McLEAN, ALASDAIR and FRASER LOVIE. 1997. *Europe's Final Frontier: The Search for Security Through Space.* Pp. 259. Commack, NY: Nova Science. $59.00.

MERCER, DAVID. 1998. *Marketing Strategy: The Challenge of the External Environment.* Pp. viii, 325. Thousand Oaks, CA: Sage. Paperbound, $32.95.

NARASIMHAN, R. 1998. *Language Behavior: Acquisition and Evolutionary History.* Pp. 219. New Delhi: Sage. $38.00.

OBERDORFER, DON. 1998. *From the Cold War to a New Era: The United States and the Soviet Union, 1983-1991.* Pp. 552. Baltimore, MD: Johns Hopkins University Press. Paperbound, $19.95.

PICCIOTTO, ROBERT and EDUARDO WIESNER, eds. 1998. *Evaluation and Development: The Institutional Dimension.* Pp. xiv, 320. New Brunswick, NJ: Transaction. Paperbound, $22.95.

PINTO, VIVEK. 1998. *Gandhi's Vision and Values: The Moral Quest for Change in Indian Agriculture.* Pp. 176. New Delhi: Sage. $29.95.

RICENTO, THOMAS and BARBARA BURNABY, eds. 1998. *Language and Politics in the United States and Canada: Myths and Realities.* Pp. xv, 357. Mahwah, NJ: Lawrence Erlbaum. Paperbound, $39.95.

ROELOFS, H. MARK. 1998. *The Poverty of American Politics: A Theoretical Interpretation.* 2d ed. Pp. xxiv, 310. Philadelphia: Temple University Press. Paperbound, $22.95.

SCHECTER, JERROLD L. 1998. *Russian Negotiating Behavior: Continuity and Transition.* Pp. ix, 225. Washington, DC: United States Institute of Peace. Paperbound, $14.95.

SCHNAPPER, DOMINIQUE. 1998. *Community of Citizens: On the Modern Idea of Nationality.* Pp. xiv, 184. New Brunswick, NJ: Transaction. $32.95.

SHOTTON, JOHN ROBERT. 1998. *Learning and Freedom: Policy, Pedagogy and Paradigms in Indian Education and Schooling.* Pp. 209. New Delhi: Sage. $29.95.

SINGH, RAJENDRA, ed. 1998. *The Yearbook of South Asian Languages and Linguistics.* Pp. 274. New Delhi: Sage. $47.00.

VERMA, MAHENDRA K., ed. 1998. *Sociolinguistics, Language and Society.* Pp. 210. New Delhi: Sage. $31.95.

VONDUNG, KLAUS. 1998. *The History of the Race Idea: From Ray to Carus: The Collected Works of Eric Voegelin.* Vol. 3. Pp. xvii, 189. Baton Rouge: Louisiana State University Press. $30.00.

VOSKRESSENSKI, ALEXEI D., ed. 1997. *Post-Soviet Policy Perspectives.* Pp. vii, 214. Commack, NY: Nova Science. $59.00.

WINIECKI, JAN. 1997. *Political Economy of Reform and Change: A Case of Eastern Europe.* Pp. xxiv, 230. Commack, NY: Nova Science. $59.00.

INDEX

Affordable

Money in the bank. It may seem like just a dream. A little price-shopping can help make it a reality. Insurance coverage offered through your AAPSS membership features competitive group rates negotiated especially for members like you.

Take advantage of one of your best membership benefits. Affordable coverage. Reliable providers. Portable benefits. Call 800 424-9883, or in Washington, DC 202 457-6820, to speak to a customer service representative. Because quality insurance coverage doesn't have to empty your wallet.

GROUP INSURANCE FOR AAPSS MEMBERS

Cancer Expense • Catastrophe Major Medical Dental Plan • High Limit Accident • Medicare Supplement • Member Assistance • Term Life

This program is administered by Seabury & Smith, a Marsh & McLennan Company.
The term life insurance plan is underwritten by the New York Life Insurance Company, 51 Madison Avenue, New York, NY 10010.
The member assistance insurance plan is underwritten by UNUM Life Insurance Company of America, 15 Corporate Place South, Piscataway, NJ 08855.
The cancer expense and medicare supplement insurance plans are underwritten by the Monumental Life Insurance Company, Baltimore, MD 21201.
The dental plan, catastrophe major medical, and high limit accident insurance plans are underwritten by United States Life Insurance Company in the city of New York, 3600 Route 66, Neptune, NJ 07754.